Contingent Citizens

Contingent Citizens

Professional Aspiration in a South African Hospital

ELIZABETH HULL

BLOOMSBURY ACADEMIC
LONDON • NEW YORK • OXFORD • NEW DELHI • SYDNEY

BLOOMSBURY ACADEMIC
Bloomsbury Publishing Plc
50 Bedford Square, London, WC1B 3DP, UK
1385 Broadway, New York, NY 10018, USA

BLOOMSBURY, BLOOMSBURY ACADEMIC and the Diana logo
are trademarks of Bloomsbury Publishing Plc

First published 2017
Paperback edition published 2019

Cover design: Adriana Brioso
Cover image: Three nurses from the Nquelezana Hospital AIDS home-care team
on their way to visit the family home of Nesta Mquanaze, Kwazulu/Natal,
South Africa. April 2000. (© Gideon Mendel/Getty Images)

A catalogue record for this book is available from the British Library.

ISBN: HB: 978-1-3500-2775-6
       PB: 978-1-3501-0809-7
    ePDF: 978-1-3500-2776-3
   eBook: 978-1-3500-2777-0

A catalog record for this book is available from the Library of Congress.

Series: LSE Monographs on Social Anthropology

Typeset by Newgen Knowledge Works Pvt. Ltd., Chennai, India.

To find out more about our authors and books visit
www.bloomsbury.com and sign up for our newsletters.

In memory of my father, John M. Hull

CONTENTS

ILLUSTRATIONS

Figures

Maps

ACKNOWLEDGEMENTS

Many people have contributed generously to this project and have helped to shape it. I must begin by thanking all of the staff at Bethesda Hospital who gave up precious time to share their experiences and insights with me. These include the nurses, nursing college tutors and nursing students, doctors and other clinical practitioners, managers, and administrative and other support staff. I have used pseudonyms for the members of staff who were working at Bethesda Hospital at the time of the research, and whose words and actions are described in this book. Despite the daunting task of grappling with so many different perspectives, and although inevitably there are disagreements, I hope that what I have written does justice to their contributions. I am grateful to Janet Giddy and Steve Reid, who supported the project from the outset and introduced me to Bethesda Hospital. Daryl and Priscilla Hackland, Helen and Jonathan Pons, and Fiona and Steve Knight gave lengthy interviews at short notice and lent valuable documents. Solomon Myeni and Elphas Myeni facilitated and supported my research in the surrounding area of Nkangala. Cynthia Gina and Thami Dlamini worked with me as research assistants and provided invaluable help, insight and conviviality.

A good friend, Fortunate Mafuleka, helped crucially during the first few months of research. She died before I finished this work. I know she would have taken great interest in the final product.

I am fortunate to have had the support and companionship of many friends in South Africa. A few of them deserve special thanks, including Catherine Burns, Jabulile Gumede, Fahad Hendrix, Kate-Louise McCay, Masa Memela, Monty Thomas, Pieter Nel and Pieter Ryan. In Durban, Eleanor Preston-Whyte gave me a home for the first few weeks of my time in South Africa. Her hospitality and stimulating conversations stood me in good stead for navigating the daunting task of fieldwork. I am grateful to Thobile Myeni,

Thabisile Dlamini, Ntombifuthi Nsele and Sibongile Ndwandwe whose warmth and kindness eased my transition into Ubombo, and to the children at the Ubombo Children's Care Village who made me feel at home on my arrival. Dawn Irons kindly provided this accommodation. Dominique Oebell gave up a room in her small park home for the rest of my stay at Bethesda. Beatrice Mbhamali and her family have taken me into their home year after year. I am grateful for their generosity, humour and patience, and for all that they have taught me along the way.

The project was funded by the Economic and Social Research Council. In 2006–7, I was affiliated to the history department of the University of KwaZulu-Natal, where I had access to the library and the weekly departmental seminars that provided an intellectual home. In 2013, I was affiliated with the Department of Anthropology in Pretoria. The Department of Health of KwaZulu-Natal kindly granted the permission to carry out research at Bethesda Hospital in 2006 and again in 2013. Members of staff at the Cory Library in Grahamstown provided access to the Methodist archives collection. Thanks are due especially to Zweli Vena, whose impressive knowledge of the archives saved me many hours.

Many colleagues and friends have helped by reading my work, or by offering their expertise and advice in small or large ways. They include Rita Astuti, Maxim Bolt, Keith Breckenridge, Catherine Allerton, Indira Arumugam, Judith Bovensiepen, Catherine Burns, Irene Calis, Leon Cardoso, Rabia Cassimjee, Girish Daswani, Ankur Datta, Katie Dow, Deborah Gaitskell, Wenzel Geissler, Maia Green, Rick Iedema, Giulia Liberatore, Shula Marks, Fraser McNeill, Julie Parle, Howard Phillips, Hakem Rustom, Andrew Sanchez, Marina Sapritsky, Fiona Scorgie, Michael Scott, Keith Shear, Roger Southall, George St Clair, Felix Stein, Hans Steinmuller, Helen Sweet and Harry West. Both Deborah James and the series editor, Laura Bear, read the entire manuscript and provided extremely helpful comments. I owe special thanks to Matthew Engelke and Deborah James for their support and mentorship over many years.

I am grateful for all the comments received by colleagues at various seminars and conferences where versions of parts of this book have been presented between 2009 and 2015. These include the Hospital Ethnography workshop at the University of Sussex; the London School of Economics and Political Science anthropology departmental seminar; the States, Public Bureaucracies and

Civil Servants and Work and Recreation: The Worlds Missionaries Made? panels at the 3rd European Conference on African Studies in Leipzig, Germany; the History and African Studies Seminar of the history department at the University of KwaZulu-Natal; the Let's Talk about Bantustans conference held by the National Research Foundation Chair in Local Histories and Present Realities at the University of Witwatersrand; and the seminar of the NRF Local Histories and Present Realities at the University of Witwatersrand.

Earlier versions of parts of Chapter Three appeared in my article 'The Renewal of Community Health under the KwaZulu Homeland Government', *South African Historical Journal*, 64 (1): 22–40, published in 2012 by Taylor & Francis; of Chapter Four in the article 'Paperwork and the Contradictions of Accountability in a South African Hospital', *Journal of the Royal Anthropological Institute*, 18: 613–32, published in 2012 by Wiley; and of Chapter Six in the article 'International Migration, "Domestic Struggles" and Status Aspiration among Nurses in South Africa', *Journal of Southern African Studies*, 36 (4): 851–67, published in 2010 by Taylor & Francis. The material from these articles has been reused with permission.

Finally, I would like to thank my friends, family and most especially my parents, Marilyn and John Hull, for their support and encouragement. The book is dedicated in loving memory of my father.

MAPS

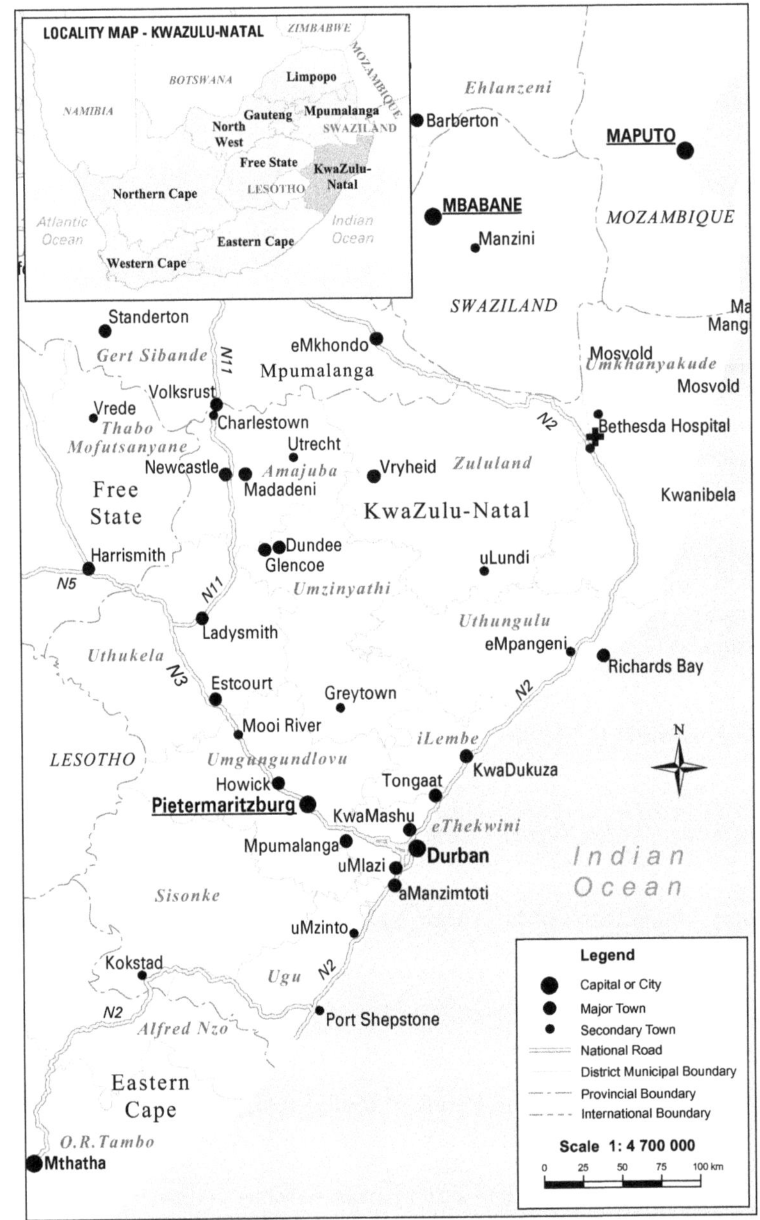

MAP 1 *The province of KwaZulu-Natal © Charles Carey, MapStudio.*

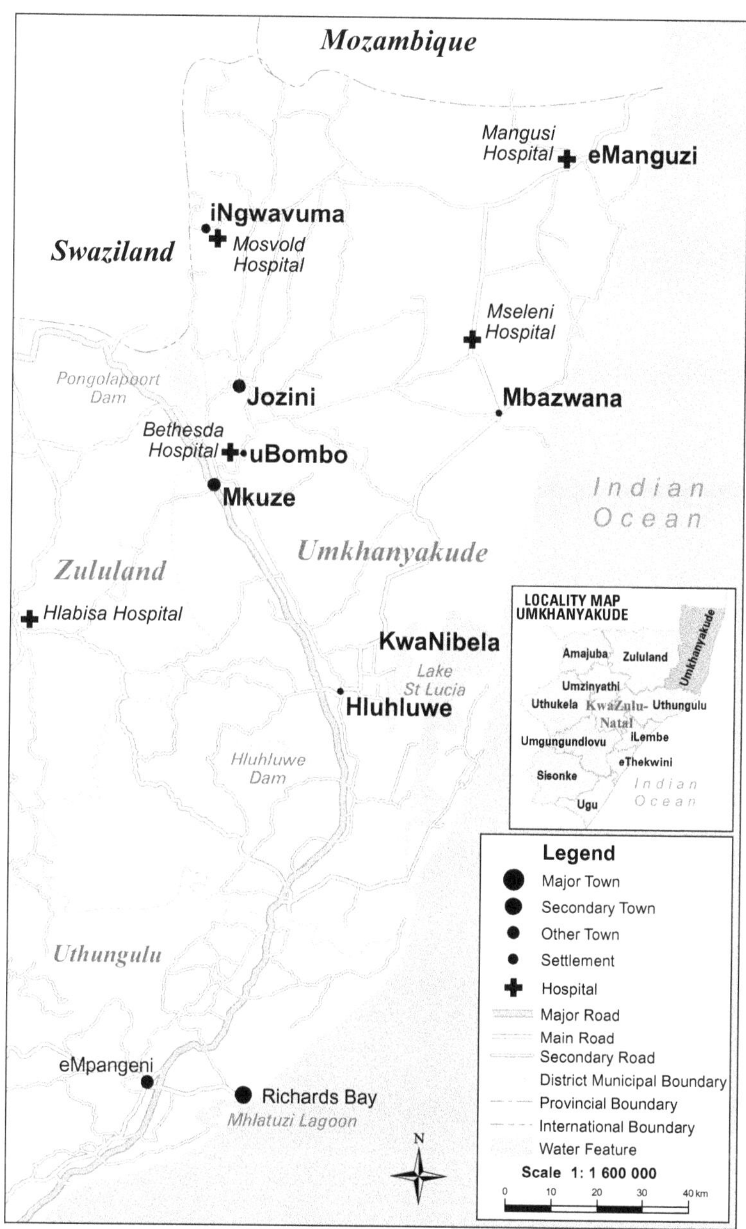

MAP 2 *The district of Umkhanyakude © Charles Carey, MapStudio.*

Introduction

On a windy day in June 2007, a crowd of 200 or so nurses and hospital labourers gathered outside the locked gates of Bethesda Hospital. Clustered together, they listened to the animated speech of a young trade union member. 'You nurses are drinking our blood!' he shouted, in an outburst of frustration as he tried to convince them to join the strike.[1] The countrywide civil servant strike had lasted for the whole month and union activists travelled across the province of KwaZulu-Natal to encourage workers to participate. At Bethesda, a rural hospital in the far north of the province, no one did, apart from a few who picketed for an hour at lunch time on certain days: a time slot allocated and approved by the hospital manager.

The nationwide strike of 700,000 public sector employees was a pivotal moment, the explosive outcome of a public sector reeling under the pressure of resource shortages, stagnating wages and a social landscape marred by poverty and ill health. Three years after the eruption and escalation of violent protests about service delivery, which have since become a regular feature of life in deprived areas of South Africa, the strikes were yet another expression of discontent, threatening to dislodge the country's increasingly fragile social order. Most worryingly for the leadership of the ruling African National Congress (ANC), the strikes indicated mounting dissatisfaction among not only the growing wageless population, but among the middle classes as well: those employed in the civil service and other formal sector jobs. In the health-care sector, the strikes signalled a crisis that had been building over several years as the severity of the AIDS epidemic grew, placing ever more pressure on overburdened staff, many of whom fled to better-paid jobs overseas or in the private sector.

For the duration of the strike at Bethesda Hospital, many people continued working but nobody came to work wearing their uniform for fear of being identified by trade unionists and forced outside to strike. Some expressed fears of physical violence. Without their neat blue and white uniforms and the familiar epaulettes that signified their professional status, the nurses blended strangely into the wider corpus of patients from whom they were usually visibly separated. The atmosphere was quiet and tense, punctuated by intermittent rumours circulating around the corridors and wards that the anonymous young male strikers were nearby, waiting for an opportunity to break through the locked gates and reinforced security at the entre of the hospital to seek out those who were working. One night there was a tussle at the gate and an attempted break-in, allegedly by one of these men.

On the large notice board attached to the wall outside the main entrance of the Out-Patients Department hung photocopied newspaper articles detailing various events relating to the strike. Among them, several bold headlines stood out: 'As More and More Unions Back the Big Strike, Get Ready for Chaos', 'Teachers to Shut Down Hospitals' and 'Baby Dies after Nurses Refuse Aid'. Regular statements by the head of the provincial Department of Health contained similar messages, condemning the strike: 'We must always remember that health is a human rights issue,' she boldly declared. Echoing the condemnatory tone of most media coverage, nurses at Bethesda explained why no one there was taking part in the strike. Striking will 'lower my dignity', one said. For another, the strike was the evidence of 'a lack of self-discipline in nursing today'. These sentiments were echoed by a union representative working at Bethesda who, unlike his fellow unionist outside rebuking nurses for strike-breaking, took the management line of opposition to the strike: 'People worry about patients because nursing is an essential service. You cannot replace your life.' He explained that his main role as a union representative was 'making people aware' of the individual consequences of strike action: their potential dismissal.

The nationwide strike of 2007 was a moment of acute threat to South Africa's young democracy. It brought social services to a halt and exposed the mounting dissatisfactions of a large middle-income tier of government sector employees, demonstrating the political clout of South Africa's formally employed professional classes. In this book, I make a case for paying renewed empirical attention to this group, whose political allegiances and social identities cannot be read easily from the economic conditions undergirding them, but will be crucial in shaping South Africa's political landscape in the years to come. Professionalism itself has become a fraught identity, highly sought after yet failing live up to or to contain the aspirational desires of its members. The book investigates both the opportunities and the constraints of professional identity in South Africa today.

Nursing offers a useful lens through which to explore this theme. A history of fragmentation and hierarchy in the nursing profession makes the social and class allegiances of nurses varied and unpredictable. They are far from homogenous in terms of either their material class basis or their social identifications. On the one hand, nurses' professional status has granted them membership of a relatively elite class. On the other hand, many are downgraded in the context of a highly stratified workplace order. This has produced two contradictory images of the nurse: as a wealthy government fat cat as well as a member of the struggling rank and file. These two contrasting representations have emerged repeatedly – often in caricatured form – throughout nursing's fractured history, reappearing once again in this post-liberation moment.

The scene of the strike reveals the moral pressures on nurses deriving from these competing identities. With whom should they align themselves and at what moral and social cost? With the strikers, who invade the sanctity of patient 'rights'? Or with the strike-breakers, who 'drink the blood' of their junior colleagues to further their own enrichment? The strike exposed both the contradictions and the fragility of professional status, and hinted at the work needed to sustain it. This book addresses the ambiguous position of the 'professional' classes in post-apartheid South Africa. I explore how the identity of professionalism creates both aspirational opportunities but also constraints. Moreover, nurses' status not only as professionals, but as citizens as well, is contingent and unstable, because of the way that citizenship in post-apartheid South Africa has been linked to one's position in the workplace. I argue that the democratic discourses designed to legitimize the ANC government and to contain and cultivate professional aspirations are increasingly inadequate to the task, signifying the failure of the post-apartheid workplace to fulfil emancipatory aspirations, and leading to new kinds of aspirational and moral formations, both in the workplace and beyond. Using the example of nursing, I suggest that a focus on professionalism offers an important perspective on the middle classes and their claims to citizenship, in South Africa and beyond.

Fear and aspiration in post-apartheid South Africa

Two decades after the inception of liberal democracy in 1994, one of the resounding features of South African society is its soaring rate of inequality. Across the world, South Africa is ranked as one of the most unequal societies. Its Gini coefficient on disposable income, increasing from about 0.67 in 1993 to around 0.69 in 2011, is one of the highest in the world (Inchauste et al. 2014: 2). This extreme scenario gives the impression of a society split between the conspicuously wealthy and the desperately poor. Media narratives display the lavish lifestyles of a new cadre of super-rich, Johannesburg-dwelling black South Africans. Incubated during the apartheid period but unable to advance under the racist regime, these so-called black diamonds (Mda 2009) flourished from the mid-1990s, often fuelled by close political and business alliances with ANC elites. A second, parallel narrative describes those 'left behind', a growing wageless population, whose precarious survival rests on a huge public programme of social protection. Overseeing this seemingly intractable social divide, the South African government plays a dual role, serving both as a mechanism for the enrichment of the new elite, as well as a redistributive technology for ensuring a minimal source of survival for the poor. The latter serves as the basis for maintaining an ever more fragile status quo.

The upper echelons of South Africa's new business-oriented elite, while highly visible, make up only a very small proportion of the population. But what about the large, educated middle tier that are joining the lower ranks of government services, those who service the country's hospitals, schools, police stations and offices? How have they experienced the first two decades of liberation? This book explores how the status of South Africa's professionals is faring in the post-apartheid context, where secure employment has become a luxury as well as the ideological terrain of an exclusive citizenship. I argue that while work has been fashioned as an integral constituent of national belonging, this form of citizenship is one that is both limited and contingent, even for those in relatively high-status positions in the workforce.

My focus on professionalism aims to shed new light on middle-class identity in South Africa. It highlights, in particular, some of the contradictions and tensions entailed in the struggle to sustain middle-class status. Throughout the twentieth century, nurses have occupied a liminal space, claiming membership of an elite class while being downgraded within their own, highly stratified and racialized, profession. Such ambiguities remain salient in the contemporary context. The strike scene is a useful place to begin with because it is at such heightened moments of political tension that anxieties and contradictions – usually forming an undercurrent below the surface of day-to-day activity – emerge and meet each other in open contestation. These anxieties, many of them concerning what is to happen in the future, also reveal central themes that have continuities with the past. One such expressed in this narrative is the strong moral discourse of the nursing profession that demands unified allegiance, even as internal hierarchies maintain significant distinctions in levels of remuneration and status between nurses. Another is the public perception of nurses as cruel or heartless, an image that has often been generalized through media focus on particular incidents.[2] Related to this is nurses' perceived status and separation from a wider (working-class) community to which they are nonetheless tied through family and other connections (Jewkes, Abrahams and Mvo 1998; Rispel and Schneider 1991; Segar 1994; L.; Walker 1996; Walker and Gilson 2004). These intertwined moral and class ambiguities were implied in the trade unionist's reference to blood drinking that in African contexts, as James Ferguson notes, signals a conception of wealth that is intimately bound together with social relations. There are 'two kinds of wealth', he remarks, 'the kind that feeds people and the kind that eats them' (2006: 73).

This book explores the ambiguous status of South Africa's middle classes in post-apartheid South Africa. Difficulties of definition arise when speaking of the 'middle class' in South Africa, as elsewhere, partly because of its heterogeneous composition and partly because neo-Weberian and neo-Marxist intellectual traditions have marked out different parameters (Lentz 2015). In his recent, far-reaching book on *The New Black Middle Class in South Africa*, Roger Southall distinguishes between the bourgeoisie, the upper middle class and the lower middle class. The bourgeoisie (or power elite) consist of a central group of key political decision-makers including the president and other senior state and corporate managers. The upper and lower middle classes are a larger and more heterogeneous group, the former consisting of middle-level managers and independent professionals, and the latter overwhelmingly of those in white-collar and service occupations, mainly operating below the level of management. Teachers and nurses form a large part of this group (Southall 2016: 62).

The lower middle classes are heavily unionized, reflecting a transformation in labour relations from the repressive apartheid workplace to a system of representative collective bargaining in the era of liberal democracy. As a consequence of collective bargaining, as well as affirmative action and other policies focused on the deracialization of the economy, Southall argues, the middle classes are key beneficiaries of the post-apartheid dispensation. In his 2004 article, Southall argued that consequently they are less likely to align themselves with working-class interests and progressive political goals. Since then, increasing numbers of strikes by this group suggest a more complex story. His recent book reflects this complexity, showing that the middle classes are not only extremely heterogeneous, but that their differing relationships to state power render their class prospects, allegiances and opportunities all the more difficult to determine. The formation of the middle classes in South Africa, he argues, must be understood in relation to the ANC 'party-state' upon which their positions are deeply reliant. It is this relationship between class formation and the South African state, I suggest, that a focus on professionalism can illuminate.

The recent history of nursing in South Africa follows the trajectory described by Southall in some important ways. Nurses are a large and influential segment of the formally employed and are highly unionized.[3] Historically, they have played an important role in labour movements, and have taken part in the unionization, industrial action and unrest of the late 1980s and early 1990s that helped to bring the apartheid system to its knees. However, like many hierarchically organized occupations, nursing has been shaped by both conservative and progressive voices, which have often existed in tension; they are far from homogenous in position, status or outlook. In this book, I show that an ethnographic engagement in the lived realities of nurses reveals an ambivalent picture. The historical trajectory of nursing is characterized by intense internal stratification and a drive among some for professional status, creating divisions and conflict despite persistent assertions of unity among those in the higher ranks.

The ambiguous and heterogeneous position of South Africa's middle classes has been recently taken up in scholarship, which shows that salaries are often spread thinly across wide networks of responsibilities and dependencies between kin. This has prompted the question of whether the formally employed do occupy a privileged space, or whether they inhabit more precarious lives, underpaid at work and carrying the burden of responsibility for dependent kin (Callebert 2015; Musyoka and Houghton 2016). Deborah James (2015) shows how middle-class lifestyles have been funded partly by borrowed credit. Formal sector salaries enter into complex chains of transactions involving moneylending and debt repayment, long- and short-term investments, and networks of consumption and accumulation that extend well beyond narrowly individual modes of expenditure and consumption. Interlinked networks of social and economic exchange suggest that the boundaries between classes are blurred and that people, who occupy similar positions within the formal workforce, may experience highly variable living standards.

These findings resonate closely with the experiences of nurses, for whom the title of success is often accorded to those who manage to invest their salaries creatively in activities that extend well beyond their remit as professionals. One nurse at whose home I lived for some time, ran a food stall in town staffed by her domestic worker, together with generating income through her work as a *sangoma* (spirit medium) and by lending money to neighbours at high interest rates. For her, 'making money go further' via these informal means was crucial for her high social standing. For her and many others, professional status alone was insufficient. International migration was another highly significant signifier of success to which many aspired, which I address in this book.

The ambiguities and limitations of professional status arise in the workplace, too. While work has become the basis of claims to citizenship in post-apartheid South Africa, the adverse social realities of the workplace render this association increasingly fragile (Barchiesi 2011). Since the remarkable transition to majority rule, subtle forms of managerial coercion have replaced the overt political authority of the late-apartheid period that was underpinned by a threat of violence. The emerging tropes of liberal democracy – such as 'accountability' and 'rights' – serve to keep workers in a fearful state of suspicion, despite the language of transparency and decentralization promising freedom from control. The rising numbers of strikes expose the growing difficulty of democratic discourses to contain these contradictions. Mounting tensions reached a climax in August 2012, when police opened fire, killing 34 striking miners near the town of Marikana. This event has emerged as a defining moment of the post-apartheid era, bringing plainly into view the limits of ANC hegemony (Hart 2013). It exposed what many viewed as a return to the violent coercion of the apartheid era, a sign that the techniques of managerial authority and workplace discipline have been insufficient to contain and control discontent.

In this book, I explore these themes as they resonate with the lives of one group of nurses living and working in an impoverished, rural part of the country. Here, I encountered feelings of deep ambivalence among nurses, and an array of aspirations arising out of both fear and hope about the future. I describe their behaviour, not as mere responses or reactions to a situation imposed upon them, but as active participants in the re-creation of these dynamics, percolated through the social and material conditions of a specific rural setting. Nurses draw on a range of strategies, from international migration to participation in informal economies to born-again faith, reappropriating democratic idioms and combining them with other values, both conservative and progressive, to formulate new material and ethical relations. The unstable category of the 'professional' arises out of – but is not reducible to – processes of state building. This generates both a contingent, but also, an engaged language of citizenship.

Towards an anthropology of professionalism

In scholarly debates about social stratification in Africa, the terms 'middle class' and 'elite' have both been used analytically to describe civil servants and other state and formal sector employees.

In a detailed discussion of the journey of these two terms, Carola Lentz (2015) shows that they represent two potentially contradictory framings, one drawing predominantly on Marxian understandings of class, and the other on those of Max Weber. During my fieldwork in the province of KwaZulu-Natal, I did not hear the terms 'elite' or 'middle-class' used to describe nurses or anyone else. Rather, the word 'professional' was commonly used as a signifier of aspirational identity and class achievement.[4] Lentz shows that at least in the Weberian strand of literature, educational achievement – a key tenet of professionalism – emerges as a crucial marker of elite status and aspiration. However, Lentz, Southall and others use the term 'professional' descriptively, rather than as a category that is culturally produced and contingent. Shula Marks's (1994) history of nursing in South Africa, which I discuss below, is an important exception. Her approach has informed my conceptualization of professionalism as a political and historical category.

Emerging in social processes through time, I understand 'professionalism' to be a category always in the making, rather than as being self-evident. The sociologist, Robert Dingwall, shows that professions and the category of the 'professional' come into being through particular configurations of power, information exchange and institutional practice. He writes that 'much of the confusion about the notion of "profession" stems from attempts at legislating its meaning rather than to examine its use' (2008: 27). Drawing on his work, I argue that it is necessary to examine how the idea of professionalism is mobilized and to what ends. As I will show, this has implications for how anthropologists approach the study of bureaucracies, public administrations and the state.

In recent years, anthropologists have focused attention on the consumption practices and lifestyles of the middle classes rather than on their working lives and professionalization strategies (Donner and Neve 2011). This is partly to do with a growing recognition of the decline of the industrial workplace as the primary site of identity formation. In South Africa, Jean and John L. Comaroff aptly characterized these changing cultural forms in their article on 'Millennial Capitalism' (2000). In the face of growing labour casualization, outsourcing and job insecurity, they argued, the workplace was no longer the key site for the creation of value. In its place was an explosion of consumerist ideology, appearing magically to offer inclusion even to the most marginalized, while also giving rise to new lines of exclusion.

More recently, James Ferguson (2015) has argued that given the proliferation of diverse livelihood activities beyond the formal workplace, scholarly attention should focus not on production but on patterns of distribution as the crucial site of political transformation in the region. However, the existence of huge public administrations populated by white-collar workers and civil servants suggests the continued importance of salaried work as a site for identity formation. It therefore becomes necessary to consider how the creation of value at work dovetails with changing worlds of meaning, livelihood, distribution and status beyond it.

Professionalism is a useful vantage point for exploring these intersections, offering a perspective on the relationship between work and personal aspirations that stretch well beyond the workplace. In Weberian approaches to class, one's 'life chances' are influenced not only by economic factors but also by a range of social attributes, including prestige level, social networks and educational achievement. Weber recognized that the formation of occupational groups with formal control over particular areas of expertise was crucial to the creation of new kinds of collective status. Such an approach avoids strict typologies and instead seeks to understand the relationship of these collective cultures to changing configurations of market, state and society.

Weberian approaches have been useful in the scholarship on African bureaucracies, particularly in characterizing the relationship between elites and the mechanisms of state power. This work has generally focused on issues of patronage, corruption and patrimonialism, rather than on formal processes of professionalization, showing that social networks are crucial for ensuring elite access to state resources. It has revealed the ways in which the personal pervades the bureaucratic, in contrast to the formalism of Weber's rational-bureaucratic norms. Scholars of African studies have generally converged around the view that the apparent 'crisis' of state governance across the continent, arising in relation to these neo-patrimonial tendencies, is the product of colonial legacies. As Jeffrey Haynes writes, 'the nature of the contemporary African state is in large part due to the legacy of the colonial era' (2002: 312). Chipkin and Meny-Gibert suggest that the internal structures of colonial rule remain firmly in place: 'the colonial state becomes a post-colonial one while retaining its original DNA' (2012: 104). Von Holdt (2010) makes a similar point in relation to health-care institutions in South Africa, evident in the patron-client style appointments to higher positions. Dominated by 'non-Weberian rationales' inherited from colonial systems of governance, he argues, South Africa's health system is prevented from achieving a form of governance more closely resembling Weber's ideal type of rational bureaucracy.

I suggest that closer attention to systems of professionalization and accreditation can shed new light on the reproduction of class and status in Africa. While wealth and status are often associated with neo-patrimonial practices, Weber recognized that contradictions also inhere in the bureaucratic model itself. Plutocratic tendencies could quickly form in modern bureaucracies, and he was aware of an intrinsic contradiction: while the meritocratic process created a 'levelling' pressure on hierarchies of social distinction, new hierarchies of privilege could easily form on the basis of technical competence. He referred to this as the 'patent of education' (Weber 1978: 1000).[5] Such plutocratic tendencies are likely to emerge because of the time and resources required for training, meaning that access to training would likely become skewed towards those already occupying positions of privilege. Although Weber did not focus specifically on the formation of professions such as medicine and law, the ideology of professionalism quintessentially characterizes the tendency that he describes.

What this suggests is a need to focus not only on patronage networks as key mediators between state power and class formation in Africa, but also on strategies of professionalization. Such an approach encourages attentiveness to emergent bureaucratic rationales, however partial or distorted these may be, in former colonial settings. Education systems have played a central role in facilitating access to the middle class strata, and in linking government to processes of class formation (Southall 2016). State accredited certification remains one of the most important mechanisms by which governments safeguard the professional sphere. It legitimizes barriers to entry, and ensures the protection of professional knowledge. Education is the key access point to the numerous work opportunities provided by large public administrations across Africa.[6] An anthropology of professionalism focuses attention on the institutional frameworks and social networks that enable people to gain accreditation and in various ways to embed themselves within protected spheres of labour.

Many anthropologists have noted the importance placed on formal education among Africa's aspiring middle classes. Despite the media attention paid to the flashy consumption habits of this group, the education of one's children is frequently prioritized over the purchase of high-status material possessions. As Deborah James shows, frugality is an important value that facilitates this longer term investment (2015: 40–41). Less attention has been paid to how these formal systems of professionalization are realized within education institutions and workplaces themselves. How are formal and informal networks and strategies of professionalization organized? How do they dovetail with aspirations and the life course beyond work?[7]

Some recent work in the anthropology of professionalism and expert knowledge begins to explore these questions. For instance, a volume edited by David Mosse (2011a), *Adventures in Aidland: The Anthropology of Professionals in International Developement,* sheds light on the day-to-day realities and dilemmas of international development professionals. The authors of the volume highlight the tensions experienced by aid workers, consultants and other development experts as they perform professionalism. Tasked with producing and maintaining the appearance of coherent, technical bodies of knowledge, they must also navigate the messy realities of their daily jobs. What emerges is that professionalism is created by the outward appearance of success more so than by the content of the work itself (Mosse 2011b: 18).[8] In health care, these performative aspects of professionalism are important. The uniforms worn by health practitioners, their use of specialized equipment, their writing practices and a wide array of verbal and bodily signifiers, all serve to demonstrate competency and to establish trust in professionals. Here, I turn attention, also, to how professional trajectories are not only about creating outward reputation but are intimately entwined with caring practices. This professional ethic is forged in relation both to historical processes and to concrete dilemmas at work. In this book, I pay attention to the labour and care entailed in forming aspirational and ethical selves in bureaucratic and work settings.

In what follows, I highlight two aspects of professionalism that are important for understanding changing configurations of work, governance and class formation in South Africa. First, drawing on

Weberian sociological work on professionalism, I address the significance of autonomy as a value that professionals hold dear. This has to do with the internal coherence of a profession and its desire to operate without interference by government, managers and so on. Autonomy is therefore an important conceptual link between professionalism and prevailing forms of governance. Second, I look to more recent literature on politics, citizenship and state building in South Africa, to consider how new values of citizenship are linked to a changing professional ethic.

The struggle for autonomy in the making of professions

Under neo-liberal regimes of audit and accountability, scholars have argued that the ability of professionals to operate autonomously is being eroded. This line of argument suggests that while the neo-liberal ideology of individualism conjures up the idea of a workplace devoid of hierarchy and driven by an ethic of personal responsibility, workplace regimes in fact introduce new mechanisms of control, giving rise to new tensions. Nikolas Rose writes that under new managerial regimes, for instance, accountability shifts to the financialized remit of management, and away from the professions (1999: 152). This creates a dynamic in which professionals are subordinate to management, and cannot operate autonomously. The literature on audit culture therefore identifies important changes in the status of the professions under neo-liberal governmentality.

However, when looking beyond studies of neo-liberalism to sociological debates on professionalism, the picture becomes more complicated. These discussions reveal that professional and managerial aims have long existed in tension. In his early study of professionalism, Weberian sociologist Talcott Parsons (1939) identified this paradoxical relationship of autonomy and dependency, which he saw as intrinsic to the professions. While the professions rely on government to legitimize their mandate through mechanisms such as state-sanctioned accreditation, he argued, their individualist desire for autonomy sat uncomfortably alongside the collectivist nature of bureaucracy.[9] For Eliot Freidson (1982), the license to operate professionally is first and foremost a license to operate *autonomously*. But despite the mechanisms in place to ring-fence professional spheres and ensure their exclusivity, the boundaries around professions are often porous.

Tensions between professional agendas and those of managers can produce highly skewed effects. Sociological literature on medicine in America showed that hospital administrators tended to prioritize status and reputation over the efficient use of resources, in order to attract professionals (Lee 1971).[10] Consider the story of the Mathibela twins at Baragwanath Hospital in Soweto, South Africa, as described by the historian, Simonne Horwitz (2013). In 1988, two-year-old Mpho and Mphonyana Mathibela, a pair of conjoined twins fused at the head, underwent a risky and highly sophisticated operation to surgically separate their bodies. The operation was hailed a success and quickly hit the headlines.

Behind the scenes, some employees were concerned that the operation represented a disproportionate channelling of scarce resources, while many more children could have benefited from simpler treatments. But from the perspective of gaining reputation, the hospital was basking in glory. Enthusiastically aided by the country's media, the hospital launched a huge public relations exercise, blotting out Baragwanath's image as a struggling government institution mopping up sickness in a Johannesburg slum. In the words of Robert Lipschitz, the leading neurosurgeon responsible for the operation, Baragwanath now became 'one of the only hospitals in Africa that is capable to do such an operation and can hold its own against any other in the world' (Horwitz 2013: 168–69). While the money might have served more closely the institutional aims of meeting the population's health-care needs, if spent on cheaper treatments, the hospital's new-found status would be essential for attracting highly skilled practitioners.

The story represents a struggle between providing efficient, cheap health care and attracting professionals. According to Horwitz, 'the operation was vital to the image of the hospital as one in which highly specialised care was available', thus raising the status of doctors and nurses themselves who were previously 'looked down on by their colleagues at white hospitals' (2013: 176). It was Lipschitz's professional expertise, displayed to the world through this landmark event, which elevated the hospital's status and drew more experts into its fold.[11]

The story demonstrates the entanglement of professional identity with institutional aims and implicitly – given that Baragwanath is a government institution – the state itself. The tensions between different kinds of institutional agendas, and the work involved by professionals in producing autonomy, are important themes in this book. Ethnographic attentiveness to the interpersonal, ethical and practical issues emerging in the daily activities of an institution means that professional and managerial practices are not as separate as have often been depicted in the literature. Boundaries are not predetermined, but are shaped, reproduced and diminished by shared projects of interpersonal ethics and care.

The story also highlights the need for historical specificity. In South Africa, the struggles for autonomy in the medical and nursing professions are closely tied to the history of Christianity, colonialism and state practices in the region. South African nursing originated in the mission hospitals of the late-nineteenth century, and was associated with religious training. Missions were crucial for facilitating upward mobility and professionalization for Africans. Missions also engaged in their own struggles for autonomy in the face of changing regimes of state governance. The concept of professionalism helps to situate nurses' contemporary experiences of workplace hierarchy and caring practices within these deeper historical processes of missionization and state formation.

In this book, I suggest that the creation of professional identity and autonomy can only be understood in the context of a historical frame wide enough to encompass these dynamics. The perceived secularization of the hospital – its transfer from mission to state control – is held partly responsible by nurses for what they believe to be declining levels of care in the democratic era. Linked to this, a focus on the precarious character of their claims to professionalism offers an important avenue for understanding the contingent nature of citizenship in post-apartheid South Africa.

Citizenship revisited

Hospitals are places in which regimes of governance are produced, normalized and challenged in various ways. Biomedicine has been an important terrain for exploring questions of citizenship in anthropology, a perspective influenced by Michel Foucault's seminal work on biopolitics. He observed that power operates at the microlevel in the daily production of subjectivities. In *The Birth of the Clinic* (1975), he showed that the medical 'gaze' objectifies disease, reducing the person to medicalized body. This biopolitical perspective allowed medical anthropology to interrogate the interconnectedness of embodied experience with regimes of knowledge, power and governance.[12] It equipped anthropology with a theoretical tool to challenge the hegemony of medical knowledge.

From within this Foucauldian tradition, the concept of biological citizenship has been important for highlighting the human biological condition as a locus of claims to citizenship. As Nikolas Rose and Carlos Novas write: 'Projects of biological citizenship in the nineteenth and twentieth century produced citizens who understood their nationality, allegiances and distinctions, at least in part, in biological terms' (2005: 441). Anthropology has taken up the idea, to show how biology is mobilized to make direct claims to citizenship and the material entitlements linked to it (Petryna 2003; Pienaar 2016). Briggs and Mantini Briggs (2003) use a related idea of 'sanitary citizens' to describe those deemed in possession of, and willing to act upon, correct knowledge about the practices of hygiene. By contrast, those failing to adhere to this knowledge become 'unsanitary subjects', and consequently undeserving of citizenship status.[13]

Many other recent ethnographic studies of hospitals are couched within this Foucauldian tradition, showing how medical settings and technologies reproduce spatialized regimes of care (Brown 2012; Sullivan 2012), the 'clinical gaze' (Gibson 2004) or the 'medical order' (Harper 2014), how bodies are rendered visible or invisible to the state (Street 2014), and how 'responsible citizenship' is produced through the myriad disciplining techniques to which hospital patients must conform (White, Hillman and Latimer 2012). In hospitals, citizenship and care are woven together as mutually justifying entitlements: 'The labor of dividing patients [according to categories of "good" and "bad"] … reproduces moral orders of good citizenship; those who transgress the order become undeserving of care' (White, Hillman and Latimer 2012: 73). Neo-liberal logics intersect with regimes of care to produce fragmented and morally charged outcomes.

The concept of biological citizenship offers a useful perspective not captured by earlier understandings of national citizenship. It provides a lens for grappling with the body as simultaneously a physical, social and political entity. However, the Foucauldian approach is both too narrow and too diffuse for understanding changing citizenship forms and inequalities of care under neo-liberalism in specific contexts. My focus is less on outward demands of citizenship that occur in direct conflict with a hegemonic biomedical ethic, and instead on more subtle affirmations of belonging entailed in the emergence of a professional ethic. These are informed by dense histories of colonialism, missionization and medicine, as well as by current constraints, obstacles and interpersonal relations at work. This allows us to conceptualize a wider terrain of citizenship formation as partial, restricted or contingent.

This has implications for anthropological approaches to the study of bureaucracies in neo-liberal settings. While bureaucracies are partly to be understood as technologies of governmentality, they are also sites of ethical production and contestation. Focusing on the creation of ethics and precarious citizenship, Laura Bear and Nayanika Mathur (2015) highlight the utopian aspirations encrypted in bureaucratic forms. They call for renewed attention to bureaucracies, not only as sites of structural violence, biopolitical discipline or hollowed expressions of market logic, but as forms of social action in which contested visions of the public good are played out. Developing this argument, I suggest that the making of professionalism as an aspirational and ethical project helps to widen the lens, focusing attention on bureaucracies not only as technologies that discipline bodies or legitimize states but as sites for the formation of collective ethical projects and the negotiation of contingent citizenship.

As various anthropologists have shown, neo-liberalism is not a monolithic project but a set of diverse and often piecemeal techniques (Ong 2006; Tsing 2005). Moreover, in its emergent forms around the world it is neither passively adopted nor 'resisted', but selectively mobilized and reinterpreted. This takes place in relation to ethical projects such as professionalism. This raises further questions about the relationship of apparently marginal places to dominant orthodoxies like neo-liberalism. At the turn of this century, Jean-François Bayart (2000) published a piercing critique of dependency theory, rejecting the myth of sub-Saharan Africa as occupying a peripheral space on the edge of the dominant global system. Africa is intricately linked in multiple webs of dependencies internally and externally, Bayart argued, but this insertion into the world economic system is managed actively and opportunistically, not passively. Rather than being simply imposed, democracy as a set of ideas and institutions is selectively appropriated.

Bayart's concept of 'extraversion' offers a more nuanced approach than the usual sterile dualisms of local/global or coercion/resistance. Extraversion refers to the process by which elites or other groups 'mobiliz[e] resources derived from their (possibly unequal) relationship with the external environment' (2000: 218). Power holders utilize external constraints and manipulate channels of influence by deploying key assets, whether political, financial, cultural or military. Discourses of democracy, for instance, have been an important source of economic rents for African elites. Moving beyond an understanding of democracy and neo-liberalism in Africa as the result of a process of diffusion, towards understanding it as a set of tools that are adopted opportunistically, has important implications for understanding its uneven emergence in the South African case. Extraversion is a useful tool for understanding collective and individual strategies by citizens, bureaucrats, professionals, institutions and governments.

This book reframes the question of citizenship in the context of the multiple articulations of middle-class aspiration. In South Africa, citizenship and work have long been interlinked. During apartheid, the colour bar prevented black people from achieving full status as citizens, vis-à-vis their white counterparts. In a detailed discussion of the contested field of social citizenship in South Africa today, Franco Barchiesi (2011) maps out this historical trajectory, showing how income security became indelibly linked to social citizenship. Due to the ways in which black people were denied work opportunities during apartheid, wage labour came to be viewed as a crucial signifier of dignified citizenship. The promise of work for all became a central pillar of the 1955 Freedom Charter. Political liberation offered the restoration of human dignity through the creation of waged employment for all, with work becoming 'coterminous with hope and fulfillment' (Barchiesi 2011: 23). After 1994, Barchiesi shows, work became the new foundation of ethical democratic citizenship. However, given a situation of entrenched unemployment, growing casualization and low wages, the 'work–citizenship' nexus proclaimed by the ANC has failed to offer the freedom it once promised.

In the post-apartheid workplace, Barchiesi suggests, the ideology of citizenship is one that demands loyalty to the nation, regardless of poor working conditions and wages that often keep workers in poverty. I extend this argument by suggesting that professionalism has historically played a similar role. As we will see in the next section, those occupying elite positions have insisted on the unified allegiance of all its members to the profession, above all other concerns. Given the similar, normative underpinnings of these terms, the task in this book is to understand how citizenship narratives intervene in the formation of professional identity, and vice versa. How might older affiliations intersect with more recent subjectivities, and inform how changing social conditions come to be interpreted? How does the professional ethic among nurses – shaped by a history of mission medicine in the region and by more recent changes to forms of new public management in the post-apartheid regime – inform processes of state building and experiences of citizenship and belonging?

Addressing the intersections of professionalism and citizenship requires ethnographic attention to the making of professional ethics within the situated, daily constraints of the contemporary workplace. For instance, a mantra that I heard on countless occasions while carrying out research among nurses was that while patients enjoyed rights under the new democratic dispensation, nurses themselves had no rights. Such comments were frequently accompanied with expressions of fear relating to issues of job security, audit and the apparently unreasonable demands made by senior nurses, doctors or managers.

These remarks, I came to realize, referenced two interconnected processes. First, they highlighted the insecurity of formal work itself in the post-apartheid period, as a contingent source of livelihood. New regimes of audit and accountability instilled feelings of uncertainty about work. Drawing on Paul Starr's distinction, these signalled a wider project of managerial authority in post-apartheid South Africa, whereby the overt political coercion of the late-apartheid period gave way, after 1994, to managerial authority as the dominant mode of governance. Political coercion, Starr suggests, is underpinned by the threat of violence or imprisonment, while managerial authority rests on the threat of dismissal (1982: 9).

Second, nurses' disgruntlement about the rights enjoyed by patients, seemingly in competition with their own, more limited entitlements, suggests that a new moral terrain of citizenship is dislodging the previous, taken-for-granted hierarchies that the nurses enjoyed as professionals. A more inclusive version of citizenship, not contained by the work–citizenship nexus, is signalled by the idea of patient rights. This brings into play a logic that contrasts with the draconian system of superiors and inferiors that have long structured the allocation of work in the hospital setting. It also represents new kinds of restrictions on what citizenship denotes.

Professionalism is a useful point of departure for thinking about the relationship between class formation, citizenship and state building. The nurses' fraught experience as aspiring professionals makes their relationship to government, and therefore their status as citizens, tenuous.[14] Here, I find Michael Neocosmos's conception of citizenship useful. He suggests that 'citizenship does not simply refer to a relationship which is given (bounded or fluid), by the state or by social relations, but to one which can also be passive, active or any shade in between, depending on circumstances' (2010: 139). Citizenship is not conferred automatically but must be actively claimed. However, whereas approaches to biological citizenship have focused on the direct claims that people make in order to secure their entitlements, I focus less on outward demands of citizenship, and instead on a range of more implicit renegotiations about the meanings of citizenship. This involves attentiveness to everyday, routinized practices and the tensions that these entail. Jean Comaroff writes that 'while most human beings continue to live *in* nation-states, they tend to be only conditionally citizens *of* nation-states' (2009: 25, emphasis in the original). In this book, I explore the nature of this contingency. A focus on professional identity – which is also, like citizenship itself, insecure rather than fixed – provides an important vantage point for considering the relationship of people to an ever emerging state formation, and therefore to the conditions of citizenship in contemporary South Africa.

Status and respectability in the South African nursing profession

In the 1950s and 1960s, before Marxist approaches came to dominate South African scholarship, anthropologists were documenting the experiences of a growing number of African 'bourgeoisie'

(Brett 1963; L. Kuper 1965; Wilson and Mafeje 1963). What they revealed was a group deeply preoccupied with maintaining status vis-à -vis their working-class neighbours. This was achieved by modes of consumption such as clothing, and by attending clubs and other elite social spaces. Concerned to separate themselves from wider black society rather than to consider themselves part of it, they would often lack interest in politics, viewing themselves as 'fence-sitters' (Brandel-Syrier 1978). In a setting where many professions employing such elites were male-dominated, the situation of nurses stood out as an exception (Cheater 1972; 1974; H. Kuper 1965;). Nursing was the quintessential high-status career for educated black women. The following description by Hilda Kuper throws light on the social milieu of nurses at the time:

> Many nurses dress smartly, wear high heels, straighten their hair, and glamorize their appearance. It is considered not becoming for a nurse to drink excessively, smoke in public, use obscene language, fight or shout in the street. Her recreational activities include tennis, ballroom dancing, parties, cinemas, and the reading of women's magazines. The training in nursing is also a training in urban sophistication. (1965: 227)

Marriage patterns also suggested that nurses were highly sought-after partners (Cheater 1972). But nurses, like other aspiring middle-class black people, quickly discovered the limitations of upward mobility due to the layers of social, symbolic and legal discrimination imposed on them by the racist apartheid regime. While conspicuous consumption may have achieved for these 'African bourgeoisie', some minor degree of compensation for the economic limitations forced upon them by the regime (Cobley 1990), ultimately they found themselves marginalized and sidelined along with other black South Africans. As Hilda Kuper writes, the nursing profession brought African women 'past the threshold of Western knowledge, but shut … the door of equality in their faces' (1965: 217). Mounting frustration led to struggle and politicization, a transition that is reflected in the literature by a shift of emphasis between the 1970s and 1990s. By the late 1990s, June Webber (2000) would describe the nurses in King Edward VIII Hospital in Durban as a politically volatile, exploited and proletarianized class. The contrast with the earlier depictions of nurses by Hilda Kuper (1965) and Angela Cheater (1972; 1974) as urban aspirational elites is striking.

These two extremely contrasting depictions of the South African nurses are products of the time in which the studies were written. They represent two opposing stereotypes of the nurses in the popular imagination that seem to be incommensurable. The complicated historical underpinnings of and connections between these two types of representation was carefully brought to light in Shula Marks's detailed history of the profession, *Divided Sisterhood: Race Class and Gender in the South African Nursing Profession*. Its publication in 1994 coincided in the same year with the publication of two other seminal works on labour in South Africa (Harries 1994; Moodie 1994). What was distinctive about all three of these studies was the ways in which they dealt with the interactions between culture, race and class. While they remained rooted in a materialist tradition, the three studies were crucial in forging a link to the Weberian approaches of the 1950s and 1960s, recognizing that the economic determinism of earlier neo-Marxist approaches was insufficiently nuanced to explain the contradictory identities, political outcomes or historical processes of South Africa at the end of apartheid. As promised by the title, Marks describes the conflicting intersections of race, class and gender, revealing that nurses occupied a precarious position on all the major fault lines of South Africa's divided society. She also traces the drive for professionalism, which runs as a thread throughout her account. Let me briefly explain some of the key elements of this history, before I turn to the setting for this book.

The strong moral discourses that have frequently characterized debates within the nursing profession have their roots in Christian values of respectability dating back to the establishment of modern nursing in South Africa. Western forms of medicine and nursing were initiated by British missionaries in the late-nineteenth century, partly in response to spiralling levels of ill health induced by the terrible working and living conditions in the towns and settlements that sprung up following the discovery of minerals in the 1870s. As well as forming a response to an increasingly chaotic and sickly industrial landscape, the expansion of medicine was also an ideological tool paired closely with the racist and moralizing agenda of the colonial project. Nurse training was to become an important terrain upon which these ideological narratives would play out.

Gender stereotypes played an important role in this. At the outset, in the 1870s and 1880s, nursing was dominated primarily by English women who migrated to South Africa to fulfil the higher demands of health care brought about by industrial change. With them, they brought the image of the 'lady nurse', which embedded ideas about caring as intrinsically linked with femininity and moral duty: 'Not only would the sisterhood provide nursing care; their purity and devotion would provide the necessary moral example' (Marks 1994: 25). The idea of the nurturing female role, a quintessential aspect of nursing, was reinforced by propaganda from the colonial government that, drawing on these images, insisted on the God-given duty of all women to provide care. These values – which supported a broader colonial strategy of labour management – were accompanied by a notion of social elegance and superiority, themes that continued to be drawn upon in nurses' struggles for professional status throughout the twentieth century.

The superior status and cultural refinement associated with these nurses made a powerful imprint on the image of the profession in South Africa, as it did in Britain, and rendered nursing an alluring option for many South African women, both black and white, from the early decades of the twentieth century. Superior mission education ensured that nurses, from the beginning, gained access to the privileged status that set them apart from the wider black population. They came to represent the desired transition from 'superstitious' traditional beliefs to 'civilized' modes of being. As Marks writes, black nurses that were trained in the early years of the twentieth century constituted the ideal colonial subject: they were 'harbingers of progress and healing in black society, a shining light in the midst of its savagery and disease' (1994: 78).

In her book about the history of black nursing in South Africa, Grace Mashaba (1995), a prominent nurse educator and academic, focuses her attention on how black nurses have 'scaled the heights' of academia and achieved a level of professional success comparable to that of their white colleagues. Given this central aim of showcasing the successes of black nurses, Mashaba's book is less concerned with the structural dimensions that held them back or that placed them at a disadvantage, although passing mention is made of such factors (ibid.: 49). But as Robert Dingwall notes in the British context, the creation of professions was as much a way of preserving the class interests of certain groups as it was about creating opportunity. Professional accreditation was crucial for sealing off areas of the labour market for exclusive access (Dingwall 2008: 80). In South Africa, this process assumed an insidious racial character. Over time the achievement of professional status became intimately entwined with ideologies of white superiority attached to particular modes of consumption, comportment and lifestyle. While black nurses were undoubtedly attracted to the respectable standing offered by their profession, they simultaneously found themselves precariously positioned within a profession dominated by the racist and discriminatory practices of a white elite, deeply concerned with the advancement of their own professional status (Marks 1994).

Tensions were exacerbated by the precarious nature of nursing's claims to professionalism, not only in South Africa but also globally. To understand this, it is necessary to consider its gendered roots. Nursing and medicine have traditionally been characterized by a stark division whereby nursing, a predominantly female occupation, developed in subordination to the male-dominated world of medicine. Florence Nightingale, founder and heroine of modern nursing, expressed this distinction as willing subordination when she said: 'We nurses are and never will be anything but the servants of doctors and good faithful servants we should be, happy in our dependence which helps to accomplish great deeds' (quoted in Gamarnikow 1978: 107). Prophetic though the intention of this statement was, the women who took up the mantle after Nightingale were not so ready to accept their subordinate role. As the twentieth century wore on, nursing developed an intense preoccupation with justifying its professional reputation as 'separate from, but equal to, medicine' (Rispel and Schneider 1991: 111; see also, Coburn 1988; Forsyth 1995; Levi 1980). In doing so, however, it faced a dilemma. How could it reconcile the technical, academic identity to which it aspired with the quintessentially feminine values of care and purity upon which the moral identity of nursing so heavily relied? Moreover, how could the demands of a rapidly growing population in need of hands-on care, which could only be fulfilled by the repetitive and banal tasks of cleaning and feeding, be met by nurses without foregoing their reputation as skilled practitioners and academics?

In the United Kingdom, South Africa and elsewhere, the answer was to be found in the creation of a formidable system of stratification. Those occupying the higher rungs of the profession carved out exclusive roles that protected them from the degrading associations of nursing with unskilled (domestic) labour – tasks which were to be carried out by the inferior and lesser qualified categories of nurses. Systems of training and accreditation became one of the key mechanisms for ensuring that these hierarchies became institutionalized and reproduced. Through them, nursing became enmeshed with the workings of the state, as government powers to issue formal professional accreditation became a tool to safeguard the interests of the professionalizers (Dingwall, Rafferty and Webster 1988).

In South Africa, as Marks shows, these institutionalized divisions assumed an insidious racial character, in addition to the class-based stratification that emerged in tandem with those elsewhere. In the early years of apartheid, the protection of white jobs was consolidated through a range of labour policies such as the notorious 'colour bar' that legally prevented black people from acquiring certain positions. Education was provided unequally, and systems of formal accreditation operated to preserve the interests of white elites. This became a central feature of apartheid social engineering during the first decade of National Party rule. The Urban Areas Act of 1952, the Bantu Education Act of 1953, and a raft of legislation ensuring job reservation for whites in 1956 and 1959, in various ways, all entrenched labour differentiation within and between racial groups.

It was during these same years that nursing became newly enmeshed in the workings of the state. An initial desire from some sectors of the profession to exclude black women altogether had long been abandoned due to the increasing levels of ill health and demands for health care, a pressure that had gathered pace in the 1940s. By the 1950s, although nursing across the country was increasingly carried out by black women, nursing was by this point controlled by an Afrikaner-dominated bureaucracy which, as Marks shows, was determined to safeguard its own elite interests (1993: 343). The Nursing Act of 1957 legislatively consolidated the entrenchment of apartheid racial ideology in the profession (ibid: 342). In the meantime, many mission hospitals continued to operate with relative autonomy, where a softer racial paternalism persisted for longer, as opposed to the harsh and dispassionate 'racial modernism' of high apartheid (Bozzoli 2004: 50–51).

In the later apartheid years, South Africa's political situation quickly unravelled. Nursing strikes were made illegal. The image of unity expressed by the proponents of professionalization became increasingly strained by the actual experience of most nurses in South Africa. This was characterized by a lack of control and autonomy, a fragmentation of tasks and therefore a deskilling of individuals that has produced increasing stratification. This downgrading of a significant proportion of nurses, for the most part, failed to result in organized resistance because, it was argued, the ideology of professionalism, serving as a kind of hegemony, asserted that 'every level of the hierarchy is united in solidarity and defence of the nursing profession' (Rispel and Schneider 1991: 119), despite the growing disparity of wages and in working conditions between nurses at different levels (Webber 2000). These themes resurfaced in nurses' responses to the recent strikes. As we saw in the opening section, they emphasized the moral deterioration of the profession, the lack of 'respect', 'dignity' and 'self-discipline' that is seen to characterize the profession in contrast to an earlier period. As the work of Marks and others reveals, these fears have a much longer trajectory in South Africa's nursing history, even if they are imagined as having only recently emerged. They signal a deep-seated preoccupation with preserving professional identity, regardless of the divisions that separate them.

The peculiar complexities arising from the intersections of class and race in South Africa meant that throughout the development of the nursing profession, the emergence of an elite African 'respectable' group occurred alongside a persistent downgrading of black nurses *within* the professional hierarchy. Nursing entered the democratic era on very shaky ground. With growing bureaucratic demands and continued efforts to preserve the status of the occupation, it was facing 'a major crisis of identity', in the words of one senior nursing professor (Marks 1994: 14). In the meantime, the pressures placed upon it would soon grow exponentially as South Africa plunged into a devastating HIV/AIDS epidemic.

In 1994, the newly elected ANC inherited a weak health-care infrastructure, characterized by excessive public spending on tertiary hospitals rather than in primary health care, and by the directing of a disproportionate amount of funds at a minority via the large and poorly regulated private sector (Schneider and Gilson 1999). Rural areas in particular bore the legacy of the worst extremes of apartheid inequalities. The government embarked upon an ambitious programme to restructure the health system. In an effort to overcome the dysfunctional, overbearing bureaucracy and the deeply inequitable distribution of public funds administered under apartheid, the government was quick to define a radically different approach, embracing the prevailing international neo-liberal model. In doing so, it promised greater efficiency, financial prudence, and public accountability, affirming a vision of South Africa as a newly democratic society within a modernizing global system.

One of the ways in which the ANC consolidated its position at the helm of the ship was to ensure the growth of a stable middle class. Government institutions were restructured partly with this aim in mind (Southall 2004; 2016), a process that has been widely associated with the entrenchment of corruption as people used state positions to pursue private accumulation. In health care, Karl von Holdt (2010) argues that the use of health-care institutions for ensuring upward mobility often acts as a barrier to effective health-care provision. The infrastructure of service delivery, he suggests, is first and foremost a tool yielded by elites to consolidate their access to professional jobs and salaries at the expense of health-care users, thus undermining democratic accountability and rights. Across the country, the new petty bourgeoisie is taking shape in the form of local councillors (Hart 2014: 149). But what about those joining the lower ranks of government services? Can formal sector employment meet their aspirations? In nursing, an ageing workforce strongly points to a growing failure of the profession to attract new students, complicating the picture painted by some scholars of formal sector work as unambiguously desirable.[15] Has the democratic transition facilitated upward mobility, as promised? How have the politics of liberal democracy affected a system of workplace stratification already firmly in place?

About the book

The book is concerned with the reconfiguration of status and profes-sionalism, and processes of moral self-fashioning, among nurses, at work and in the wider social and political context of post-apartheid South Africa. Specifically, it provides a historical ethnographic account of the views and activities of nurses working in a rural gov-ernment hospital in northern KwaZulu-Natal. I look particularly at how nurses respond to, and negotiate their positions in relation to, changes in health-care systems and the wider debates of post-apartheid public discourse. Much of the literature suggests that it is the squeeze on resources that accounts for why there is regular recourse within health delivery settings to seemingly old-fashioned, draconian systems of hierarchy. In this book, I agree that resource shortages are a crucial constraint in the continued reproduction of workplace hierarchies. But rather than attributing this to 'lack of capacity building' and other shortfalls of 'good governance', I argue that the situation can only be understood through a lens which is wide enough to encompass the histories of Christianity, colonialism and apartheid in South Africa. I attempt to uncover the deeper processes at play that create and recreate situations of individual, institutional and political constraint.

This book is neither an acclamation nor a critique of the hospital and its staff. It does not expose wrongdoings in the hospital nor make assessments about the competency of staff or the quality of care provided, beyond relaying the comments and opinions of the people who participated in the research and wished for their views to be included. It is intended, instead, to provide a deeper analysis, both historical and ethnographic, that sheds light on nurses' experiences of the contemporary workplace. It reflects on their perceptions of their roles and aspirations in the context of a society in flux. I use the example of nurses to describe the intersections between processes of post-apartheid state building and the formation of lower middle-class aspirations. The book is focused upon the particular locale of an institutional workplace but is not confined to this; it is concerned fundamentally with the relationship of that workplace to a wider set of regional, national and global processes. The book, therefore, is not an ethnography of an institution. Rather, the hospital and its surrounding area serve as the context for an ethnographic investigation specifically of nurses, their changing experiences of work, and what this might tell us about their position as contingent citizens in post-apartheid South Africa. I focus on bureaucratic procedures only to the extent that I encountered them in my observations and conversations with nurses.

In the book, I use pseudonyms for all nurses. For junior nurses, who were often my peers, I use first names. When referring to those in more senior professional roles, I mostly use the title 'Sister' followed by a pseudonymous surname. I have chosen to make this distinction because it is in keeping with the choice of language

I used during fieldwork. In some cases, I have changed arbitrary details about my interlocutors in order to ensure anonymity. I have omitted data about the work context that would clearly expose the identity of nurses, and have excluded various conversations and observations for the same reason. All of this data, however, form the basis for the arguments presented here.

The geographical and historical context for the research is provided in Chapter One. Here, I begin to map out the contours of autonomy and control that shape experiences of professional identity, which are shaped by both temporal and spatial dynamics. I provide some insight into the research process, and reflect particularly on the implications of producing anthropological knowledge in a setting characterized by an emerging culture of audit. I also include here an explanation of the structures of training and formal stratification, and how these are changing in relation to debates about professionalization.

In Chapter Two, I describe the contemporary experience of nurses as one of insecurity in a context in which formerly taken-for-granted hierarchies are loosening, and in which a growing preoccupation with patient rights generates fears of culpability for wrongdoing. The concern that patients might utilize complaints procedures in order to generate financial gain echoes the uneasy form assumed by democratic idioms in South Africa today, and especially in former homelands, where economic and moral spheres are frequently entwined.[16] Although nursing remains a high-status occupation, nurses express ambivalence about it in relation to other activities, which they view as more lucrative and less rule-bound. With nursing and teaching no longer the exclusive routes to professionalism for black women, the status of the professional is challenged both from inside and outside the workplace.

In Chapter Three, I describe the lead up to the democratic transition. This provides the historical context for present day nostalgia that is widely felt among older nurses, which is often interpreted in terms of a decline of religion. Founded by Edinburgh-trained doctor, Robert Turner, in 1937, the hospital was run by the missionary society of the Methodist Church of South Africa until its takeover by the government forty-five years later in 1982. In the hospital's final years under Methodist control, missionaries drew on a shift in international focus towards primary health care, enabling a reinvigoration of the original aims and ideologies of the mission even as imminent government takeover loomed large. I argue that while the hospital was nominally governed by the KwaZulu homeland government between 1982 and 1994, nurses and doctors experienced considerable autonomy, which informed later experiences of healthcare restructuring. Closely resembling, but not entirely explained by, a Weberian shift from patrimonial to bureaucratic authority, this history is important for understanding the nurses' interpretation of current events. In this chapter, I depart from an earlier dominant narrative about homeland rule simply as tyrannical and oppressive. I offer a more nuanced perspective, identifying moments of cooperation, optimism or perceived progress, as a consequence of the relative autonomy and increase of funds achieved by the hospital during those years.

While processes of bureaucratization were well under way by 1994 in large urban hospitals, at Bethesda the significant moment came after the inception of ANC rule, when the homelands were disbanded and health services in rural areas underwent major restructuring. Moving into the contemporary period, in Chapter Four, I look at how discourses of accountability take shape in the ward context, and how these affect the behaviour of nurses at work. I consider how projects of care and professionalism are built alongside the creation of new practices of audit and managerialism. I draw a comparison between the paperwork practices of the hospital with those of South Africa's border control agencies, to suggest that citizenship is both demarcated and rendered contingent by these documentary practices. Religion emerges from this secularized institutional setting as a source both of nostalgia and of renewed moral concern.

Chapter Five explores why nurses blame 'democracy' itself for a perceived decline in care in recent years. I examine how these narratives dovetail with and influence hierarchical relationships at work. Here I develop the theme of secularization and its significance at Bethesda and in the nursing profession. I consider ways in which the nurses' memories of the hospital's missionary past are constructed and creatively deployed in the contemporary production of moral discourses relating to work. This discussion is foregrounded (as is the book as a whole), by the profound feelings of moral and professional discomfort and sense of disorder felt by nurses, compounded by high workload and the severity of ill health in the region. I argue that religion and the secular are important signifiers of wider processes. An ongoing social commentary about the relationship of the hospital to its missionary past and a perceived 'secularization' of the institution informs contemporary issues of workplace hierarchy, professionalism and ethics.

While earlier sections of the book deal with the historical trajectory of the hospital and with idealized notions of the past, Chapter Six emphasizes nurses' hopes and aspirations that are projected into an imagined future. International migration offers new and powerful forms of status acquisition beyond the post-apartheid workplace, while born-again Christianity offers renewed moral purpose within it. While narratives that bemoan the decline of religion challenge ideas of democratic liberalism on their own terms, I argue, born-again faith offers a critique formed from an ontologically alternative position. I suggest that religious practices and migration constitute different ways of grappling with the hegemonic discourses of state building in the workplace. Albeit dependent on the state for their livelihoods, nurses are engaged in the creation of new modes of action and citizenship that either compete with, or reclaim, the workplace as the dominant site of belonging, status and worth. I argue that professionalism is a necessary, but insufficient route to middle-class status.

In the Conclusion, I draw together the various strands of argument, reconsidering what it means to be aspirational during precarious times. A flexible concept of citizenship is needed to understand how nurses' narratives and experiences both challenge and feed back into hegemonic state processes. I reflect on what the example of South African nursing offers our understanding of the intertwined projects of accumulation and care among the middle classes globally. For lower-middle-class South Africans, life is precarious. But despite the pressures they face, nurses are seeking new ways of asserting claims to citizenship.

CHAPTER ONE

Geographies of Autonomy

Bethesda Hospital sits at the top of one of the southernmost mountains of the Lebombo range. It is located in the village of Ubombo, an eighteen-kilometre drive from the town of Mkuze that lies at the foothill of the mountain. Behind it, one looks out across a large plain stretching as far as the Indian Ocean to the east, which is just visible on a clear day. The hospital is connected to KwaZulu-Natal's major transport infrastructure, with the national N2 road running through Mkuze, reaching the town of Pongola and continuing into the province of Mpumalanga and eventually Johannesburg to the west, while to the south it runs parallel to the coastline through the large peri-urban centres of Richards Bay and Empangeni, until it reaches the city of Durban some 350 kilometres away. To the northwest of Ubombo, beyond the large Pongolapoort Dam, lies the national border between South Africa and Swaziland, and due north of Ubombo, a little further, is situated South Africa's border with Mozambique.

There is a steep stretch along the winding road that travels up the bush covered mountainside from Mkuze to Ubombo which is known locally as *shaya indoda* – 'beating/killing of men' – a name that residents believe refers to the slaying of men on this mountainside during the battles that raged between the English and the Zulu. Now the name warns of current danger: many car accidents have occurred on the precarious hairpin bend that appears unexpectedly on the road's descent. An adjacent, distinctively shaped peak is called Ghost Mountain, a reference to the graves that are thought to have been located there, the burial place of many Zulu men killed in war. Their ghosts are said to dwell on the abandoned mountainside, where lights flicker mysteriously at night. The hilly regions surrounding the hospital, located in the former KwaZulu bantustan, are dotted with homes, which form a fairly densely populated catchment area of over 90,000 people spread across an area of 1,500 square kilometres.

The road beyond *shaya indoda*, rebuilt with tarmac about fifteen years ago, continues to wind its way up the mountainside, reaching the hospital on its right-hand side after a sharp bend to the left. A short distance beyond the hospital, it leads to the police station and magistrates' court at the mountain peak, just before the tarmac reaches an abrupt end, and the dusty road continues along and back down the other side of the mountain into the low veld below – a flat plain stretching out between the mountains and the sea. The unfinished road is a reminder of the incomplete state of service delivery in the area, exaggerated by local hearsay claiming that a government bureaucrat pocketed the money allocated for the completion of the road.

The hospital covers an area of about 500 metres by 200 metres, and is separated from its surroundings by a tall perimeter fence. Its developed infrastructure of solid, brick buildings with electricity and water supplies distinguishes it from the surrounding area. On the frequent occasions of electricity blackouts, usually coinciding with heavy rains, the hospital's own internal reserve generator is automatically switched on and can be heard from some distance away. These visible and audible imprints on the landscape indicate a concentration of resources, setting it apart from an area otherwise devoid of such features. Opposite its entrance is a row of several shops, including a general food and clothes stall, a petrol pump and small bar, outside which are often seen several men sitting and drinking beer. Others mill around, waiting for the buses and minibus taxis that shuttle people up and down the mountainside. Slightly further, an expensive bed and breakfast set back in a wood-circled clearing attracts a trickle of tourists to the area. Along the side of the hospital, lining its tall wire fence, is a row of smaller stands where women sell fruit, vegetables and sweets. There are several churches nearby, including the small Methodist mission, which has close historical links with the hospital.[1]

In this chapter, I trace the historical and political contours of the region, and the hospital's place within it. It is well known that the remoteness of such areas from cities contributed to their political and economic marginality; today, it remains one of the poorest regions in the country. In this chapter I describe how its peripherality was also characterized by various claims to autonomy. In the nineteenth century the area was one of the last to be missionized due to the strength of the Zulu polity that was located there. In the twentieth century, the wider region of Zululand would become the heartland of Zulu ethnic nationalism. Later, the mission hospital of Bethesda was the last in the country to be taken over by government. I argue that the experiences not only of marginality but also of autonomy are important for understanding nurses' nostalgic reflections on earlier times. These also influence their experience of professionalism – an ideology also deeply concerned with questions of autonomy.

A magistracy was first established in Ubombo in 1892, just prior to when the area – then known to the British as 'Amatongaland' – was put under British protection, prior to its annexation to Zululand.[2] In 1927, it was constituted as a full magistracy and transferred to the control of the Department of Native Affairs.[3] The name 'Ubombo', which then referred to an administrative area, is now used colloquially to denote this region. The Zulu word for the area is 'Obonjeni', meaning 'on the big nose' (referring to the mountain ridge).

The idea for a hospital in this remote area of Maputaland was proposed in the mid-1930s by a mission doctor, George Gale, who was working at the Tugela Ferry Mission Hospital further south at Msinga in Natal. Gale was a well-known figure, later taking up the position of South Africa's secretary of health in 1946, where he would pursue the progressive community health ideas of mission work, albeit temporarily, in the heart of government (see Chapter 3). He appealed to Scottish philanthropist Lord Maclay, who agreed to provide the initial costs for a hospital at Gale's chosen site of Ubombo. The Methodist Church took on the project and Gale recommended Edinburgh-trained mission doctor, Robert Turner, to set it up. After meeting Lord Maclay and receiving his approval, Turner took up the post of district surgeon in the village of Ubombo in 1937 (Gelfand 1984: 214–15). This was a government position, indicative of the collaboration between mission and state from the very beginning of the project.

When Turner arrived in October that year with his wife, Lena, and their two young daughters, they had to travel the last arduous stretch of a three-day journey from Durban, up the dirt track to the home of the local magistrate at the mountain peak. The magistrate showed them to the only available accommodation in the mountaintop village: a 'shack' of two rooms, 'running with rats and cockroaches'. A nearby sweet potato field on six-and-a-half acres of government-owned land was soon to become the site of the new hospital. Lord Maclay donated £2,500 towards the initial building costs, and the project was to be managed by the missionary arm of the church: the Zululand and Maputaland missions of the South African Methodist Church.

This small mission hospital was quickly drawn into a wider government system of health care and labour control. With government support, in the context of declining health and the threat of communicable diseases such as tuberculosis, the hospital grew quickly.

Uneasy dependence between mission and state

In the middle decades of the twentieth century, in a climate of declining colonial power, missionaries experienced increasing antagonism from governments around the world, writes David Hardiman. Mission hospitals throughout China, India and Africa were closing down or being taken over so that, by the 1960s, their 'reputation as a beacon for health care in poor countries … was in crisis' (2009: 219). The additional burdens of financial constraints and rapidly changing approaches to health care meant that the churches were forced seriously to reconsider their role: 'It was seen that the much ill health in mission regions was caused by poverty, malnutrition, poor sanitation, a lack of education and social deprivation. Hospitals could hardly provide a solution to these multiple problems' (ibid.: 220). Many missionary branches were realizing the necessity to divert their efforts away from medicine to other pursuits.

It is interesting, then, that Bethesda Hospital was established just at the moment that mission medicine in general was in decline. Some forty-five years later, in 1982, it was the last mission hospital in South Africa to be taken over by the government.[4] However, mission and government formed overlapping modes of governance from the outset. When Bethesda Hospital was established, it was immediately incorporated into a wider political economy of health-care provision that, from the beginning, meant it was entwined closely with the workings of the state. The government's interests in rural health care in the 1940s was prompted by growing unrest and the spread of infectious diseases. Expansion in the mining and industrial centres had brought about rapid industrialization, while the labour migration system became increasingly entrenched and the government's segregationist agendas consolidated. Poor health in the reserves was closely linked to a deteriorating rural economy as malnutrition, and TB and other infectious diseases – virtually unknown prior to colonial expansion – became increasingly wide-spread. In Zululand, the additional scourge of malaria compounded these problems (Marks and Andersson [1983] 1992; Packard 1989). Efforts at salvaging the reserves through 'betterment' schemes largely failed, and worse yet served to increase political tensions between peasants and chiefs.

By the mid-1940s maize production was at a minimum, and periodic droughts and floods compounded agricultural instability. Increasing political pressure and the need for a sustained workforce eventually compelled the government to turn its attention to the scale of African ill health. In rural areas, otherwise lacking in any form of health-care provision, the government acted to co-opt a growing network of mission hospitals to address health needs. In the hospital's opening ceremony on 4 July 1940, Mr H. C. Lugg, the chief native commissioner, expressed 'the deep and practical interest of his Department in the plans of the Church for medical mission-ary work'.[5] As this quote suggests, the presence of Mr Lugg was not simply ceremonial, but, from the very outset, marked a close involvement of the Department of Health with Bethesda Hospital.

This involvement, driven by the crisis of the 1940s, was reflected in the speed of government-funded growth at Bethesda. When Robert Turner began his medical work in Ubombo, his wife Lena, herself a trained nurse, was his only assistant. They soon employed an African nurse, trained at McCord Mission Hospital in Durban. Mission funds were used to build the initial infrastructure, which by 1940 consisted of a 14-bed ward, 3 rondavels, 6 cubicles, an operat-ing theatre and the doctor's house (Gelfand 1984: 214). Soon after, the Chief Native Commissioner's remarks were quickly transformed into action. Within a year of the hospital's opening, the Department of Native Affairs made a grant of £300 towards the cost of a nurses' home, while the Department of Public Health began providing a regular grant for the treatment of infectious cases. Throughout the 1940s, with increasing reliance on state funding, the hospital grew rapidly. The total number of patient days[6] rose from 2,833 between June 1940 and June 1941, to 17,565 between June 1947 and June 1948.

For the duration of its existence as a mission hospital, between 1937 and government takeover in 1982, Bethesda served as a conduit for state funds. Despite the antagonism that emerges in the hospital's archives, which draw a sharp ideological line between the hospital and the institutions of the state, Bethesda Hospital operated not outside of the state, but integral to, and within, it. Paradoxically, then, nurses and doctors experienced feelings both of isolation as well as suffocation by the administrative demands made upon them by various branches of government. While their work was dependent on state funds and being unable to function without them, they were also cut off from apartheid's white-dwelling metropoles that benefited disproportionately from access to state resources.

Much of the area surrounding Bethesda later formed part of the KwaZulu homeland, one of the nominally semi-independent homelands set up by the apartheid government in the 1970s, formed out of various and separate pieces of territory including parts of Zululand and Maputaland. From April 1972, the magistracy of Ubombo became an office of the KwaZulu government service, with Ubombo nested inside the then newly demarcated homeland boundary. The creation of homelands was a policy intended, in part, to generate legitimacy for the apartheid state by appearing to support ethnic political self-determination. Part of the government agenda, at least in rhetoric, entailed supporting and funding institutions of welfare and industry that would enable the homelands to develop self-sufficiency. As part of this agenda, the government began its takeover of mission hospitals in these areas in 1973, mostly with the assent of the missions because of the severe financial difficulties they faced. Bethesda Hospital was taken over by the government in 1982, and transferred to the control of the KwaZulu homeland government.

These descriptions undoubtedly give the impression of a region gripped by various, entangled forces all vying for control: those of successive colonial, apartheid and homeland governments, missionaries, traders, Zulu ethnic nationalists and more recent government forces have all engaged in power struggles over the past century. Paradoxically, the area is also one that has been powerfully shaped by political claims to autonomy. This has partly to do with its remote geography. It was one of the last in the region to succumb to missionization, even while areas further south were firmly established as mission strongholds. Later, its Methodist-run hospital was the very last to be subsumed by the state. Over the period of transition to democratic rule, a former doctor described how the staff would ignore instructions from the newly formed provincial Department of Health. 'We did things differently,' he said. For instance, the four hospitals in the region would meet every six months of their own accord. One administrator in the provincial office jokingly called them the 'Four Northern Rebels'. The doctor bemoaned the gradual domination of the hospital by its growing administrative wing. This was the last straw, he explained, leading to his departure.

This geography of autonomy and control is important for understanding experiences of professionalism among nurses in this former homeland region. James Ferguson and Akhil Gupta (2002) have suggested that one of the defining features of the state as an imagined entity is its perceived spatial separation from, and position 'above', local contexts. In this book, I will argue that the particular historical and geographical configurations of power and autonomy shape how nurses perceive their work today. While the disintegration of homelands and their absorption into a decentralized, democratic nation appeared to resemble the devolving of power, previous experiences of autonomous professionalism produced a different outcome, with nurses and doctors feeling that control had been taken away.

Politics and professionalism

By the time the hospital was taken over in 1982, Zulu ethnic identity had emerged as a major social and political force. The KwaZulu homeland became the site for a resurgence of Zulu ethnic nationalism led by Chief Mangosuthu Buthelezi of the Inkatha Freedom Party (IFP), who established a powerful grip over the region (Maré and Hamilton 1987; Harries 1993).[7] In the early 1990s, the area suffered a wave of violence that swept through the cities and countryside of KwaZulu as conflict between the Zulu nationalist IFP and the United Democratic Front (UDF) aligned with the African National Congress (ANC) escalated.

Mostly nurses spoke only vaguely and reluctantly about this period of violence that broke out in the years prior to the elections in 1994.[8] But on one occasion, a nurse recounted to me a memory from that period. On a wet evening, she recalled, a bus crashed on the national N2 road near Mkuze. Many injured passengers were brought up the winding, dirt road to the mountaintop hospital, and the nurses and doctors who received them worked frenetically through the night. The patients were terrified when they arrived at hospital, she remembered, not only because of the injuries they had sustained but because they feared that they might be refused treatment or even harmed. The bus that crashed was carrying ANC activists and, like many deep rural regions of Zululand, the area surrounding Bethesda Hospital was a renowned IFP stronghold.

No doubt the fear harboured by these injured passengers was shaped by the dangers pervading urban settings at that time. After more than a decade of deepening economic hardship and escalating conflict between the IFP and the UDF, the sprawling townships and huge squatter areas that had rapidly emerged following the removal of failed influx control laws in the mid-1980s were in turmoil. By the early 1990s, these densely populated urban spaces had been divided into political territories whose boundaries were guarded and patrolled by heavily armed gangs of men. To cross into another territory was to risk violent attack or even execution. The intimidation and rape of women was common, and the homes and families of politically aligned young men were frequently targeted (Bonnin 2000). In urban hospitals such as Prince Mshiyeni Memorial Hospital in Durban, patients not aligned to the IFP were sometimes refused care.

With the passage of time, as conflict escalated, violence spread deep into the countryside. In the regions around Bethesda Hospital, people carried their children into the bush every night to sleep for fear of attack, returning to their homes as the sun rose. Others would send their young men some distance from the home to keep watch throughout the night, alerting the family to impending trouble so they could wake up and flee when required.[9]

Under such circumstances the injured passengers, hurt and unable to protect themselves, would have felt distressed to enter an area that was well-known IFP territory. However, much to their relief, when they arrived at hospital the patients received 'first class care', the nurse explained to me. She told me the story as an example of the professionalism of nurses, a value that she held dear. She spoke with pride as she recalled the gratitude her patients had shown that day. What stood out from our conversation was the way that she spoke about work as a part of her life that enabled the transcending of political rivalries and which offered alternative forms of identification beyond the ethnic or political. The hospital was far away from the growing labour unrest among nurses and other workers in the cities, and unlike other (formerly) mission-run institutions that have been described as hotbeds of resistance, the attitudes of the doctors that ran Bethesda were guided by a position of non-partisanship linked to their identities as professionals. Former medical superintendent Daryl Hackland described Bethesda Hospital as a 'haven' from political unrest. Less concerned about criticisms of political allegiance than with the practical desire to be as effective as possible, he would later accept a position at the head of the Department of Health in the KwaZulu homeland government.

This experience of autonomy, of professionalism as an identity that sits apart from politics and conflict, is important for understanding the contemporary perspectives of nurses. During my initial research at Bethesda in 2006–07, conversations with older nurses revealed overwhelmingly that the dominant self-proclaimed identity emerging from the earlier period was that of the mission-trained professional. Experiences and memories of work during that time affected the ways in which many nurses approach their work today, where feelings of nostalgia were strongly present.

In the literature, such apolitical identifications among South Africa's so-called middle classes have contributed to the denouncement of rural-dwelling government employees as homeland-incubated elites. The homelands were nurtured through an alliance between local despots and the central apartheid state. Viewed as complicit in the corrupt system that confined black South Africans to these ethnically homogenous areas, the aspirations of the so-called narrow educated stratum (Mamdani 1996: 76) were generally deemed unworthy of scholarly attention, if not dismissed altogether as politically irrelevant. Unlike their urban counterparts who engaged in union activism and anti-apartheid struggle (Webber 2000), they instead quietly benefited from these nefarious regimes. In this regard, professionalism resonates with ideas of 'respectability' that were prominent in earlier descriptions of the African bourgeoisie. In her ethnography of sixty elite black men of the pseudonymous Reeftown, Mia Brandel-Syrier described a situation of political disengagement, in which values of respectability and the imitation of white lifestyles were prioritized as avenues to wealth and prestige. These men partook of 'typical capitalist pursuit', whereby ownership of money constituted the 'new badge of identity' (Brandel-Syrier 1978: 181). Politically disinterested, 'they were fence-sitters, and could turn in any direction which promised them greater opportunities' (1978: 180). They lacked involvement in politics, and their lifestyles expressed a commitment to socially and economically distinguishing themselves from their black working-class counterparts.

The ideology of professionalism shares some of the same associations with these earlier modes of respectability, encouraging an 'opt out' attitude to politics that Brandel-Syrier describes. During the apartheid era discussions about the political role of the black middle classes, for instance, Blade Nzimande argued that an ideology of professionalism was counterproductive to the anti-apartheid struggle, offering the working classes the promise of a bourgeois alternative to political emancipation. He wrote that 'the ideological influence of the black middle classes … legitimates an ideology of professionalism and careerism; and reinforces the belief within the working class that their only salvation out of shop-floor exploitation and repression is by becoming professionals' (1986: 40). This observation is borne out in the history of nursing in South Africa, described by Shula Marks (1994), where the drive for professionalization has often been antithetical to progressive politics.

But the view that professionalism simply offers an opting out of politics also overlooks a more complex reality. It does not explain the alternative ethical attachments that an identity of professionalism facilitates. Instead, it takes for granted that social status and private gain are the primary or only motivations in the creation of professional trajectories. I do not make this assumption here, but instead, pay attention to the deep histories of work and Christianity out of which nurses' professional ethic emerges. At Bethesda, this is connected with the hospital's mission past. During the mission period, hospitals operated in tension with government agendas, but nurses and doctors utilized their relationship of mutual dependency with the government to advance a programme of community health care (see Chapter Three). Trajectories of professionalism were interwoven with projects of care. This was hinted at also in the story of the bus accident, in which an ideology of professionalism allowed the nurse to construct an ethic of care based on valuing human life that transcended political affiliations. In the contemporary post-apartheid setting, values of professionalism are drawn upon as an ethical alternative to practices of corruption and patronage.

The mid-1990s witnessed an astonishing transition to majority rule. Over the course of this transformation, the homelands were dissolved and their hospitals reintegrated within the national health-care infrastructure. At this time, the newly formed province of KwaZulu-Natal was redivided into eleven municipal districts (see Map 1). In this book, I consider the nurses' experiences of transition in this former homeland area of rural KwaZulu-Natal. I examine what lies behind the nurses' perceptions of disintegration and decline, and what accounts for the nostalgia that many of them feel for the pre-1994 situation. To situate nurses' narratives in a longer historical trajectory demands that questions be asked about the forms that such discussions take, the purposes they serve, and the processes which they represent – sometimes in caricatured form – in the current context of wider social change.

During the years of homeland rule black nurses began to occupy senior positions and the draconian and racialized governance of nurses' private lives became less overt. Nonetheless, the strict medical and nursing hierarchies along which accountability flowed – overseen by the medical superintendent at the helm – remained in place. The bureaucratic transformation after 1994 prompted a seismic rupture in these institutional norms. It produced what Weber (1978) referred to as a 'levelling' pressure on formerly taken-for-granted hierarchies. Each individual employee was to enact their responsibilities, not under the discerning watch of a scrupulous matron, but in accordance with their official duties laid out by the scope of practice. The separation of managerial and medical spheres was a blow to clinical autonomy, a gap that was mediated increasingly by paperwork and meetings. It was these modes of communication, rather than face-to-face contact on wards, that increasingly constituted channels of authority through which orders were given, policies distributed and medical information collated.

It is important to note that in South Africa as a whole, the movement in this direction long predated the inception of liberal democracy in 1994. Bureaucratic norms and practices were consolidated in government hospitals during the 1950s and 1960s, as the apartheid government drove ahead with ideological and organizational transformation. After the National Party victory in 1948, policy governing the rural reserves was rapidly centralized: a departure from the piecemeal and idiosyncratic governance that had characterized the earlier 'segregationist' years (Evans 1997: 233). This marked a period of state-led repression, only possible as a result of the rapid tightening and sophistication of its bureaucratic machinery (cf. Breckenridge 2005). Apartheid therefore gave rise to what Belinda Bozzoli has called 'racial modernism', replacing the 'welfare paternalism' that preceded it (2004: 50–51). This began to unravel in the 1980s, as administrations disintegrated under the pressure of mass political opposition and economic crisis (Evans 1997: 303).

However, due to Bethesda Hospital's geographical remoteness and, consequently, the relative autonomy enjoyed by nurses and doctors there, the patrimonial style authority of mission medicine remained prominent for longer than in the large urban hospitals (see Chapter Three). After 1994, these mechanisms intensified in a context in which 'accountability' has become a central principle of public services. The style of bureaucracy shifted from one based on interventionist, state administration to one modelled upon the international principles and values of private sector management. But far from one system simply replacing another, the narratives of fiscal austerity, transparency and decentralization characterizing contemporary systems of governance combined with enduring relations and practices inherited from the intersections of multiple histories – those of nursing and medicine, missionization, and the administrative and policy regimes of the former KwaZulu homeland and apartheid governments.

Spatial hierarchies

Bethesda Hospital now falls under the district municipality of Umkhanyakude and within that, in the local municipality of Jozini.

A further four hospitals are located in the district of Umkhanyakude, all similarly former mission hospitals (see Map 2). Bethesda is a small district hospital serving a population of over 90,000 people, who are scattered throughout the 1,500 square kilometre catchment area.[10] It is a 240-bed hospital, providing a range of district level services, and operating a referral system to other hospitals for specialized consultations and treatment.[11] It also coordinates a network of eight primary health care clinics spread throughout the region, and two mobile clinics. With a nursing staff of 150 when the research began in 2007, there was a 34 per cent vacancy rate among this group. Eleven doctors were employed at the hospital, though this number fluctuated, and there is generally a high turnover of medical staff. The hospital as a whole was running at roughly 60 per cent of its capacity due to staff shortages. The problem of staff shortages was compounded by the migration of nurses to England, particularly between 1998 and 2002. Most significantly, the onset of HIV/AIDS has ushered in an era of profound ill health throughout the region, placing an additional and extreme burden on the health system. Abigail Ntleko who was working as a nurse in KwaZulu-Natal at the time wrote that the HIV crisis 'reached a dimension that simply crushed any system in place' (2012: 99). It is this recent history of HIV, coupled with a chronic shortage of staff, which undergirds the observations in this book.

Projects of care intersect with those of professionalization, which in turn are mediated by the spatial and temporal arrangements of the hospital. Bethesda Hospital had a self-contained feel that reminded me of the 'company towns' described by Peter Carstens and others, albeit on a smaller scale (Carstens 2001; Rolston 2014). Enclosed in its own compound surrounded by a fence and guarded by security, it accommodates roughly half of its staff. Every morning and evening, nurses and other employees follow the well-trodden road – rebuilt with tarmac after 1994 – between the rows of accommodation on one side of the compound and the wards and offices on the other. Neatly kept flower beds adjacent to the main hospital entrance gave the impression, as one nursing manager suggested, of an institution that was 'alive', despite the challenges it faced.

The red-brick blocks of accommodation units and houses that now comprise a large section of the hospital grounds – differently sized but similar in design – were built after the ANC came to power in 1994. Prior to that, the small number of houses were mostly reserved for doctors and their families – in addition to the nursing college dormitories. Like the company town of Kleinzee described by Peter Carstens, whose 4000 inhabitants are employed as mineworkers by the De Beers company, workplace hierarchy is etched into the hospital's physical layout. Carstens writes that 'housing, and its cost to the employer, is a significant indicator of each employee's status in the industry, determining and reinforcing the nature of the relationship between employer and employee' (2001: 4). Rooms and apartments at the hospital are generally allocated according to occupation and skill level. Students sleep in shared dormitories. Staff nurses and some registered nurses are housed in single rooms in single-sex barracks. These are small with a single bed, storage cupboards and a small fridge and electric stove, as there is no kitchen. Showers and toilets are shared as well as a washing room with sinks and scrub boards. Specialized clinical staff that work at Bethesda for one year for their community service – such as doctors, dieticians, physiotherapists, occupational therapists and dentists – usually live in smaller self-contained apartments sometimes shared by two. Nursing matrons, doctors and senior managerial staff reside in larger apartments or houses that include a living room, a fully equipped kitchen and two or three bedrooms.

General labourers, security staff, kitchen staff and other unskilled workers and a number of nurses are employed from the surrounding area, and so are deemed to live close enough to travel each day from home. Some assistant and staff nurses apply for residence but are generally unsuccessful. As the hospital manager explained to me, only those who fall under the 'scarce skills' category can be assured of accommodation: 'Without doctors we cannot function as a hospital. Without registered nurses, we cannot function. But we can function without nursing assistants.' This prioritizing of senior employees occasionally caused dispute and resentment among more junior staff, for while some housing stood empty, reserved for skilled clinical staff whose posts were yet unfilled, other junior staff struggled to find a their own accommodation outside the hospital.

The hospital manager explained this as follows:

The problem is that with a staff of 600, you cannot possibly accommodate everyone. You would have something like a small

FIGURE 1.1 *Staff accommodation © Elizabeth Hull.*

township if you did that ... But people feel that if they work here, they are entitled to accommodation. It does not work like that. But they feel that it is their entitlement.

I found this remark intriguing, not least because labour regimes in South Africa historically have relied on the creation of townships – located close to mines and industrial complexes – precisely to ensure a reliable supply of labour. The alleged attitude of 'entitlement' may be linked to this deeply embedded spatial logic around which the migrant system was arranged. The insufficient accommodation at the hospital signals the severity of underfunding for rural government institutions like Bethesda. It also implies the rejection of these so-called claims of entitlement, especially by workers who are deemed dispensable. This spatial logic sits alongside wider experiences of contingency and the differential value of labour in contemporary South Africa. I now turn to the systems of training that reproduce structures of work and formal hierarchies in nursing.

FIGURE 1.2 *Staff accommodation: doctors' homes © Elizabeth Hull.*

Structure and training

Nurses advance their careers by progressing through various stages. There are eight categories, organized hierarchically from 'nursing manager' to 'enrolled nursing assistant', positioned along an incremental salary scale. Nursing assistants (one year of training) have limited responsibility and carry out basic tasks, including feeding and washing the patient, recording vital signs and other noninvasive tasks. 'Staff' or 'enrolled' nurses (two years' training) have additional tasks such as administering medicine and taking blood. 'Professional' or 'registered' nurses (four years' training) observe, assess and record the symptoms and progress of the patient, take direct instruction from doctors, and deal with more complicated cases, as well as performing some administrative duties. Senior and chief professional nurses do the above, in addition to managerial tasks including human resource management on individual wards. Nurses are considered to have reached the full status of professional nurse only once they have completed the four years of training, either the diploma or the degree.

Inherited from nursing's historical roots in the ministry, female registered nurses are frequently addressed with the title 'Sister'. Nurses in senior managerial positions are often referred to as 'Matron'. Male nurses assume the normal title of 'Mister'. Hereafter, I use the term 'junior nurse' to refer to those employed in enrolled (two years' training) or assistant (one years' training) roles.

Since 1986, there have been three routes to becoming a fully qualified, registered nurse. The two core pathways are a university degree programme and a college-based diploma, with the former being widely recognized as the more prestigious route. A third route is offered via a two-year bridging course, providing staff nurses with an additional two years of training to receive the diploma and progress to the position of professional nurse. Small training colleges, including those situated in rural hospitals like Bethesda, offer this training programme.

This system is set to change in the coming years. It is useful to briefly explain these anticipated changes because, as in previous moments in nursing's embattled history, they expose long-standing debates about professionalization. Most significantly, recent legislation will create new restrictions for accessing senior positions. Under the new legislation introduced in the 2013 Framework for Nursing Qualifications in South Africa, yet to be implemented, there will be only a single route to professional accreditation, via a four-year professional degree (BA) in nursing (Blaauw, Ditlopo and Rispel 2014).[12] The bridging course will no longer run and colleges that formerly offered the diploma may apply to be upgraded in order to train to the BA level. It is likely that many will not be granted this status, thus restricting the training of registered nurses to the universities. Through this legislative shift, enrolled and registered nurse training are being reconstituted as separate, mutually exclusive career paths, without the option of progression from one to the other that was previously provided by the bridging course.

This raises the question of whether obstacles to career progression will intensify, particularly for nurses from disadvantaged rural areas. The South African Qualifications Authority acknowledged euphemistically that 'the typical target populations for each category will almost certainly be quite different'.[13] The risk is that such changes may reinforce class-based inequalities in nursing as divisions between the university-trained and college-trained, and the professional and enrolled, categories become further entrenched. The long-standing image of rural areas as pools of flexible labour, characteristic of the bifurcated system associated with the apartheid era, resurfaces here. The reinforcement of geographically demarcated class hierarchies, however unintended, may perpetuate the skewed character of health-care provision in South Africa, particularly between rural and urban areas.[14]

The proponents of the new degree programme argue that it is a necessary step to face the growing complexity of demands on nurses, to produce practitioners who have undergone a more rigorous training than that which currently exists. Part of the impetus behind the new legislation has to do with the direction of nurse training internationally. Various high-income countries have recently made the baccalaureate degree a requirement for registration (Blaauw, Ditlopo and Rispel 2014: 9). The nursing elite in South Africa evidently is eager to keep up with their global counterparts.[15] However, others suggest that the struggle for professional status continues to dominate such decisions. The changes have been motivated, they argue, by 'the desire to enhance the professional status of nurses, attract high-quality students, escape medical domination, and allow for more autonomous nursing practice' (Blaauw, Ditlopo and Rispel 2014: 2). The question is whether further measures to professionalize nursing are either the most cost-effective or the most suitable in the context of a national health system in dire need of increased retention and more equitable service delivery. The change will seal off access to the senior positions of the profession by prohibiting the progression of enrolled nurses to the status of registered nurse.[16] These are long-standing themes in the history of nursing, in South Africa and elsewhere, reflecting tensions between elitist agendas and the demands of meeting the health needs of the population.

In 1994, Shula Marks suggested that the future of nursing would hinge on the debate about the training of enrolled nurses. It epitomizes, more than any other, the long-standing conflict between the ideology of professionalism and the need for basic nursing care. Marks predicted the direction of these debates when she wrote that 'there are clear hints that the Council is hoping to limit their entry into the more privileged ranks of the registered nurses', adding that 'this elitist professional model of nursing care pays scant attention to economic realities and has little hope of serving the needs of the majority of the people' (Marks 1994: 202). It is notable how persistent such hierarchies have remained even to the present day. How they will play out, especially after the introduction of the long-awaited National Health Insurance system, remains to be seen.

Anthropology and audit

This book explores the contradictions of the post-apartheid workplace from the point of view of a group of workers, whose status positions and aspirations are by no means assured. When I began research at Bethesda Hospital, I quickly became aware that many nurses harboured intense fears in relation to their work. These concerns were amplified by my own presence as a researcher. The nurses' fears of audit were accompanied by a sense of confusion and insecurity at the quickly changing protocols and policies that, with limited resources, they were tasked to implement.

When I began my research in 2006, accountability and audit were not as central to the study as they became later. But my encounters with nurses, and especially their fears about participating in research during the early stages, ensured that these issues made their entry into my field notes and re-emerged repeatedly thereafter. Many nurses were nervous about the research. Access to junior nurses invariably depended on the willingness of the registered nurse in charge to allow the research to go ahead. In this respect, the contours of research and issues of access mirrored normal workplace hierarchies. In wards where the registered nurse was reluctant to participate, I would meet with a wall of silence among other nurses on the ward. Conversely, in wards where a nurse manager was open and curious about the research, and willing to allow it to go ahead, junior nurses would become less reticent, and in some cases would enthusiastically express their views and opinions. Others would appreciate the opportunity to air grievances.

With those whom I gradually came to know better, the relationship was never stable; small events could augment the dynamics of my interactions with them in enduring ways. For instance, to observe a dispute between a nurse and another member of staff could result in my being called upon privately as witness, or alternatively to being distanced, the act of being observed itself enhancing a feeling of culpability. While growing familiarity strengthened some relationships, others were constantly shifting. They were interrupted by unexpected events and the unavoidably political nature of observation, in a context where workers were subjected to audit. Nurses occasionally expressed a fear of 'getting into trouble' that, at times, made it difficult to talk with them at all. Like many people whom anthropologists encounter, nurses were adept at 'managing what is to be known, and to whom when' (Strathern 1999: 13). At other times, nurses indicated their cautious approach to the disclosure of information by the choice of language they adopted, concealing certain views and opinions behind bureaucratic jargon.

During the earlier phases of fieldwork, I found this frustrating. I faced what David Mosse describes in institutional settings as the multiple mechanisms for 'filtering and regulating the flow of information and stabilising representations' (Mosse 2005: 12). I could not help but feel that there was a reality that was hidden to me. It was only through the gradual and reflexive process of fieldwork that I was able to work through the epistemological challenges that these experiences presented. The methodological constraints themselves exposed the struggles and contradictions for nurses of being and working in the institution. As Michael Burawoy writes, 'The limitations of method become the critique of society' (2000: 28). At Bethesda, the institutional filters that nurses enacted had to do with maintaining a contingent professionalism, a status that was made and remade daily.

During graduate training in anthropology, one learns that fieldwork involves a gradual process of transition. The successful ethnographer transforms, over time, from the status of 'outsider' to one – albeit only ever partially – of 'insider'. As I came to discover, anthropology in institutional settings works partly in the reverse. In an institution like a hospital, an anthropologist begins research not with an outsider status, but rather as a specific kind of insider. To many nurses, I occupied a role within the broader culture of surveillance and accountability, as something akin to an auditor. It was easy at first to disregard this assumption as a simple misunderstanding. But it played on my mind. I began to question whether the line between anthropology and audit was hazier than I was admitting. How closely did my actions emulate those of an auditor, carefully scrutinizing and documenting the activities of staff? How unequal was the relationship, where nurses were unable to control the interpretations being made? That the government did not employ me was of little comfort to some nurses, who would remind me that the research outputs could be read and used by government officials. I recognized, in these moments, that the ethnographic document was one among – and equivalent to – many documents produced within the hospital. By unintentionally assuming the persona of an auditor, especially during the earlier stages of research, I inadvertently – often uncomfortably – confronted questions about the relationship between anthropology and audit, and about the production of hospital paperwork vis-à-vis the production of anthropological documents. As I explain in Chapter Four, a primary mode of accountability for nurses emerges in the juncture between observation and writing. So too, the ethnographic text must be looked upon as another kind of document that is produced in, and not external to, the institution (cf. Riles 2006).

For nurses, the category of 'research' is a familiar one, and most have undergone at least some basic training in research techniques and methodology during nurse training. Some of the more senior nurses had carried out research projects themselves, and had an opinion about the procedures and processes that research entailed. Nursing students are schooled in a deductive method of research. They learn that research occurs in stages, beginning with a hypothesis. They were often surprised that my research was not limited to a single, fixed hypothesis that I had set out to confirm or dismiss. I would explain to them, instead, that I generated tentative hypotheses in the process of and in response to, as well as prior to, data collection – as is typical with inductive methods. The uniform and rote style of teaching was made plain to me, when I was asked to teach a research methodology class to students at the nursing college at Bethesda. The syllabus encouraged students to envisage a single 'correct' methodology that was fairly narrow. I began to appreciate the nurses' unfamiliarity with, and suspicion of, techniques that fell outside of this carefully prescribed approach.

On the one hand, my legitimacy as a researcher relied on conforming to expected behaviours. For example, I would carry out a certain number of interviews regularly. I produced my official letter of permission from the provincial Department of Health dozens of times during the course of fieldwork, as formal and symbolic verification of my official role. On the other hand, many of my fieldwork experiences emerged out of my effort to disturb the role that, from the nurses' perspectives, I closely embodied. I pursued some minor volunteer roles, including giving some lectures as part of the research methodology and sociology course in the nursing college, computerizing patient files in the HIV/AIDS clinic, assisting in the nursing college library and helping nurses with various small administrative tasks.

The first period of data collection for this book took place during a ten-month stay at Bethesda Hospital in 2007. I have returned to the surrounding region almost every year since, living with three different families in nearby villages and working on various other research projects, culminating altogether in just over four years spent in the region since 2006. I returned to the hospital for a two-month period of follow-up research in August 2013. During this period, I found that quite a few of the nurses who had participated in the earlier research had left, and others had replaced them. But several of the familiar ones were still there. I discussed my earlier research findings with them and adjusted these in light of our discussions. I also carried out several additional interviews.

Over the years that I have returned to the region, my knowledge about the hospital has deepened as I experienced it through various roles. I was an outpatient myself seven times. On one of these occasions, four months into fieldwork, I was rummaging through old files and objects piled in a heap inside a garage in the foreground of the hospital. Returning a file to a pile of miscellaneous things, a forceful squirt of thick liquid splattered across my face, drenching my left eye. Opening the other one, I saw a snake – which I would later discover, was a Mozambique spitting cobra – rearing tall in front of me, hissing. Nurses and doctors in the Resuscitation Unit treated me for several hours. A visceral reminder of my naivety, the experience jolted me suddenly out of my position as outside observer and without warning into the world inhabited by patients. It attuned me first hand to the different temporal and emotional registers within the hospital: the sensation of time suspended during acute illness or injury; the monotony of pain; the restless waiting of patients in sharp contrast to the hurried activity of staff; the constant hum of fans marking out time's continuous passage; feelings of vulnerability and unpredictability tamed and contained inside a regimented and routinized work space and time.

Over the years, I accompanied friends to the hospital on numerous occasions, particularly in the more recent years of fieldwork, when I lived in surrounding villages and my car was a vital asset, one of the main ways in which I reciprocated the time and generosity shown to me by others. I visited sick friends and new-born babies. I rushed children to hospital for rabies jabs, waited for HIV results and collected the death certificate of a friend at the mortuary with his bereaved family. Yet, while my experiences of the hospital accumulated over time and gave me insights that I had previously lacked, the earliest challenges of access have become just as important. Both intimacy and estrangement, in no small measure, have influenced the research journey on which this book is based.

Remaking respectability in a changing world

A couple of months after the beginning of research, I visited Mrs Biyela, a retired nurse who had spent much of her working life at Bethesda Hospital. She lived in a large house situated on the edge of an area known colloquially as White City – named after the magistrates, missionaries, traders and other white people who had clustered at this mountaintop peak, far above the reach of malaria which was endemic in the lower regions. While I waited for Mrs Biyela to arrive, I spoke to a young woman sitting outside. She was Mrs Biyela's granddaughter. Three children played next to her, pushing empty crushed plastic bottles along the ground like toy cars, eagerly shouting out 'Hello!' to me in English. I glanced around at the neatly trimmed garden with a brightly coloured flower bed in the centre. Nearby a small, netted patch of ground grew vegetables. In the drive, a Toyota four-wheel-drive was parked next to a small, white car.

Mrs Biyela arrived, a woman of about seventy, wearing a blue and white pinafore dress and a furry, black hat. I introduced myself and she invited me in. We sat down in a living room on sofas arranged around a coffee table. Many carefully positioned objects filled the room making it busy to the eye, including photographs, shiny ornaments, and decorative bowls. A corner of shelves was full of books, among them a set of about twenty encyclopaedia books and a thick textbook on nursing. Through one arched doorway I could see into a dining area, and beyond that, another spacious room.

Born in the then Transvaal Province, Mrs Biyela studied nursing and midwifery at King Edward Hospital in Durban, where she worked for several years, after which she went to Polokwane to pursue further studies. She moved to then northern Natal, because her husband had a job as a teacher in the Manguzi area. Eventually they moved near to Bethesda, where she subsequently worked for many years. She told me fondly of the few months she had spent in England, working at the Birmingham Central Hospital. Since I had grown up in Birmingham myself, we had much to talk about. She went there during leave one year and had liked it very much, wishing that she could have gone back. Remarking how it was odd that one tended to remember particular moments very clearly, she recalled seeing a woman with a beautiful coat: 'I bought the very same coat so that I could look like that lady!' she told me laughing. 'I also bought a skirt. It didn't fit me – back then I was quite large – but it was so nice that I bought it anyway. I have it here.'

She went on to explain that it was her son who encouraged her to go to England. He had been the first to make the journey, having gone there to study medicine. As she spoke, she reached up to the top of a tall, brown cabinet in front of me and handed me a photograph of him. She explained that he had since died. In the photograph, Mrs Biyela and her son were standing next to one another, he smartly dressed in a suit and she in graduation clothing. Another picture showed Mrs Biyela wearing a different graduation outfit. The third photo showed her daughter who, she explained, had also died.

This is a scene that resonates with the stories of hundreds of black South African women who, despite all the constraints imposed during apartheid, were able to pursue a career in nursing and to establish comfortable lifestyles, investing in their homes and educating their children in careers such as medicine and law. The story of premature deaths among the younger generation is, sadly, also more broadly resonant.

This upwardly aspiring group is usually associated with the urban centres, where many stayed or moved to seek work opportunities. In contrast, the rural areas has long been characterized as the site of an impoverished underclass. The mission stations that provided education and health care to rural communities, dotted far and wide across the South African countryside, were seen as stepping stones enabling aspiring professionals to get training and a foot in the door of their chosen career before disappearing to the city. The reverse migration of people like Mrs Biyela from town to country, attracted by the jobs created in these rural outposts, is not so well documented. Mrs Biyela, and many like her chose, to stay and work in rural areas, albeit interrupted by stints of work in the city or even overseas. Some spent their whole careers at Bethesda Hospital, witnessing the changes wrought by the transition from mission to state control during the homeland years, followed by the dramatic restructuring that has characterized the post-apartheid period. Rather than leaving for the city, they have built their permanent homes nearby, creating a base for their children who travelled away to boarding school and university. Investing in these rural abodes, government employees such as nurses and teachers engage in modes of consumption that are largely beyond the reach of many of their neighbours. Mrs Biyela's home was suggestive of an older 'respectable' status, a way of life that was nurtured particularly by mission education.

Nurses expected that with the dawn of a new democratic era in 1994, access to the elite rungs of the profession would accompany the transition to a de-racialized society. Black nurses were finally promised the status and seniority that was historically restricted to whites. But, as they headed for the goal, they found that the posts were moving. Democratic politics was having a levelling pressure on workplace hierarchies and new forms of status acquisition were emerging in rural areas, to compete with the high-status image that nurses had previously enjoyed. The older respectability of the traditional professions was becoming anachronistic. Aspirational trajectories were to be mediated, interrupted and reconstituted by quickly changing environments, from the crippling effects of AIDS to new post-apartheid narratives about what it should mean to be aspirational. In the next chapter, I draw out the contours of nurses' ambiguous status in the contemporary setting.

The Limits of Professionalism

I interviewed Sister Gama in a small room that doubled as an office and storage space near to the TB ward. Aware that it was an opportunity to air views that she couldn't usually express formally and assured of the anonymity of the interview process, she became eager to speak to me. She had worked at the hospital for most of her working life. She had therefore experienced many of the changes that this book describes. But like many of the hospital staff I spoke to, she struggled to put into words what these changes meant. As in so many conversations with nurses, the word 'democracy' quickly appeared in her efforts to explain. 'Because of this democracy, now people have opened their eyes,' she told me. 'We are afraid if you talk to a patient.' She was referring specifically to me in my role as a researcher. The fear nurses felt surrounding my research and what it might uncover was by now familiar to me. So, too, were comments about 'democracy' being implicated in the transformation and deterioration of the workplace over the last two decades. It was a catch-all phrase that people struggled to define, a trope that signalled a wide range of issues.

Sister Gama was concerned that if she made a mistake, even or especially one she was not aware of, this might result in her liability: 'Patients have rights and they can complain about you.' Raising her voice and speaking in a more animated tone, she told me that she had recently heard a radio advertisement by a legal firm targeting heath-care users. It declared that if a patient has been mistreated in hospital, the firm would assist the patient in seeking compensation by suing the hospital in question. After describing this advertisement, she said: 'They are looking for money from the government. The patient wants money. That's why nurses are afraid.' In a monologue that was now fast and uninterrupted, she told me that patients are able even to speak directly to the minister of health via a free national telephone number. 'They can report a lie, because they want money,' she repeated. In the case of a complaint being made, the inquiry would be submitted to the hospital's public relations officer, who would write a statement about the incident. A nurse could lose her job on the basis of this statement.

During a pause, I asked Sister Gama if she had encountered any instances of this at Bethesda Hospital. She said she couldn't recall it happening here, but that she believed it has taken place in other hospitals. Although, as these final comments suggest, such instances of dismissals of nurses are rare, the fact that her fears of liability have not materialized in practice is beside the point. Sister Gama's comments are an example of how public sector employees feel – both that they are the objects of scrutiny, and that service users have new rights and powers that put their own situation in jeopardy. Fears of accountability procedures are a mode of expressing these interlinked feelings that produce uncertainty.

In this chapter, I argue that the professional status of nurses is challenged in two ways. First, changing regimes of audit and accountability within the workplace undermine taken-for-granted hierarchies, creating a feeling of needing to be prepared for contingencies at work. Second, while nursing and teaching used to provide exclusive access to elite status for black women, the new routes to wealth creation beyond the formal workplace create a source of perceived competition. Sister Gama's fears, about how patients might profit financially at her expense, hinted at this dynamic.

What interested me most about Sister Gama's account was the way that her story linked together these two seemingly unrelated threats to professional status. She depicted the accountability structures that created a feeling of contingency for nurses as the same that patients might mobilize deceitfully to generate financial gain. This suggests that, while formal institutions place increasing stress on accountability, there is an experience of vulnerability deriving from a sense that power might be misused. Such a feeling may be especially pertinent in this former homeland context, where neo-liberal tropes of transparency and accountability have overlain and combined uneasily with existing systems of governance involving patronage networks. During the former homeland era, such practices transformed state bureaucracies into mechanisms for private gain (Hyslop 2005), entrenching the idea that state bureaucracies were sites of struggle over resources.

Would it not be better to disregard such conspiratorial stories as insignificant hearsay, and to focus on more serious questions of health-care delivery and working conditions? However, I suggest that such stories are an important window into these issues. They signal the pressures of high workload, experiences of underappreciation by managers, and the underlying contingencies that frame the experience of work in post-apartheid South Africa. In their discussion of the seemingly oppositional narratives of transparency and conspiracy theory, Todd Sanders and Harry West write: 'Amid all this talk of transparency, many people have the sense that something is not as it is said to be – that power remains, notwithstanding official pronouncements, at least somewhat opaque' (2003: 2). Conspiracy theories, they suggest, emerge out of the dissonance between narratives of transparency and the concealed ways that power operates under conditions of modernity.

The contradiction is expressed in Sister Gama's allusion to how new avenues of profiteering beyond the formal workplace cast a shadow over the traditional routes to status acquisition. Mechanisms of accountability intended to embed democratic principles of transparency and patient rights are refashioned as an opportunity for despondent rural-dwellers: to be mobilized and rechannelled into avenues for illicit gain. Liberal democratic ideals such as accountability are reconstituted in this narrative as an opportunity for financial self-advancement. Impunity and accountability are strangely twinned through the same broken paths of government discourse. Echoing the paradoxical experience of power to which Sanders and West allude, Jean-François Bayart writes that, 'every phenomenon or event is permanently shadowed by its double in another sphere' (2000: 255). Rather than systems of accountability reducing cultures of impunity, the two appear to reproduce one another. Accountability is a node of ambiguity, tension and possibility.

This is a good place to begin in making the argument that the experiences and identities of South Africa's lower middle classes cannot be confined either to the workplace or to life beyond work. Instead, it is important to look at both, as well as the intersections between them. In this chapter, I suggest that as the contradictions of neo-liberalism deepen, professional identities are challenged, both inside and outside of work. These points might appear insignificant, given the fact that nurses do enjoy secure employment compared to the swathes of people forced to survive in a state of permanent wagelessness. However, as Roger Southall has suggested, the future of South Africa's fragile status quo may rest on the extent to which the African National Congress (ANC) can sustain the loyalty of the middle classes. The fragility of professional identity that I detail throughout this book, therefore, has wider bearing on South Africa's political trajectory moving forward.

Nurses experience a double-edged sword, of intensifying regimes of accountability at work alongside inchoate opportunities for wealth creation beyond the remit of the formal sector. This is mirrored by an ambiguous and fraught process of state building, of the strengthening of state control alongside the cracks in its hegemony. Reflecting these contradictions, professionalism is both a necessary, but also, a fragile avenue to status in post-apartheid South Africa. To understand the nurses' positions in relation to these processes of state building, it is necessary to consider the restructuring of health care since the transition of the 1990s.

Health care through transition

The elections of 1994 marked the end of apartheid and the inception of a new democratic era in South Africa. Amid the fanfare and triumphant celebrations, the newly elected ANC soon awoke to a momentous challenge. Faced with a society in turmoil and an economy brought to its knees, the government adopted a massive social and economic policy programme known as the Reconstruction and Development Programme (RDP). This was an ambitious economic agenda based on a set of fiscally expansionist policies aimed at promoting growth, reducing poverty and creating jobs, housing and infrastructure. However, within months the ANC began to change direction. By 1996, the government abandoned the RDP and replaced it with a programme called the Growth, Employment and Redistribution strategy (GEAR), which was closely aligned to global neo-liberal orthodoxy. The reasons for this shift have long been debated, but key factors included political differences inside the ruling party and economic instability prompted by a sudden currency devaluation. It was a controversial U-turn that many viewed as a betrayal of the aims of the resistance movement and a consolidation of corporate interests at the heart of South Africa's government and economy (Bond 2000). The new programme favoured fiscal control, privatization, trade liberalization and the promotion of foreign investment and export competitiveness.

The programme achieved some economic stability in the short term. But, ultimately, it failed to meet the needs of the majority of the population. While unemployment was endemic by 1994, GEAR's economic policies proved unable to redress this. Indeed, given the ANC's focus on strengthening productivity and profits in the formal sector while failing to create jobs, the problem grew exponentially. Unemployment increased from 13 per cent in 1994 to 30.3 per cent by 2001. Some areas fared much worse. In the district of Umkhanyakude where Bethesda Hospital is located, the unemployment rate was 66.5 per cent in 2001, the highest rate in all the ten districts of KwaZulu-Natal.[1] Today unemployment in South Africa sits at around 25 per cent. In rural areas such as Umkhanyakude, with a formal job market impenetrable to the majority of people and limited scope for agricultural production, many families rely on government grants, which may be supplemented by income earned through various informal activities.[2]

The impact of GEAR on service delivery was also massive. The ANC implemented a range of economic and structural reforms in conformity with neo-liberal models of decentralization and fiscal reductionism. The resulting reform of the public sector involved many of the techniques of New Public Management (NPM), an administrative model developed in Great Britain under Margaret Thatcher. It was characterized by two core principles. The first was the application of business objectives to the public sector – such as cost reduction and productivity – through the introduction of competition, increased use of the private sector through contracting out and a downsizing of bureaucracies.[3] The second characteristic was to reformulate the relationship between national policy formulation and local operations through a process of decentralization. Political decision-making about service delivery became increasingly separated from practical implementation, by decentralizing administrative and financial processes and emphasizing managerial autonomy. This was accompanied by strategies that encouraged self-monitoring, including procedures of audit, accountability and performance management (Gow and Dufour 2000).

In South Africa, these changes had already begun in a limited way before 1994. In the 1980s, influenced both by severe budget deficits and by emerging international trends, the apartheid government began edging towards the neo-liberal model. In particular, it introduced significant contracting out to private companies, so that by 1995, 9.4 per cent of the public hospital budget was taken up by such contracts (McIntyre et al. 2006: 437). However, a large and inefficient bureaucracy hindered further attempts to reduce costs. Alongside the escalation of political and social turmoil during the 1980s, state-owned enterprises suffered a massive decrease in revenues (L. Smith 2004: 382). This financial crisis formed the rationale for a bureaucratic transformation in South Africa. As elsewhere in Africa, the poor and inefficient performance of government services and the limited financial resources available to the government convinced many that such changes were inevitable and necessary. Its proponents demanded an overhauling of managerial practice as part of a wider reformulation of the role of government in the economy and public services (Dunleavy 1991; Hughes 2003; Kaul 1997). But critics argue that the intentions of improving efficiency are impaired by chronic staff shortage and poor capacity (Bateman 2006; Schneider, Barron and Fonn 2007).

Ten years into democracy, the crisis of ill health in South Africa was deepening. The HIV epidemic had escalated beyond control, after a notorious period of denialism by senior members of the Mbeki administration. TB was on the rise. Since then, despite the milestone legislation of the National Health Act of 2003 that aimed to consolidate the constitutional commitment to equity and the individual's right to health, uneven access to health care has continued. The presence of a powerful private sector has played a central role in further entrenching inequality in the post-apartheid period. The government found itself pulled in different directions, by a powerful private health-care industry on the one hand, and a growing equality agenda on the other hand, led by organizations like the Treatment Action Campaign. Analysts have repeatedly pointed to the failure of the health system to keep up with progressive changes in legislation. Despite the legislative promise of equity, the reality falls way short of this aspiration.

The ideological narrative accompanying NPM has been central to its consolidation in the public sector. Its proponents are aware that NPM relies upon 'more than simply a set of administrative techniques. [It] implies values and an administrative culture' (Gow and Dufour 2000: 578). In South Africa, these ideas are embedded through programmes such as *Batho Pele* ('People First' in SeSotho), laid out in the 2007 White Paper on Transforming Public Service Delivery. This is a set of principles by which health workers are expected to abide. It promotes a shift away from seeing patients as 'welfare recipients' and towards their reconceptualization as 'customers' or 'clients'. This shift is a widely recognizable feature of neo-liberalism around the world. In South Africa, the process quickly assumed a political character. In the aftermath of apartheid, the formation of a new moral order achieved through the symbolic and technical reconstruction of state institutions contributed to the forging of a redemptive break with the past: 'Where the previous state had been authoritarian, repressive and oligarchic in nature, the new state is intended to be democratic, developmental and committed to a culture of human rights' (Cameron and Tapscott 2000: 81). The restructuring of social services, and the state's attempts at generating a new workplace ethic within its institutions of service delivery, has been integral to this wider ideological project of state building.

In a wide-ranging discussion about the impact of neo-liberalism, Nikolas Rose argues that NPM has eroded professional autonomy. In particular, it has

> transformed the governability of professional activity. Whilst apparently devolving more decisional power to those actually involved in devising and delivering services in local sites, it renders those activities governable in new ways. The enclosures within which expertise could insulate themselves from 'political interference' in the name of 'professional autonomy' are punctured. New grids of visibility have been established. (1999: 153)

Earlier sociological work by Talcott Parsons (1939) and Everett Hughes (1971) suggests that the tension between the individualist and autonomous identity of the professions and the collectivist nature of bureaucracy long predates much of the dynamics that Rose associates with neo-liberalism. It suggests a more fundamental dilemma for the management of organizations, not specific to the neo-liberal project. Nonetheless, Rose's point is valuable in highlighting the ways that this conflict may be intensified by NPM and its accompanying techniques of audit and accountability. Sister Gama highlighted this when she evoked the experience of diminishing control, in the context of new modes of governmentality.

In writing about neo-liberalism in Africa, anthropologists run the risk of reproducing representations of the continent as a passive recipient of ideas and models invented elsewhere. Here, I draw on Bayart's concept of 'extraversion' to suggest that, rather than being absorbed passively through a global diffusion of ideas from Washington to South Africa, elements of neo-liberal ideology are mobilized actively. Methods of managerial authority such as NPM are techniques of extraversion. They are actively and selectively appropriated in the process of consolidating managerial power and procuring foreign aid. South Africa's health-care system is relatively better protected from external pressure than other African countries because the bulk of its funding comes from the South African Treasury (Ijumba and Padarath 2006: vii). Elsewhere in Africa, governments are much more beholden to the stipulations of international agencies and global orthodoxies, due to the financial resources garnered from overseas sources of funding (Lee et al. 2009). For Bayart, the proliferation of democratic idioms in many postcolonial countries is also evidence of extraversion. The ruling ANC has used discourses of democracy – including the centrality of work as a modality of citizenship – to shift the mode of control, in Paul Starr's words, from techniques of 'coercion' to those of 'persuasion' (Starr 1982: 9–10): from political authority that characterized the latter years of apartheid to managerial authority underpinning post-apartheid governmentality.

The relationship between governance and professionalism in South Africa cannot be understood only through the lens of neo-liberalism. It is necessary now to consider the particular configurations of state power in South Africa, and how these intersect with and, at times, mobilize certain elements of liberal discourse, while not being reducible to them.

Severing the bond: government and the professions after 1994

By the late 1980s, there were grave concerns that an ANC-led transfer of power would destabilize the nursing establishment

(Marks 1994: 203). Recognizing the inevitability of change, the South African Nursing Council (SANC) asked the government to amend the clause in the 1978 Act that made striking illegal. This change came into effect in 1992 (ibid.: 206–7). Yet, as the transition began, the ANC's allegiance to its working-class comrades was far from assured. In 1994, Nelson Mandela publicly rebuked nurses for going on strike, declaring it to be an irresponsible disservice to patients and, by implication, a disloyalty to the newly formed nation (von Holdt 2010: 250). For some nurses, especially those active in union politics, this was a difficult pill to swallow. They saw it as a betrayal, a sign that the ANC had forgotten the important role that nurses had played in the resistance to the apartheid regime. It also gave a loud signal that citizenship, which black South Africans knew only too well had been fought for and not conferred upon them automatically, was now to be earned through their role as responsible workers. Consequently, work and citizenship are indelibly linked in the post-liberation period (Barchiesi 2011). The image of Mandela having abandoned the rank and file is suggestive of a common story about the ANC: one of a severance from the black working-class majority.

In the meantime, the ANC was working hard to consolidate support among the middle classes. In the final decade of the struggle against apartheid, as Roger Southall explains, the ANC increasingly co-opted the black middle-class constituency. This was to lay the foundations for 'the transformation of the ANC into a predominantly middle-class, rather than multiclass, organisation and the scaling down of its institutional ties with organised labour' (2016: 40). The ANC, like other elite African governments, came to operate in broadly clientelistic terms, nurturing a professional class and a black elite, while averting political crisis and social upheaval through the provision of social grants to the poor. In these respects, the ANC has become an organization of, and for, the black middle classes.

However, looked at through the lens of professionalism, the story becomes more complicated. Even those in the elite branches of nursing complained of a drop in their status as professionals. At the Nursing Summit in 2011, one of the pressing concerns raised by attendees was the alleged de-professionalisation of nursing. Little attention has been paid to the ways in which the professions have felt threatened by processes of state building in the transition to post-apartheid democracy.

The pressures of democratization created inevitable tensions, especially in a context where fiscally reductionist economic policies were squeezing the health sector of resources. Moreover, despite the emphasis on decentralization, the counter-tendency of centralizing of state power was in play (Wunsch 2014). As Gillian Hart explains, the ANC 'creat[ed] the conditions in which the state can hold not only its agencies but also non-state bodies to its principles' (2014: 184). In the case of nursing, two issues guided this process. First, the new cadre of ANC elites viewed the professional bodies inherited from the apartheid era as institutional nodes of a racialized power that required immediate reform. A special branch of the Truth and Reconciliation Commission exposed the unjust monopolization of the profession's institutions by a white minority, and the decades of unfair treatment suffered by black nurses as a result. This led to legislative reform in 2005, allowing the minister of health much greater power over appointments to the SANC – the profession's central regulating body.[4]

The arguments presented in favour of this change included the poor voter turnout in previous elections and 'the challenge of transforming a council when the membership of the profession was as yet not reflective of the demographics of the country' (Gray and Pillay 2006: 8). This euphemism implied that the nursing profession was still in the hands of a cadre of white elites concerned to use SANC to further their own interests. But for others, the changes implied a sinister entrenchment of centralized state power. One journalist reacted scathingly, accusing the Act of forcing, with little public consultation, 'the centralisation of unbridled power' into the hands of the minister.[5] The attack was directed at the then minister of health, Manto Tshabalala-Msimang, who was by that point suffering a crisis about her reputation for her controversial and widely publicized claim that foods such as beetroot, lemon juice and garlic could prevent the progression of HIV to full-blown AIDS.

A second key issue that allowed government to make inroads into the autonomy of the nursing establishment was the need for a revitalized public accountability across the public sector. Practices of corruption and patronage that had been embedded in state apparatus especially in the homelands meant that new systems of accountability were seen as imperative. The moral impetus also derived in large part from the findings of the Truth and Reconciliation Commission, which decried the abuse of patients by health workers as a continuation of institutionalized apartheid in the health-care sector. It recommended various accountability mechanisms and human rights training for health workers (SATRC 2003: 337). A series of media publications also focused on negligence and cruelty of nurses (Pillay, Marawa and Proudlock 2002: 9).

The new Nursing Act reflected these concerns. It included measures to increase the accountability of health-care providers and to enhance mechanisms for dealing effectively with professional misconduct. It allowed SANC to carry out an inquiry into 'unprofessional conduct', with or without a formal complaint or allegation having been submitted. The Act specifies the potential consequences of unprofessional conduct, including dismissal from the nursing register either temporarily or permanently. While many regard more rigorous accountability mechanisms as crucial for consolidating the democratic rights of South Africans, the concern is that such mechanisms generate a form of accountability that operates unidirectionally.

My concern here is to move beyond the official stipulations and formal narratives, towards a consideration of how these new workplace logics began to shape the material and ethical worlds of government employees. In 2006, the year that I began my fieldwork, this legislation was coming into effect. Media focus on the inadequacies of health-care provision had intensified the anxiety that nurses felt around the subject. One told me emphatically that nurses could be video recorded secretly while at work. She was referring to a highly publicized event in 2002, following a flurry of negative media attention, on the alleged cruelty of nurses. A nurse working in a public hospital in the province of Mpumalanga was reportedly captured on a hidden camera that had been planted in a maternity ward for a month by the television programme *Carte Blanche*. The footage allegedly showed her forcing abortion patients to remove the foetus themselves and to 'clean up the mess'.[6] The footage created an outcry after it was shown on the popular investigative news programme, after failed attempts by SANC to withdraw the piece from the programme. When the nurse was brought before the court, the evidence provided was insufficient to convict her. Despite this, she was charged with a gross violation of patients' rights by the SANC and underwent a disciplinary hearing. This resulted in her removal from the nursing register, permanently preventing her from working legally as a nurse in South Africa. At the time that the incident took place, the hospital was severely under-resourced and had no medical superintendent. Nonetheless, it was the nursing profession that received the brunt of criticism. Through careful use of language, one media report gave the impression that the incriminating behaviour had been carried out by several nurses instead of one, and that this was a normal, rather than exceptional, type of behaviour on the ward.[7]

The videotape is an apt metaphor for the gaze feared by nurses, and for the skewed character of current audit practices, which have the appearance of being controlled secretly and at a distance. Undergirding new regimes of accountability is the threat of dismissal, which in a society characterized by increasing levels of casualization and work insecurity, further severs the bond between nurses and the government. It creates contingency around the nurses' feelings of entitlement to work, status and citizenship.

In the hospital, normative state agendas are partially incorporated into the temporal and spatial logics and quotidian practices of work. One medium was the hospital's comments box. The hospital's complaints procedure includes a comments box in which patients and other visitors can write comments, appraisals and complaints. The comments box is indicative of the patients' newly empowered status in post-apartheid South Africa as clients with citizenship rights, rather than merely as recipients of state services. It also had the potential to expose lines of hierarchy and exclusion in ways that were concealed by normal politeness in face-to-face encounters. Akhil Gupta writes that 'more than any other genre, it is in the complaint that subaltern resistance and bureaucratic corruption become most visible' (2012: 166). Many nurses expressed concern that the box was used inappropriately, and could even be used to threaten and intimidate staff. 'People like myself view it positively,' said a senior nurse. 'Although at times, because people are not educated, when they complain they could destroy a person … They do not make positive, constructive criticism.' For this matron, the alleged misuse of the comments box had to do with lack of education among the patients. The extent to which hospitals receive appropriate or 'destructive' comments, she told me, 'depends on the community that you are serving'. During my time at Bethesda, rumours also circulated about both patients and hospital employees using the complaints box to intimidate or threaten staff. In extreme cases, nurses and doctors have allegedly received direct threats, either from other staff or from patients. Other rumours suggested the use of mobile phones to issue threats to members of management. The alleged 'misuse' of the comments box is an example of how the discourses of democracy and the formal mediums introduced to channel these discourses are inadequate to contain discontent.

Alongside this, nurses are increasingly aware that they no longer have a monopoly on status. Moreover, as I explore in the next section, there exists alternative avenues of enrichment. Such competing routes to status acquisition give an anachronistic feel to the mission-style respectability represented by Mrs Biyela in the final vignette of the previous chapter.

Democracy commodified

Sister Gama's comments about patients utilizing complaints procedures expresses an awareness of the increasing articulations of popular discontent in South Africa today. Her vivid depiction of the anonymous patient with a direct line to the minister of health, who can utilize patient rights to generate financial gain at the expense of workers, evokes Bayart's characterization of 'trickery' as one particular strategy of extraversion. This narrative disrupts former, established nurse–patient hierarchies and locates the managerial power of dismissal, not in the formal structures of accountability but in the clandestine world of informal economic activity that dwells beyond it. Formal systems can be mobilized by these forces, she implies, to generate financial gain. In a former homeland context in which clientalism and corruption were common, Sister Gama's account seems strangely to mimic the murky practices of the elites' access to state resources, where citizenship, rights and democracy become reimagined as tangible commodities.

The comments demonstrate an understanding of the limitations of discourses of democracy and rights, and their failure to improve the economic prospects of the rural poor, and the way in which such frustrations give rise to skewed and unpredictable expressions of popular discontent. The tensions between those with and those without work are palpable (Ashforth 2005; Comaroff and Comaroff 2000). In a context of growing inequality and diminishing hopes of a better life after apartheid, there is a widely held perception that, as Adam Ashforth describes, some people are out to make money regardless of the consequences or ill-effects this may have, directly or indirectly, on others. This ideology of malevolent self-advancement manifests itself differently across South Africa's class spectrum. In Sister Gama's account, the idea that patients could have a direct line of communication to the minister of health, and that moreover this could be used deceptively as a way of eliciting cash at the expense of lower level public sector workers, is a striking metaphor for the ways in which the South African state is seen both as a nexus of resources to which people allegedly feel 'entitled', and for the clientelism that increasingly characterizes elite access to state resources. It is an apt expression for the opaque operations of power and the uneasy forms taken by its representations, especially in the context of a former homeland, where clientelism and corruption became the norm.

The object of fear is personified most vividly in the character of the unemployed, rural youth. As Bayart writes:

> [T]he strategy of extraversion through democracy has shown its limits. It is, indeed, unable to incorporate either economically or institutionally, in terms of either education or ideology, ... young people and rural communities, in spite of the fact that these two excluded categories actually compose the majority of the population. (2000: 227)

This begins to offer an explanation as to why Sister Gama and many other nurses embrace seemingly anti-liberal views, holding democracy itself responsible for current problems at the hospital. Her concerns suggest that the limits of democracy in South Africa are exposed in the crisis of work, not only for those who find themselves chronically without it, but also for those who feel the threat of dismissal. These anxieties are compounded by a feeling that nursing is no longer a protected status, that the poor can hold nurses accountable and, in doing so, generate wealth. Linked to this is a growing awareness that there are ways to make money quickly outside of the traditional professions like nursing and teaching.

What Sister Gama's story expresses first and foremost is a fear of dismissal. Her comments conveyed a picture of the workplace where previously taken-for-granted hierarchies between nurses and patients no longer carry the same social capital, and where systems of law can be mobilized by patients to sue the hospital and lead to job losses. The story hints at the way in which nurses no longer have privileged access to middle-class status and lifestyles. On the contrary, nurses are all too aware of the new ways of generating wealth that have mushroomed outside of the traditional structures of state employment. Such observations are gleaned not only via the media frenzy that makes visible the flashy, consumer lifestyles of the new class of so-called black diamonds (James 2015; Mda 2009). In this poverty-stricken region of rural KwaZulu-Natal, one encounters occasional stories of local residents who – within the interstices of an otherwise stagnant rural economy – have managed to generate income quickly. This is often achieved by winning a government tender or procuring irrigated land and/or government funding for agriculture.[8] These uneven and often conspicuous pockets of accumulation have provoked feelings of ambivalence among nurses and have given rise to new kinds of aspirations that cannot easily be met by a career in the formal government sector.

'I do not even have one cent'

Nursing is one of the few career paths that facilitates upward mobility in an area characterized by widespread poverty. According to the deprivation index of the Health District Barometer of 2008/ 09, based on a range of demographic, socio-economic and health data, the district of Umkhanyakude was the second most 'deprived' of the fifty-two provinces nationally during the period that I began research (Day et al. 2009: 197). However, despite the inequalities that create deep fissures in rural communities, imprinted on the visual landscape by the vastly contrasting housing sizes and styles, the nurses' lives are intertwined intricately with those of their patients and the local population. Like Mrs Biyela, whom we met in the previous chapter, many have experienced the death of close family members, especially in the context of the HIV/AIDS epidemic, which at its height in 2003 was taking the lives of 770 people per day in South Africa (Hunter 2010: 24). By the time I arrived at Bethesda Hospital in 2006, the antiretroviral treatment had been available for only three years. By this point, nurses had experienced at first hand the devastating effects of the disease; they had treated, comforted and cared for many of its victims. Few nurses escaped the effects of HIV/AIDS in their personal lives. Many had themselves succumbed to the disease.

In other respects too, the nurses' lives are entwined with those around them, rather than occupying a sealed, middle-class lifestyle. Though nursing offers a regular income from the beginning of the training programme, many divide this income among family members. In some instances, entire extended families rely predominantly on the single salary of a nurse. Consequently, the lot of nurses varies substantially, a scenario that exacerbates the tensions produced by the hierarchical structures dominating the workplace. There is an assumption that: work creates and sustains the rest of life; that production precedes consumption; and that the salary of a worker enters, sustains and builds the home. But how do the experiences of home and community shape those of work, and serve as a basis for interpreting workplace relationships? In nursing, the connection has always been implicitly drawn by the gendered associations between nursing and domestic labour, and linked to this, the analogy between the nurse-doctor and wife-husband relationship, which serve to reinforce and naturalize the sexual division of labour in the work setting (eg. Gamarnikov 1978; Littlewood 1991; Savage 1997). But for South African nurses, the relationship between the world of work and the world beyond it has also been characterized historically by a jarring dissonance between the senior status that black nurses have achieved in their communities and the frequent downgrading they have endured at work under a system of racialized workplace stratification. The intensely stratified character of the hospital setting, and of the nursing profession itself, means that the social position and experiences of nurses are extremely heterogeneous.

But during much of the twentieth century, nursing was a path that offered unusual access to high status for black women in South Africa. Now, many nurses look around them at other kinds of income generating activities and they find nursing wanting. Thandi was a 32-year-old staff nurse. She had previously worked at the nearby Mosvold Hospital for two years and, at the time of fieldwork, was a student at Bethesda Nursing College, pursuing the first year of her two-year further training to become a registered nurse. She had a young child who lived with her grand mother in Vryheid, a town about three hours away by bus. Thandi stayed at the hospital for her training, usually visiting her son about once a month, although she wished that she could see more of him. When she finishes her training and gains some experience as a registered nurse, she would like to specialize either as a theatre nurse or as an AIDS coordinator, feeling that these are the two areas that suffer most from staff shortage: 'At my hospital [Mosvold] there is an HIV coordinator but only one … If maybe the staff can be increased, people won't die because of this.' Her own experience of the death of her son's father was further motivation to help people who were ill, dying or raising children alone.

However, despite her philanthropic incentives for becoming a nurse, Thandi also expressed dissatisfaction with nursing. 'The money is much too little,' she said. 'I am trying to budget, but it is not enough.' In response to a question asking whether she envisaged a lifetime's career in nursing she said, smiling, 'I don't want to die being a nurse! I am regressing as a nurse. I'd like to be a farmer. My grandfather was a farmer. As a farmer you can earn much more money.'

'Really?' I asked, encouraging her to continue.

'There's a lot of money in the soil, I am telling you,' she said, enthusiastically. 'I think certain types are better than others as well, like chickens. If I can be a farmer concentrating on chickens, I can gain a lot of money rather than staying here.' Although farming was prohibitive for most due to expensive start-up costs and limited access to land, the government had various funding schemes to support those with the means to produce food commercially. Many families and groups were forming farming cooperatives in the hope of accessing these funds, and the nearby Makhathini irrigation scheme had afforded substantial gains for a small number of farmers, who had managed to gain access to a plot. She proceeded to switch without a pause to another observation: 'You know there are these women who are selling things, like second hand clothes from outside, from other countries. They are getting a lot of money. Those mothers, they say [to me] "you put in a lot of time and are gaining nothing!" Yet they get two thousand Rand per week!'

The feeling among nurses that their job was temporary or that it had to be supplemented with other wealth accruing activities was common. As Deborah James (2015) has shown, a formal sector salary frequently feeds into multiple short- and long-term cycles of investments, loans, indebtedness, and accumulation that traverse the established categories of formal and informal economic spheres. Nursing salaries could fund a range of additional income creating practices. One registered nurse employed a woman to run a street-food stall in a nearby town. She was also a *sangoma* (spirit-medium) and, intermittently, a *mashonisa* (moneylender), both of which generated further income.

While speculating about how else she might generate income more quickly than her staff nurse salary would allow, Thandi raised international migration as a further possibility, but admitted that she was deterred by rumours about terrorism and diseases such as severe acute respiratory syndrome (SARS) and pneumonia that, so she had been told, were prevalent overseas. International migration, however, was an aspiration held by many, and a small number succeeded in doing it (see Chapter Six).

Thandi expressed a feeling of ambivalence about nursing, that while it did enable an escape from the poverty suffered by many, there were other significantly more lucrative activities that required less effort. Her comments suggested that nursing, despite its historical reputation as a high-status career, was no longer the most desirable way of earning a living.[9]

Such frustrations applied not only to junior nurses but also to those in senior and managerial positions. I got to know Sister Dlomo well and would frequently visit her. Sister Dlomo was born and grew up in the province of Mpumalanga, where she had pursued her assistant nurse training in 1982. Realizing that 'there is no future as a nursing assistant', she returned to school to repeat her matriculation (standard school leaving qualification) in order to improve her results so that she could go to university. After this, she went to the University of Zululand to do a four-year degree in nursing, and then worked at various hospitals as a professional nurse before starting at Bethesda in 1997. I asked her why she decided to pursue a university degree in nursing rather than follow the nursing college route and she explained: 'You are at a better advantage. You do all the subjects at a degree level. This means I could go straight into a Masters now if I wanted to pursue my studies, whereas those who are doing the diploma, those courses are not recognised. If you choose to study further, you must have a university degree.' She explained, in addition, that with the degree course, you gain all the essential qualifications at once (including Basic, General, Midwifery, Psychology and Community), whereas to achieve additional qualifications beyond Basic in the diploma system, you have to take time out of work to pursue your studies. The process is therefore longer and more complicated. But for those who do not have enough money for university education, she explained, this is the only option. At the previous hospital where she worked, she continued, 'I was the only person from the comprehensive course. Even the matron said to me, "I don't know how to handle this one!" because I had come from that course'. She spoke about how the initiation of an academic course in nursing in 1986 in South Africa had provoked a fierce debate, with some people complaining that nurses would be 'too educated'; that the focus would no longer be on the practical side of nursing. 'To me,' she added, 'nursing is nursing. You do it with your hands.' Yet, despite this apparent affirmation of nursing as a practical skill (as opposed to an intellectual pursuit), she nevertheless demonstrated a keen awareness of the benefits of a university degree.

Despite being highly educated, Sister Dlomo felt that her salary did not reflect these skills, a sentiment that was conveyed in a statement that was typed and pinned to her office wall on an A4 piece of paper: 'The Lord look [*sic*] at My work And he was very pleased Then he look again And saw my salary. He turned away Bowed his head And he wept. How do you survive? He cried and I cried.'

She told me, 'We are in need of money. We are really struggling here. People look at me and think that I am rich. But I do not even have one cent. I am in debt and we are not getting paid until the 15th … It is because I drive a car. They think that means I am rich. But it is the cost of that car that has wasted all my money. Now I have nothing …' She continued after a pause: 'Yet some of the people are very poor. You see those people who walk long distances for water. Some of them walk a long way to go to school, and they are not wearing shoes.' These comments suggested that Sister Dlomo saw herself as an upwardly mobile professional, occupying a fairly high-class status in relative terms. Yet, she defensively claimed that others were wrong to assume that she was rich. Aware of a wider popular discourse that views nurses as 'fat cats' living comfortably off generous government salaries, she insisted that her salary was unable to cover a modest lifestyle including car ownership.

Sister Dlomo frequently talked about going abroad, particularly because she had a close friend who had secured a nursing job in the United Kingdom. Her friend had left her children in her care with the intention of travelling for a year. Having earned a good salary and having saved money, the friend bought a house in England instead and finally brought her children over to live with her. Her friend's experience was a reminder that her own aspirations were not met, even as a senior nurse in South Africa, and she frequently spoke of her intention to seek greener pastures elsewhere.

What comes across in Sister Dlomo's account is that dissatisfaction at work and changing opportunities beyond it call into question governmental representations of formal employment as the site of social citizenship. A feeling of professional insecurity created beyond the workplace exacerbates this challenge to the workplace order. This is expressed clearly in Mazo Sybil T. Buthelezi's account of Nonhlanhla Nxumalo, a 'nurse pioneer' who had worked briefly at Bethesda in the 1980s. Buthelezi writes that Nxumalo

> ... represents the liberated post-Mandela Government African nurses who have to pay for mortgages, buy their cars, equip their homes with the latest gadgets and send their children to the best schools. They can no longer meet these demands with the peanuts that the apartheid government paid African nurses. They can no longer be captives of archaic traditional African practices which assigned subordinate roles to African women. These are the nurses who positively respond to the gradual globalization of opportunities and will go anywhere in the world in order to realize their potentialities. (2004)

In the next section, I explore further how the professionalism offered by the South African workplace stands in the shadow of competing routes to enrichment.

Getting rich quickly

Noreen, a would-be nurse whose ambitions had so far been thwarted, was thirty-five years old and lived in a village separated from Bethesda Hospital by a steep, dry valley covered in thick bush. She had grown up and spent most of her life in the village, apart from occasional trips away for short periods of work. I first met her early in 2007 when I was visiting the *induna* (the chief's headman), who lived near her, to seek permission to pursue research in the area. At that time, she was unmarried and lived in her parents' home with her two sons and fourteen other family members, including her siblings, nephews and nieces. Her father, who had retired, had spent his working life as a groundsman at the hospital, and Noreen and her siblings had been raised on his salary. The family were well known in the village: they were closely related to the *induna* who was also the most powerful *inyanga* (witch doctor) in the area. Another senior relative lived nearby with his three wives and was also a highly respected figure. The cluster of homes where they lived on this corner of the mountain road was known to all as a place of political power and spiritual potency. But despite her family's firmly established status, its younger members suffered the same lack of opportunity that was endemic in this area. With so many family members to provide for, the pension of Noreen's father didn't go much further than providing the basic food requirements, and the buildings they lived in were old and in disrepair.

When I first met Noreen in March 2007, she was unemployed and looking for work, selling mobile phone credit from her home in the village in the meantime to get by. She bought the credit in bulk from the nearby town of Mkuze and made a profit of R1 (about £0.10) for each voucher sold, patiently saving the money eventually to buy small items like clothing for her two sons. In the past, she had done other types of informal jobs such as buying and selling clothes. She was a confident and ambitious woman with a strongly independent streak. Many women relied on men for money, she would tell me, but she didn't want to rely on anyone but herself. 'It is better that way,' she would say, stubbornly rejecting the idea of dependence on men, whom she comprehensively dismissed as irresponsible. Noreen desperately wanted a job, and would pray every night for help. She bemoaned that a year previously, she had trained as a paramedic – a course for which she had paid R3000 – and yet she had failed to identify a single vacancy in the role. She had applied for the nursing course at Bethesda and several other hospitals but, despite having her matriculation (school leaving) certificate and very good English skills, had not been admitted to the course which was heavily oversubscribed. When speaking with her and her sister about the lack of jobs in the area, Noreen pointed out despondently that the few jobs that existed seemed to go to people with connections (cf. James 2015). Her sister interrupted:

> I heard recently that *another* of the chief's daughters got a job at the hospital. It's not fair really … Now the chief has five children that are working. Some are there in the hospital and some work

at Spar [supermarket] in Jozini.[10] There are nineteen of us in my family and none of us are working … There are no opportunities here. Even the *induna*: six of his children are working! – because there was another one that started working there at the hospital in May. They are the ones that are getting all the jobs … Everyone here is angry about it.

In an otherwise stagnant local economy that lacked private investment and enterprise, jobs at the hospital were extremely sought after. Nurses, who receive a salary from the first day of training, are among the highest income earners in the area and usually enjoy a level of economic security far greater than most, suggestive of Seekings and Nattrass's characterization of the semi-professional class of nurses and teachers as 'privileged elite' (2005: 269). Predictably, nursing posts were desirable, and Noreen had applied several times without success.

Her anxiety over failing to find a job was exacerbated by what she perceived as the superior attitudes of those in employment. We were driving to town one day after having dropped in to visit a nurse, Grace, who lived near to her. Grace was someone I had recently befriended, but my arrival in the company of Noreen had received a cold response from Grace and I made sure, on subsequent visits, to go alone. In the car afterwards, Noreen grumpily commented that 'the teachers and nurses think that they are better'. I asked her what she meant and she recalled an incident that had taken place at the hospital involving Grace. Noreen had taken her son to hospital and had waited for a long time in the queue to see the doctor in the Out-Patients Department (OPD). When they finally saw him, he referred them to the physiotherapist. She took her son immediately to the physiotherapist who treated him and told them to return to the doctor. On their return to OPD, she saw Grace who had been working there all morning. Given that she had waited for such a long time earlier that day, she asked Grace, 'Do I have to wait in the queue again, or can I go in to see the doctor when someone comes out?' Grace replied, 'No, you must go and wait in the queue.' So again they had to join at the back of the queue and wait for a long time. 'She didn't help me even though she knows me!' Noreen said in an annoyed voice. But while they were waiting, another nurse acquaintance of Noreen's, who lives in the same village, saw Noreen and said, '*Hawu*! You have been waiting all morning. You mustn't wait again. Come with me, and you will see the doctor now.' She sent Noreen to the doctor as soon as the next patient came out. 'You see? She helped us, because she knows us. She is only a staff nurse, but yet she helped us. But Grace is a professional nurse and she wouldn't help. It is because she likes to be better.' A 'professional nurse', also known as a 'registered nurse', has received the full four years of training, unlike their junior counterparts, 'staff' or 'enrolled' nurses, who have completed one or two years of training. I asked Noreen whether she found that nurses in the hospital behaved in this way generally. She replied that 'the thing is that I *know* her. So I can see it more with her'.

It was not that she had to wait twice to see the doctor that, in itself, made Noreen angry. Rather, as she emphasized following my final question, it was the fact that Grace failed to provide the help to which she felt entitled on the basis of knowing her outside of the hospital context. For Noreen, an expectation of reciprocation and social obligation was undermined by Grace's refusal to help. The fact that the second nurse, despite being 'only a staff nurse', was willing to intercede on her behalf, demonstrated to Noreen that Grace was not compelled by the formal regulations of her work to send her to the back of the queue. Rather, she had refused to help in order to assert her status vis-à-vis Noreen, 'because she likes to be better'. Noreen's interpretation was supported, she claimed, by Grace's general attitude of self-importance and the social distance that she displayed in relation to Noreen and others in the village.

The story reflects the complex negotiations that take place in attempting to reconcile or, at times, reinforce the contrasting roles that nurses assume as both 'public servants' and 'private citizens' (Gupta 1995). Thus, Noreen had an expectation of favour from Grace on the basis of 'knowing her' in the village context. She anticipated that Grace would honour their social connection by allowing her to move to the front of the queue. By not doing so, Grace reinforced her position as a professional and consequently undermined her private relation to Noreen. Noreen subsequently rejected Grace's implicit claim to superior status in the village context, saying, 'She behaves in this way yet she does not even have a nice house. It is so dirty inside.' Having been unable to challenge Grace's assertion of professional status in the hospital context, Noreen criticized her home environment, a powerful symbol of status and respectability.

As I got to know Noreen better, I came to understand that such feelings of animosity were partly an expression of personal dissatisfaction created by long-term joblessness. Noreen told me about yet another incident in which she felt that someone close to her had let her down. Her cousin was a teacher in a nearby school. She offered Noreen a job at the school, to work as a biology teacher. Noreen told her that she would be capable of teaching biology because she learnt it while training as a paramedic. Later, however, Noreen discovered that her cousin had given the job to someone else without telling her: 'She is my own cousin,' said Noreen, despondently. 'People are jealous. They are happy when you are not working.'[11] In her usual indignant tone, frowning deeply and speaking in a firm voice, she continued:

> That is why I am going to go to Mpumalanga to get a job. I am going to build a nice house *here*, in *this* village. When I have built that house, I am going to get a very nice car, to show them. Just to show them.

Aware that few opportunities existed for escaping poverty in this region, I couldn't help feeling a sense of doubt as she said this. But over the course of the next five years, my scepticism was proved spectacularly wrong.

I returned to the area in April 2009 after an eighteen-month absence. Taking the familiar sharp right turn onto the rocky path that led to Noreen's home, I saw her outside the front of the main house in the shade washing clothes in a large bucket. She walked towards me slowly, very surprised and grinning widely. Everything seemed much like before. We sat down on the bed inside and drank coke. She told me she still didn't have a job, but that things were looking promising. She had heard that the government was contracting tenders and she was preparing to apply for one. This was no easy task. She had to form a company – which she was doing with two friends – that had to be registered officially with the South African Revenue Service before an application could be made for a tender. The process was long, particularly because each step was bureaucratic and costly. Yet, something in Noreen's voice had changed, and she was hopeful.

When I returned a year later, Noreen's certificates were all in place, and some months after that, she won her first contract: a government tender to build a children's home. The job was a success, and earned her a sizeable sum of money. In 2012, having been granted permission by the *inkosi* (chief) to build her own house on a patch of land opposite her parents' house, she employed relatives and neighbours to lay the foundations. By the time I returned for fieldwork again in June 2013, they had completed the construction of the house, which was larger than any other in the village; it was a remarkable transformation. On 8th July, she showed me around the new house. It was spacious and the ceilings were high. The house was tiled throughout, and unusual features like a showerhead exuded an air of sophistication. There was no water infrastructure in the area, so warm water would have to be prepared and filled manually to operate the shower. There wasn't much furniture yet, but the house was tiled throughout with a shiny, white marble effect. A Hardbody Nissan, which she had recently purchased for work, was parked outside in the spacious drive. She and her two sons were unable to move into their new home yet, because she still had furniture to buy, the roof to complete and, finally, she wanted to buy a new car for nonwork purposes.

By the following year, sure enough, all of these tasks were accomplished and the family had moved in. A brand new people carrier sat in the garage, which she showed to me proudly. In a further act of conspicuous display, she had personalized the number plate with her mother's surname as a way of thanking her for all that she had done. During a long research interview in December 2014, she described the construction of her home right next to her family's house as a gift to the rural area where she grew up, which she felt demonstrated her loyalty to it. We spoke about the possible jealousies harboured by neighbours (a key motivation for witchcraft), and she explained that she wasn't afraid of this. I asked why this was, and she explained that her behaviour towards her neighbours had not altered as a consequence of her success:

> I am [Noreen] that I was before. I didn't say, 'Oh now I've got money, I must go to the suburb, to Durban.' No! I must build in my area, in order for the area to go up [develop] ... Oh, in rural areas, there are good things. Everyone will see.

In these comments, Noreen expressed a sense in which her own material success created a feeling of prestige that could be shared by all. Even the style of her house, with its triangular shaped roof, was being imitated by others in the village: 'They like my style, they want to copy me,' she said, smiling.

This was different, she continued, from the behaviour of teachers and nurses, who moved to urban areas as soon as they were financially able. She alluded to a distinction between older modes of status, associated with the government professions, which she implied were focused on the pursuit of private success at the expense of others and from which she herself had been excluded, and her own version of accumulation which was, she urged, a collective good. The commitment to a rural abode was integral to this depiction.

Expressing relief that she had not followed the nursing route, she went on to compare herself directly to those working in government positions: 'It is surprising because I am not working, but look at my car. I have my dream car. Others are nurses but they do not have a car.' She expressed a dislike for the very long shifts required of nurses, and though she spoke about the advantage of the financial benefits that come with public sector employment – such as pensions and medical aid – she said that her private insurance policies covered these necessities. The only thing she lacked was medical aid, but she was perfectly content with the service provided at Bethesda and thought that private health care was overrated. She used this point to turn the conversation back to a celebration of rural life. 'I trust the government hospital. Even if I want to clean my teeth, they give me the date,' she said, laughing. Clearly she was pleased to be free of the burden of viewing the hilltop hospital as a potential source of much needed employment.

What the example shows is that nursing and teaching are no longer the exclusive or even the most desirable routes to wealth and social recognition that they once were for black women. On my most recent visit to Noreen's, she denigrated nursing for its long working hours and expressed relief that, years earlier, she had not been accepted into the nursing course. Instead, she is one of a small number who have managed to successfully compete for government tenders, regarded as one of the quickest ways of enriching oneself over a short space of time. The traditional 'respectable' professions of nursing and teaching, while undoubtedly remaining high-status positions, lack the glamour of new avenues to enrichment. In terms of the distinction that Gillian Hart makes between two distinct kinds of bourgeoisie in rural South Africa today, the traditional routes to social status increasingly stand in the shadow of newer ones.

Conclusion

Noreen's experience indicates how new opportunities for entrepreneurship such as those provided by winning tenders, that may partly utilize state resources but do not fall under such tightly controlled regimes of managerial authority, are increasingly attractive to many. Nursing, with its long hours, draconian hierarchies and stressful working conditions, pales in comparison. Moreover, Noreen described her new-found status as inclusive in contrast to the exclusive superiority she associated with the traditional professions. *Her* wealth would be used not to declare personal achievement and to separate oneself from one's neighbour – a tendency she attributes to nurses who abandon the village for the city – but rather, is an inclusive status, one shared by all. In comparison, professional status is anachronistic, signifying an apartheid mentality in which people sought to escape or transcend black society by adorning themselves with the signifiers of otherness – of whiteness. In contrast, in post-apartheid South Africa, new ways of making money are represented symbolically as beneficial to all black people, as Deborah Posel (2010) describes in relation to the consumption practices of the ANC elite. Noreen alluded to these kinds of reasonings when she commented that her new home was a sign of rural upliftment, a new and important symbol to be shared by the whole community. Instead of cutting herself off, and forging an exclusive citizenship synonymous with professionalism, Noreen viewed her accumulation of private wealth as a collective good.

This disregard of professional status also resonates in the stories told by Sister Dlomo, who feared that new channels of accountability would make nurses vulnerable to exploitation by patients in search of financial gain. The concept of 'patient rights' in this framework spells new forms of state loyalty: a wider and more inclusive version of citizenship than that formerly offered by professionalism. Whereas the nursing profession was promoted and protected by the apartheid state through mechanisms like formal accreditation – and hence state power was a resource used by the profession to ensure its own status and exclusivity – nurses now find that the government serves the interests of its new 'clients', the patients. In contrast, nurses are recast in these accounts as victims, both financially and professionally, of the democratic transition. This begins to explain why many nurses hold 'democracy' itself in such low regard. This is a theme that I explore in more depth in Chapter Five. But first, it is necessary to consider how history and nostalgia inform nurses perceptions of professionalism. As we will see in the next chapter, the turbulence of state building that plays itself out in the corridors and wards of rural hospitals today is a far cry from the sheltered paternalism of the mission era.

CHAPTER THREE

Autonomy and Control From Mission to State

The Out-Patients Department (OPD) is located inside the main entrance of the hospital and provides one-to-one consultations between patients and doctors. It is typically a hive of activity. Patients cluster around the large, glass-covered reception desk at the entrance waiting to collect their yellow appointment cards, for which they usually pay a user fee of R20, before making their way to the rows of wooden benches that form a central waiting area. Here they queue to see one of the nurses in the front area of the room, who takes their blood pressure, temperature and weight. Queues of people, sitting on long wooden benches extending down the adjacent corridor wait, sometimes for hours at a time, to be called by a doctor into one of the several small rooms behind the wall where the nurses are working.

Earlier in the morning, there is a different scene. A small number of patients, usually between about five and twenty, wait quietly for the day to begin, having arrived early to avoid the queues. At seven o'clock promptly, all the nurses working in this department, usually about twenty, form a neat line in the front portion of the room, standing equidistant from one another and facing the patients. The line of nurses is sometimes too long to fit into the room, and extends down the corridor, and out of sight. The majority are women, wearing knee-length blue skirts, white shirts, stockings and black shoes. They are distinguishable from one another by the epaulettes that indicate their level of training. These are small, rectangular, metal bars fixed above the shoulder, enamelled in various colours: red, for general nursing; green, for midwifery; blue, for psychiatry; and white, for nursing tutor. The male nurses, of whom there are usually two or three, are wearing black trousers and white shirts. Student nurses stand out in their plain white dresses or in shirts, with no epaulettes.

This daily event begins with a song, which is usually initiated enthusiastically by two or three of the older nurses, stalwarts of the hospital, who have been working there for many years. They sing loudly in harmony, often accompanied with clapping, or swaying to and fro. Levels of enthusiasm are always variable. Some nurses clap and dance, their voices rising above the others, while others – often the younger staff nurses – lean against the wall behind them, with arms folded.

After one or two songs, one of the nurses addresses the audience in Zulu, saying a prayer or short sermon, or telling a biblical story, which is then followed by spontaneous prayers muttered by everyone present, both nurses and patients. The simultaneous, communal praying merges together to create a soft hum of sound, intermittently broken by an animated shout or drawn-out lamentation. This lasts for a minute or so, tailing off until the final couple of voices peter out. A short pause is usually followed by another song.

At the close of the singing, one of the nurses steps forward towards the seated patients. She initiates a new conversational tone, with the typical greeting of *Sanibonani* ('Hello') and *Ninjani?* ('How are you?'). The nurse introduces a topic related to some aspect of health or hospital legislation. Topics that have come up repeatedly include procedures for seeing a doctor, awareness of patient rights *(amalungelo)*, how to fill in a complaint card, how to recognize common TB symptoms, and how to prevent mother-to-child transmission of HIV. The nurse presents the basic issues relating to the topic, and sometimes encourages the patients to participate by asking questions. In one session, a nurse was discussing *amalungelo*. She explains to the patients that they are entitled to complain, if they feel that they are not receiving correct or adequate care. For example, if a nurse is shouting and treating you badly, she tells them, you have the right to report it. Or, if you don't want to sleep in the hospital the night before a transfer, you are permitted to raise the issue with staff and to request another place to sleep. She goes on to explain that they could do this by speaking to a senior member of staff like the ward sister or matron, or if they are unsat-isfied with an aspect of the service, they could fill in a complaints card. She then describes where these cards could be found, how to complete them and where to submit them.

During this pedagogical exercise, the other nurses wait, motion-less in the line until the lesson is complete, at which point they break away, and a hum of chatter and laughter begins as they gather in another room to begin their regular morning work meeting.

The morning prayer session is a habitual feature of life at the hospital, part of the nurses' daily routine. It is a common practice in hospital wards and clinics across South Africa, and evokes the early mission influence that shaped them. It appears as a fragment of the past: an enduring appeal to religious authority, yet juxtaposed against a new secular discourse of rational bureaucracy and rights that has marked the historical transition of secularization from a mission hospital to a state institution. The hierarchical relationship between nurses and patients are inscribed in words, uniforms and behaviour. As Lewin and Green describe in one Cape Town clinic, morning prayers created feelings of unity through shared participa-tion in worship and also 'enacted and facilitated power relations' (2009: 1468). A nurse, who had worked at Bethesda for many years, was taken aback when I asked her the reason for participat-ing in the morning prayer session, and told me that she had always thought that it was 'compulsory'. It is not the management but the nursing profession that ensures the continuity of morning prayers, and requires that its junior members be present. Nurses enact the contradictory elements of their relationship with patients, who are associated with them through their role as 'culture-brokers' sharing in the language and cultural idioms of patients (Digby and Sweet 2002), while also separated from patients by their professional status.

In these morning events, medical and administrative matters are dramatized, resembling what Erving Goffman described as an 'insti-tutional display', in which language and performance are structured, enabling institutions to 'present themselves to the public as rational organizations, designed consciously, through and through, as effec-tive machines for producing a few officially avowed and officially approved ends' (1961: 73). On the occasion described above, the nurse's talk about *amalungelo* was not only a lesson to the patients, but also served as a reminder to the nurses that their behaviour at

FIGURE 3.1 *Nurses about to begin morning prayers* © *Elizabeth Hull.*

FIGURE 3.2 *Hospital entrance* © *Elizabeth Hull.*

work is expected to correspond to a set of codified rules and regulations, and that they may be held accountable for actions that fall outside of these prescribed norms. Nurses can no longer take for granted a superior status in relation to patients, in a context where patients' concerns and opinions are increasingly prioritized.

While providing information about patients' rights and other institutional or administrative matters, morning prayers also evoke nursing's historical connections with Christian prayer and worship. The active participation of older nurses, in contrast to some of their junior counterparts, embodies the nostalgia many of them feel for an earlier period when prayer was more central to hospital ethos. These feelings of nostalgia are replicated in conversations with older nurses, many of whom felt that Christianity no longer plays a significant part in the life of the hospital.

In his book *Native Nostalgia*, Jacob Dlamini asks the unsettling question: 'What does it mean for a black South African to remember life under apartheid with fondness?' (2009: 13). This question is pertinent in the context of Bethesda Hospital, and all the more unsettling in one of the former homelands, which were notoriously marginalized and exploited under the apartheid regime. Many of the older nurses recalled with nostalgia the days prior to 1994. They frequently complained that nowadays nobody stays at work for longer than their contractual hours. In contrast, when the hospital operated as a mission hospital, and during the period of homeland rule when government only nominally ran it, staff activities seemed frequently to blur the boundaries between work and leisure. Older nurses spoke enthusiastically about the numerous occasions they recalled from the past: decorating the wards; receiving presents from management and holding parties at Christmas time; going on trips arranged by the doctors to nearby tourist sites such as Sodwana Bay; gathering regularly for shared meals and barbeques, and invitations to Dr Hackland's home on Easter Day; none of which, they readily pointed out, still occurred.

One nursing manager summed it up, saying that they had felt 'that *unity* – initially, when it was still a mission, we all felt as a family ...' Nurses often used fictive kinship terms such as this, to describe their relationships with each other during that time. Dr Hackland was described, for example, as 'a father to us, although he was very strict' – encapsulating the then patrimonial style of hierarchical management. Nostalgia pervaded these accounts: work was described as 'a jolly place', 'a hobby' and 'good fun', in contrast to descriptions of work in the current setting that repeatedly emphasized feelings of stress, pressure and isolation. Such recollections were intricately bound up with perceptions of the work process then and now. As one nurse said to me: 'Even on a day off, if somebody needed your help, you would say, "I will assist you, no problem"… Now they say, "Oh, who will give me money for that?"'. Such comments hint at the 'formalistic spirit' of Weber's rational-bureaucratic systems of governance, where one is obliged to perform stated duties but, in turn, is not required to do more (Weber 1978: 217–18).

Such descriptions cannot be treated as unmediated descriptions of the past, but are instead ways of interpreting the present. They express the sense of loss that is widely felt among older nurses, when they talk about the hospital's missionary past, and hint at the feeling of moral disintegration – the breakdown of 'unity' – that pervades these narratives. Their accounts are consistent in their celebration of the hospital's past under missionary leadership, in contrast to an equally negative portrayal of the current workplace, the two often spoken about in tandem. In this chapter, I draw on archival material from the period prior to 1994, not in order to confirm or negate the positive representations that the nurses hold of the period, but to gather some insight into the tremendous changes that they evoke.

In this chapter, I suggest that the mission period (including the period from 1982 to1994, when the hospital was not formally run by the mission but when the mission ethos remained prominent) is associated for nurses with experiences of professional autonomy. This may seem glaringly inconsistent with the extreme paternalism that characterized mission training, which subjected women to strict regimes of control and discipline, an experience that seems anything but autonomous. My argument must be understood in relation to two main points. First, christian missions infused nursing with the moral ethos that became integral to its professional identity, and which stood apart from alternative modes of control. For instance, women's entry into nursing facilitated financial and professional independence, allowing an escape from marriage – even though it also meant subjection to a different version of patriarchy.

The second point relates to the specific context of Bethesda Hospital. During the period of homeland rule, when the KwaZulu homeland government nominally controlled the hospital, the nurses and doctors were left to their own devices, allowing them to advance a progressive programme of community health. While the literature emphasizes the oppressive character of homeland governance, the Bethesda experience highlights, paradoxically, what many nurses and doctors described as an exciting period of autonomy and creativity. Ironically, it was in the transition to a decentralized system after the end of apartheid that some nurses and doctors experienced a feeling of increasing intrusion by the state.

Rewriting the homelands

In 1996, Mahmood Mamdani published an influential book called *Citizen and Subject: Contemporary Africa and the Legacy of Late Colonialism*. In it, he explained that the creation of the homelands was a project intended to demarcate zones of custom controlled by the decentralized despotism of the chieftains, separated geographically and politically from urban regions that were structured and managed, in contrast, through systems of wage labour. Rural dwellers were governed by rigid and highly effective structures of neo-traditional rule. What he referred to as 'the narrow educated stratum' – nurses, teachers, traders and so on – were seen as elite and passive beneficiaries of the repressive system. As such, they were largely overlooked in his account.

In contrast, some scholars saw the nurses not as beneficiaries but as the victims of homeland policies. For instance, Cedric De Beer (1984) showed that nurses were constrained and their movements, and their autonomy, was restricted by the creation of separate ethnic nursing associations. He wrote that nurses in the Bantustans were 'bound to particular ethnic government institutions in a relationship of financial dependency. The Bantustan bureaucracy is a very real thing in their lives', a reality further exacerbated by their forced departure from the South African Nursing Association and subsequent affiliation to ethnic nursing associations (ibid.: 183–84).[1] Shula Marks suggests that while some nurses in South Africa supported the 'Africanisation' of nursing marked by the creation of these associations, overall 'black nursing opinion … was overwhelmingly against the formation of homeland associations' (1994: 184). The IFP used methods of coercion to demand loyalty, such as by forcing nurses and doctors to swear allegiance (ibid.: 196). In Chapter One, I recounted the story of a nurse's experience of treating ANC activists following a bus crash. She proudly remarked that the patients were treated with 'first class care', despite the hospital's location in an IFP stronghold. What the story pointed to is that nurses found forms of identification beyond the tribal conception of culture that Mamdani viewed as so totalizing.

In these contrasting depictions, we find again the two opposing perspectives of nurses that mirror those in the account of the 2007 strike with which I began this book: on the one hand, nurses belong to a category of elites who benefited from the corrupt homeland system that provided them with secure jobs in return for political allegiance; on the other hand, they are its victims, limited to ethnic categorizations that undermined their professional and personal freedoms. What both perspectives share in common is an assumption about the despotic control wielded by homeland governments. An important aspect overlooked by these accounts is the limits of the state's power, which led to tentative bargaining and agreements, and enabled institutions like Bethesda Hospital to operate with relative freedom. Grasping this is crucial for understanding how nurses interpreted the later transition to liberal democracy and the changes this brought to the health system.

Existing scholarship on health care in the homelands has focused overwhelmingly on the enormous financial constraints, the inadequacy of service provision, and the immiseration that this produced. For instance, Max Price argued that 'the political priorities of "independence" ... over-ruled the interest in improved health care', and at the same time, 'allow[ed] the White government to deny responsibility for both ill health and poor services' (1986: 165–66). However, despite these realities of grossly unequal distributions of resources at the national level, the experience of the nurses and doctors at Bethesda Hospital was somewhat different. What their stories reveal is that the period of homeland rule also provided a certain degree of autonomy from the prescriptions of the central state, along with a relative increase of funds which, though inadequate, nonetheless created an opportunity for these hospitals to develop and implement a progressive model of community-based care. This meant that despite the government's takeover of the Methodist-run mission hospital in 1982 and its handing over to the KwaZulu homeland government, the hospital continued to operate in much the same way as it had done previously, structured around the patrimonial-style leadership of the medical superintendent upon which the earlier missionary model had been based.

The KwaZulu government lacked the will to intervene more actively in its operations. Though nominally the hospitals had been taken over by the government, health care was essentially outsourced to the missions in the context of chronic under-government. Like the apartheid state that governed rural areas vicariously through chiefs and homeland administrations, the KwaZulu homeland governed hospitals indirectly via former religious institutions that were the tail end of the mission period. The missions occupied a 'mediator' position that was characteristic of colonial administration in rural Africa (Olivier de Sardan 2014: 414). Therefore, whereas hospitals in the urban areas were gradually transforming in accordance with new managerial styles, the mission model persisted for a longer period in parts of the homelands. The elite professional status of nurses may have meant that they identified more closely with urban dwellers than with their fellow rural inhabitants. However, their professional identity – informed by the Christian ethos of the mission rather than by ethnic politics – sustained a progressive health-care agenda that involved moments of cooperation, optimism or perceived progress, however muted, that have thus far been concealed under a dominant narrative of the homelands as illegitimate and oppressive.

The autonomy experienced by health workers during this time created the space for a resurgence of energy and idealism, which drove forward a progressive programme of primary health care. In doing so, it shaped fundamentally the modes of authority, accountability and professional identity by which nurses understood their work. But before turning to this, we must first go back further into the past to understand how both control and autonomy have long shaped the nursing experience in South Africa.

The history of nursing at Bethesda

By the 1920s, in South Africa, nursing had become a 'highly prestigious occupation for the daughters of the westernised elite' (Marks

1994: 88). In rural areas, this transformation took longer, and nurse recruitment was often more challenging. Work was seen as improper for women, and women who worked often found their marital prospects diminished. In 1943, Dr Turner complained of the difficulty of recruiting women from the area surrounding Bethesda Hospital, breezily expounding the issue declaring that 'marriage fills their horizons!' The light-hearted tone suggested that it was the naivety of women's own unthinking behaviour that led them into marriage instead of a career. On the contrary, many women struggled against family and community expectations, and endured neighbourhood opprobrium, to pursue a nursing career. In her autobiography, Abegail Ntleko, a nurse who worked in a rural hospital in northern KwaZulu-Natal for several years in the 1970s, describes her struggle as a child growing up in a rural area in the 1930s. Against the will of her father, she managed to pursue an education and career. After witnessing the abuse suffered by her sister at the hands of a violent husband, she wrote:

> I was determined never to be treated like that; I would never be a man's slave. An education would give me independence. I thought, If I am educated, I can still get married. If things don't work out with a man, at least I have other options. (Ntleko 2012: 29)

During the period in which Ntleko was growing up, seismic changes were under way. As a result of diminishing agricultural capacity and cattle rearing at the beginning of the twentieth century, many men sought employment as the only route to marriage, in order to meet the demands of the *ilobolo* (bridewealth payment) (Hunter 2010: 41). Nursing could both enhance a woman's opportunities for marriage, especially in urban areas where they entered a growing African bourgeoisie, but it also offered the possibility of escape from the reliance on men. Several decades later, the idea that women would choose a career instead of marriage was quite familiar. Nursing provided escape from the trappings of marriage and other family pressures.[2]

But though it offered a route to financial independence, mission education was no escape from patriarchy. Educational and occupational training was formal and disciplined, especially for women and girls. It was part of a broader pedagogical instruction that covered every aspect of life, including religious practice, lifestyle, leisure pursuits and good manners. Mission education was a training, not only in work but in moral and social conduct, elocution, dress and other aspects of 'civilized' lifestyle. Deborah Gaitskell's discussion of Anglican and Methodist Church hostels for women in Johannesburg offers an interesting example, showing how missionaries were motivated both by the need to fill the capitalist labour market for domestic servants as well as by a desire to nurture the 'moral purity and security of women' in a dangerous urban setting that, they felt, put at risk the 'intrinsic value' of womanhood (1979: 45).

Nurse training encapsulated similar sentiments, and usually entailed a draconian set of rules by which nurses were expected to live, according to the wishes of their senior matrons who assumed a variety of roles, both kindly and maternal as well as firm and superior. As Marks observed, the nursing hierarchy in the 1940s and 1950s in South Africa was extremely rigid (1994: 103). Bethesda was no exception. The hierarchical relationship between senior staff on the one hand, and junior nurses and patients on the other, reflected powerfully a racial divide. In a letter to Miss Evard in 1952, a white nursing sister then working at the King Edward Hospital in Durban, Dr Farren – medical superintendent between 1944 and 1953 – conveyed characteristically the sense of racial superiority that was commonplace: 'Although our patients are primitive, they are a cheerful lot. You would find an absorbing interest in the training and "mothering" of the nurses.'[3]

Revealing a disturbingly harsh version of the maternalism that pervaded hierarchical structures during mission training are the memoirs of Lena Turner, the hospital's first matron and the wife of Bethesda's first doctor. She dedicates several pages to describing the behaviour of nurses, what she describes as their 'cheek and insubordination'. The tone is light-hearted, carrying an air of amused disapproval as though speaking of children. After discovering that a nurse had given birth during the night, Lena told her husband: 'Well she can stay there [in the side room] and have no visitors. Otherwise the others will think she is very clever.' Nurses were repeatedly penalized and sometimes dismissed for leaving the premises without permission, for entering romantic relationships and, on one occasion at the nearby Manguzi Hospital, for assisting a friend with an abortion.[4]

In some mission hospitals, doctors regularly monitored the nurses' weight; those deemed too large or too thin were subjected to tests for pregnancy, TB or other health conditions. Pregnant women or mothers were prevented from joining the occupation, part of the reason why marriage and nursing often were seen as mutually exclusive. Such concerns reflected a wider unease. As Marks describes, 'the virginity of young African girls was a recurrent preoccupation of missionaries, administrators and Christian Africans in twentieth-century South Africa' (1994: 104; see also Kumwenda 2005). The control of women's bodies was part and parcel of the civilizing process that would render them fit for duty. Both the bodies and the minds of black women had to be transformed by a strict programme of training. As Mr Oram, nursing tutor and senior nurse between 1965 and 1979, wrote: 'The black nurse has a different attitude to life than that of her white colleague but her skill has blossomed out with a higher standard of training' (Oram (unpublished): 38).

During the 1970s, Dr Daryl Hackland was running the hospital, by which time some of the most conservative strands of taken-for-granted mission-style hierarchy were loosening. During an interview, Priscilla and Daryl Hackland described aspects of hospital life under the Turners that they were eager to do away with quickly. 'Things were organised in a very old fashioned way that fell in line, in some ways, with apartheid,' Priscilla said. 'During meetings, all the whites would sit separately down the side of the hall. That had to change. We got rid of that straight away.' They wanted to avoid the earlier system as they saw it, in which 'authority was very much in the hands of the superiors'. Over time, they introduced a system they called 'participative management' by, for example, holding open staff meetings on a weekly basis.

Modes of discipline, however, remained draconian in character. The following is an extended quote from a research interview in which another nurse was describing her memories of the nursing tutor, Mr Oram, who had worked at Bethesda between 1965 and 1979 and had a reputation for being extremely strict:

> I can tell you my story. I was with a friend and we were in the kitchen. We were there because we were expected to make cocoa for patients sometimes. While we were doing that, we

were talking in Zulu. We were not allowed to speak Zulu at all during shift time. While we were speaking to each other, Mr Oram caught us and said, 'Go to my office'. In his office, we pleaded with him that the shift is over. He said, 'You are still wearing your uniform. Therefore the shift is not over!' He gave me the punishment that, from 7 until 8 every morning, I had to go to laundry and be assigned a different task each day. This lasted for a whole month! Just for speaking Zulu! He would give all sorts of punishments; working with your cap off, working with your shoes off, washing the walls, and always for one month. The punishment always lasted that long. It was so cold to be working with no shoes!... I remember one time when Mr Oram locked me in the linen room, I had to stay there for hours. I couldn't eat anything. When I wanted water, I had to knock loudly on the door and wait for someone to come.

Evoking the paternalistic attitudes of the time, she ended with the following assessment: 'they treated you like children. But we were adults.' Added to the extreme paternalism of the mission were the effects of changing systems of state governance, as rural areas became increasingly subject to apartheid social engineering.

Coercion and change in the countryside

The focus on territorial separation became a much more central component of National Party policy than under the previous government. The Tomlinson Commission of 1956 recommended the development of independent homelands, viewing the alternative – complete integration of the two racial groups – as unthinkable. The focus had shifted from maintaining the system of migrancy upon which South Africa's rapid industrialization had been based, to controlling and curbing it so as to limit the growth of cities. This was to be achieved by the creation of industry in rural areas to attract labour away from the cities. These areas began increasingly to be identified as the sites for separate ethnic homelands. The government set out to consolidate the rule of the chieftains in these areas, which was to provide the ideological foundation upon which the peripheral and divided, self-governing homelands would rest. The provision of rural health care became all the more necessary for the viability and legitimacy of this project. Even though rural African areas continued to be neglected, rural infrastructure received more careful consideration under apartheid via a tightened bureaucratic apparatus. Throughout the 1950s and early 1960s, although government grants to the hospital did increase, the overall picture was one of escalating ill health, caused especially by the spread of TB, alongside dire resource constraints.

In rural areas, mission hospitals provided some degree of shelter from the more overt forms of racial discrimination. Nonetheless, apartheid policies that placed restrictions on staffing severely undermined the already limited capacities of rural hospitals, in a context crippled by escalating rates of TB. This was evident in a statement by the Bethesda Hospital committee in the minutes dated 23 August 1968:

> Dr Turner had made enquiries of the Nursing Council concerning the possible appointment of an African Matron. The Council replied that it was policy to employ Bantu as much as possible for the nursing of Bantu patients, but no White person could be employed under the control of anyone other than a White person. Dr Turner reported that after much thought, he could not see any way to fulfil this regulation without impairing the efficiency of the Hospital.[5]

The statement referred to a law that had been enshrined in the Nursing Act of 1957. The Act legislated for representatives of both the South African Nursing Council (SANC) and the South African Nursing Association (SANA) – to which it was compulsory for all practising nurses to belong – to be elected by white nurses and midwives. Other racial groups were to be represented by subsidiary Advisory Boards that were governed by SANC. Separate nursing registers were to be held for the different racial groups, and SANC was given the power to decide upon differential training and uniforms according to race (Marks 1993: 343). Finally, no white nurse was to be supervised by a black nurse. This legislation, which created barriers to professional advancement for black nurses nationally, was the same that exacerbated disproportionately the problems of health-care delivery in peripheral rural areas already struggling to recruit staff.

Despite the political unrest of the 1950s in which nurses played an important part, the 1960s was characterized by the increasing entrenchment of apartheid ideology within nursing. This included unequal salaries across the racial groups and the attempted exclusion of black nurses from the profession altogether, partly through inadequate basic education for black South Africans and, more directly, through unnecessarily rigorous accreditation processes and examination procedures. Nurses were encouraged to acquiesce to unequal pay and conditions through the socialization of the training process which presented the nursing ethos as dutiful and compliant, as well as offering a system of rewards for those willing to conform (Marks 1994: 178).

Despite the racial paternalism evident in the previous section, missionaries were aware of the social and educational inequities that placed African nurses at a disadvantage. In a report written in June 1970, Mr Oram noted that twelve of thirteen nurses had recently passed their examinations as compared to a national average of 59 per cent, a success he attributed to the quality of teaching at Bethesda. In his typically crass yet serious style, he continued:

This prompts me to comment on the low standard of education resulting from the Bantu Education Act. The general knowledge of the African has deteriorated rapidly since the introduction of the present system in 1955. At the present time nurses with a Junior Certificate cannot calculate the simplest subtraction or multiplication without using the palms of their hands as a slate! Their general knowledge is less than a Std. IV white scholar. They have told me that their teachers instruct them when calculating in fractions to work to the nearest half! When coming here they are unable to express themselves in simple English.

In the realm of education 'divide and rule' has brought all it was designed for. This education system is an indelible blot in the history of a so-called Christian country. We as Christians must resist this insidious lowering of the education of the largest portion of the population.[6]

Oram's statement, devoid of the formality and even-temperedness of other entries in the hospital's reports and minutes, provides a window into a more subversive commentary that was perhaps more frequently spoken rather than written down. Such comments reflect an engagement with wider trends of political opposition in South Africa in the 1970s as the number of boycotts and protests against Bantu education in schools grew (Maré and Hamilton 1987).

The late 1970s marked an important turning point. Across the country, many years of trying to enforce apartheid segregation within the nursing profession had eventually become unsustainable, due partly to increasing political pressure that developed throughout the 1970s, and even more because of the huge, nationwide shortage of nurses that ultimately necessitated the recruitment of black nurses to all levels of the profession (Marks 1994: 189). In the context of growing political upheaval, including increasing activism among nurses, the government responded with repressive legislation in the form of the Nursing Act No. 50 of 1978, that made nurses' strikes illegal.

In the context of this upheaval, the government was pushing forward with its plans to form separate homelands. In part, this involved co-opting the African bourgeoisie in the homelands. An African middle class was needed to pioneer the project and serve as the fuel for its administration, industries and services. Instead of forcing professionals to conform to discriminatory legislation that held them back, they were instead to be given status and seniority. In 1977, a Bethesda Hospital report states, the hospitals were told 'quite emphatically' by the president of SANC that the restrictions on appointing senior black nurses no longer existed. On the contrary, the government wished actively to encourage the employment of skilled Africans whenever possible within the homelands. As the homelands project wore on, it became clear that the promotion of Africans to senior positions was not only necessary but also desirable.

Another part of this plan involved taking over the hospitals in the homelands, which had until now been run mostly by missionaries, and placing them under the control of the homeland governments. In 1982, Bethesda Hospital was the last hospital in the country to be taken over.

The renewal of community health under the
KwaZulu homeland government

On 6 October 1979, a new 300-bed hospital was opened in Manguzi, a rural area of the then homeland of KwaZulu. The event was celebrated with an address delivered by Chief Buthelezi – leader of the IFP and prime minister of the then KwaZulu government – attracting a crowd of 2,000. This appearance was one of many such publicity efforts by a leader adept at making use of public platforms and the media. The event also signalled – if less publicly – the cooperation between Buthelezi and the central apartheid government for, while it was funded by the latter, the hospital was used during this event as a political instrument in ongoing efforts to legitimize the homeland. Formerly a Methodist-run mission hospital – the sister hospital to Bethesda – the expansion and reopening was part of a nationwide process of government takeover after which many mission hospitals such as Manguzi and Bethesda were handed to the control of homeland governments.

But the celebratory tone of the event also disguised an underlying controversy about the need for such a large hospital in the area. Against the advice and wishes of the medical staff of the small mission hospital which had preceded it, the expansion of Manguzi Hospital was symptomatic of a tendency within central government towards cheap, curative, hospital-based care, contrary to the growing popularity in medical circles of preventive, community-based approaches. Furthermore, the staging of the hospital's opening with Buthelezi as the centrepiece – evoking the well-known reputation of the IFP leader being joined with the apartheid government in mutual interest – implied a degree of commitment by the homeland administration to the state's centralized approach to health-care delivery.

Here, however, I argue that quite the opposite was the case. The period of homeland rule in fact provided a certain degree of *autonomy* from the prescriptions of the central state, along with a relative increase of funds, which created an opportunity for mission hospitals to develop and implement a model of community-based care. Literature on health and health care in the homelands has tended to focus on the enormous financial constraints and the overwhelming inadequacy of service provision in these areas (e.g. De Beer 1984; Marks and Andersson 1988; Price 1986). What has been largely neglected thus far, however, was the relative gains made by mission hospitals working in KwaZulu due to the homeland government's willingness to pursue and to fund their more progressive community health initiatives – despite Buthelezi's overtures at the opening ceremony of an expensive regional hospital. This has important implications for understanding how nurses experienced professionalism, then and now. Nurses describe their work as having been more autonomous than it has been in recent years. Any dichotomy of this kind, based on a nostalgic recollection of the past, should be treated cautiously. We have already seen that mission education was highly disciplined and controlling. I am interested, therefore, in what such narratives tell us about contemporary experiences of professionalism. To do this, it is important to make sense of these assertions in the context of changing regimes of governance over the last fifty years.

The 1970s and 1980s thus bore witness, both to a consolidation of the intensely controversial homeland system twinned with the rise of the Inkatha movement, and the development of a radical global vision of primary health care encompassed by the World Health Organisation (WHO) mandate of 'health for all' – a model that was anticipated in South Africa, and largely failed due to political opposition, some thirty years previously.

In 1981, just over a year after the new hospital at Manguzi had opened, attention turned to Bethesda Hospital. Dr Hackland, medical superintendent of Bethesda, reported that the Department of Co-operation and Development had drafted plans to establish a regional hospital with 600 beds at Bethesda. The board received this news with 'great apprehension',[7] stating that it was 'concerned that development totally unsuitable may take place at Bethesda and at all costs wanted to avoid the situation which is now a fait accompli at our sister hospital Manguzi'.[8] The plan for a regional hospital at Bethesda never came to fruition. Nevertheless, such disputes indicated a repeat of the arguments of the 1940s, in which radical plans for community health came up against the hospital-centred focus of the state.

South Africa's earlier test of social medicine was also a crucial forerunner, pre-empting this global shift to primary health care in the 1970s and 1980s. During the 1940s, a group of progressive doctors and members of government attempted to initiate a programme of radical reform, shifting the country's health-care system towards a model of community-oriented social medicine. Many of these figures, like George Gale, had long-established roots in mission hospitals. An important vehicle for this agenda was a report that was commissioned in 1942 to investigate the basis for a National Health System. The debates marked a period of considerable tension between different levels of government. For while provincial authorities struggled to fund the increasing hospitalization of Africans in urban areas – a problem that provided the initial impetus for health-care restructuring – they became reluctant to give up control of hospitals to the central government, which was recommended as part of the proposals of the National Health Services Commission (NHSC) in 1944.

The final report was radical. It suggested the creation of an inclusive National Health Service which would serve, racially and geographically, all areas of society. Linked to this was the central proposition of a shift away from a hospital-focused, curative treatment, to an emphasis on preventative care. Such care would be provided primarily through small, local clinics and health centres. Henry Gluckman, who headed the NHSC and would soon after take on the influential role of minister of health between 1945 and 1948, just before the National Party came into power, stated it thus: 'Our job is to formulate a plan where hospitals would be kept empty' (quoted in Digby 2008: 492). This coincided with similar reforms in the United Kingdom, with the Beveridge Report of 1942 and the creation of the National Health Service in 1944. It was this vision that would serve as the basis for disagreements some thirty years later over the creation of the Manguzi Hospital.

But the National Health Service failed to materialize. The proponents of the report faced resistance from members of the medical profession, who feared being undercut by the proposed health centres, and were eventually unable to follow through with many of their more radical plans for reform.[9] Nonetheless, the impact of these ideas was significant, both at the time – with the setting up of health clinics across the country – and in years to come as the international health-care community shifted towards a primary health-care agenda in the 1970s and 1980s. The impact of these national discussions on the global stage was significant. The Pholela Clinic, set up by Sidney Kark in South Africa in the 1940s, was an early example of the model later adopted by the WHO (Litsios 2004: 1980). This demonstrates the important influence of South Africa's health system on global debates.

The apartheid government was quick to adopt the language of primary health care which was fast becoming a global priority, yet, as some authors predicted in 1983, this revival of the *rhetoric* of the earlier aims of the 1940s Gluckman Commission was largely unmet by a commitment to its implementation (Marks Andersson [1983]1992). In 1986, for example, indicators suggested an 'overwhelming dominance of high technology curative medical care consuming about 97 percent of the health budget with only minor shifts towards community-based comprehensive care' (Jinabhai, Coovadia and Abdool-Karim 1986: 163). Rather, Marks and Andersson, among others, interpreted this shift as a form of state propaganda amid attempts to secure legitimacy for the homelands (De Beer 1984; Marks Andersson 1988; Price 1986). Whether or not this was true, faced with the continual struggle of financial constraints, concerted efforts were made by missionary doctors and nurses working at Bethesda to implement a primary healthcare strategy, creating a resurgence of missionary identity and ethos at the very moment when governments were taking over the hospitals.[10]

'A whole-man type of ministry': reassertions of faith amid impending takeover

In the years leading up to Daryl Hackland's arrival in 1970, hospital reports suggest that his predecessor, Dr Robert Turner, had become tired and frustrated with the hospital's ongoing financial difficulties and with the ever-increasing encroachment of government demands on hospital affairs. He emphatically stated at one point, 'Bethesda was begun as a MISSION hospital, and we are still seeking to make that title real'.[11] Such sentiments were compounded by, perhaps also helped to produce, a feeling of inertia with regard to the spiritual work of the hospital that was expressed repeatedly through complaints to the board about the lack of a hospital evangelist.

When Daryl Hackland and his wife, Priscilla, arrived, they were free of the burden carried by their predecessors of years of hard work and limited financial resources. They brought with them a new lease of life. In Hackland's first report of March 1970, three months after his arrival, he commended Dr and Mrs Turner for having 'served to their uttermost', and the staff for facilitating a smooth crossover. Yet, he wasted no time in laying out his own initiatives and the changes he intended to bring about:

> Conscious that we are not only called to preach and to heal but also to teach we have a concern to commence this programme. We have started in a small way with Occupational Therapy

work, but this must be extended to include Health and Hygiene programmes at our Clinics and even basic agricultural projects on the 5–6 acres we have available. The problem is we have *no clinics* – we must start and we require a further vehicle for this purpose. (Emphasis in the original)[12]

Thus began a renewed effort to provide medical outreach and an attempt to widen the breadth of the hospital's work, as well as its geographical reach, with a more holistic approach to health care.

By 1971, preventative medicine programmes were in place throughout Bethesda's catchment area, including immunization of under-fives and health education. In addition, a Family Health Clinic had been set up at the hospital, seeing 256 families regularly. Coupled with these initiatives was a greater focus also on 'spiritual outreach'. Hackland, who was himself a trained minister, initiated 'a definite evangelical preaching programme by Staff of the Hospital to their areas'.[13] For Hackland, the community health approach and the aims of the mission were inseparable.

A year later, Hackland reported: 'Clinics continue to gather momentum and emphasis on prevention [is] particularly thrilling'. Signs were also showing that the government was beginning to take a more active role in supporting the clinics. Hackland reported one preventative measure by the state health department which had recently been extended to Bethesda: the Kwashiorkor Scheme that provided free subsidized milk powder.[14] By 1973, the hospital was applying to take part in the government's Comprehensive Medical Care Scheme. On 1 May 1973, it was agreed during a meeting that the state health department would fund an additional doctor's post at Bethesda to make the scheme feasible. This was granted and the necessary funds for the scheme paid to the hospital later that year.

Yet, the government-initiated Comprehensive Medical Care Scheme quickly developed difficulties with financing, and was rarely prioritized by government. During the following few years, funding for the clinics was sometimes forthcoming and at other times delayed or not given at all. Once again, there appeared a dissonance between professed intentions and effective implementation. Part of this was to do with the confusion around whether accountability lay with the central state health department or the KwaZulu government. For the state had now begun the process of trying to pass on the responsibility for health-care provision and financing over to the KwaZulu homeland government. At Manguzi Hospital, a report from November 1976 identified an urgent need for more clinics, a frustration that was compounded by the KwaZulu government's failure so far to put its words into action: 'Permanent clinics run by Kwa Zulu [*sic*]. Government show no signs of being established though talking has been going on for years.'[15] Likewise, at Bethesda during the same year, plans for a clinic in Madonela were stalled by the central government's continued negotiations with KwaZulu: 'The state is at present holding discussion with the Executive Council of Kwa Zulu [*sic*] re a clearly defined policy.'[16]

Meanwhile, both hospitals continued within their limited means to provide outreach, and it is clear that over the course of the decade, this aspect of their work became prioritized by the mission staff themselves, as a focus of exciting and innovative change and expansion motivated by the increasingly popular notion within the international medical and nursing professions of holistic, community medicine. In 1977, Bethesda Hospital's outreach work was grouped together under the title 'Go Ye in Christ' and incorporated clinics, immunization schemes, agricultural projects, health education, a soup kitchen, literacy support at the mission, and evangelizing. The new title re-emphasized Christian faith as the driving motivation behind all these initiatives. The hospital report of March 1978 exclaimed:

> 'Go Ye in Christ' 1978 was worked out, and is at present being implemented. The thrilling moments have been to see Jesus preparing ahead of us each step of the way, one jump ahead of us.[17]

Health education was delivered alongside bible study, as in the case of a five-day residential course for mothers.[18] Later that year, a further step was taken towards systematizing and standardizing the community health structure when formal nurse training, leading to a Bethesda Diploma of Primary Health Care, commenced. A meeting with the KwaZulu government confirmed that a primary health care course would soon receive official recognition.[19] This was an indication of the increasing interest shown by the KwaZulu government towards the hospital staff's work in developing primary health care: a show of support that would soon prove vital in enabling the continuation of this work after government takeover.

Nurses were the backbone of the community health-care system.[20] They were responsible for the day-to-day running of clinics, with help where possible from doctors, who would move back and forth between the hospitals and clinics. Mobility was aided by an aeroplane service named Zumat that began at the hospital in December 1975. This was established with the financial support from one of the doctors, Pat Garde, and the employment of a pilot, John Stevens. On days when doctors were due at the clinic, the nurses would go ahead and screen all of the patients. The doctor would arrive later by aeroplane.

Critiquing the notion that missionary education served to distance nurses from the beliefs and lifestyles of their communities, Anne Digby and Helen Sweet suggest that the process was a kind of 'cultural osmosis' characterized by a gradual interchange and flux of cultural idioms. The nurse became more effective not by distancing herself from her patients but by being 'both in and of the local community' (2002: 121). In many cases, nurses' skills as cultural mediators enabled community involvement, where suspicion and distance would otherwise have obstructed the relationship between residents and medical practitioners. In her autobiography, Abigail Ntleko described the local population as a pool of knowledge and skills available to be tapped. Unlike some of the white doctors with whom she worked, Ntleko had subtle appreciation for the potential to expand medical care by harnessing local methods and by equipping people with additional skills. She negotiated with representatives of five tribal wards and set up a two-month training program for Traditional Bed Attenders, based on knowledge gathered from women about local techniques for assisting with deliveries (Ntleko 2012: 67–68).

The nurses I interviewed, who had worked at the clinics spoke about the pre-1994 period with strong feelings of nostalgia, describing their work as rewarding. The discussion often veered towards the considerable autonomy they had enjoyed. Often this autonomy was the consequence of necessity, due to the sheer scale of need and the very few doctors on hand to help. Some nurses would be stationed at clinics far from the hospital. But they generally spoke well of the support they received from the doctors, matrons and senior midwives based at the hospital. Though mistakes could be made, doctors would provide regular, written feedback that would help them to improve. Comparing this process to the kinds of feedback nurses receive today, one said that 'it was helpful, because you were not afraid'. Although infrastructure like roads was poor, the hospital-based members of staff were available via radio communication. Nurses conveyed an overwhelming impression of having felt supported and respected but also independent in their work, suggesting that by the 1980s, the racial paternalism of earlier years had softened.

Invariably, these heightened recollections of the past were juxtaposed against the different attitudes and dispositions, as they perceived it, of their junior counterparts today. 'Something has been lost,' said one nurse who had worked at Bethesda since 1986:

> [Junior nurses] don't know that if you learn something new, you must practice it … even if you are under stress – because they always say, 'We are overworked'. Even when you are overworked you can do it correctly … I think they have got no confidence in themselves.

As we see in the next two chapters, the problems which are frequently attributed to the individual attitudes of junior nurses have their roots in the changing fields of governance that produce modes of accountability in the workplace. A key difference in the contemporary setting is that nurses fear that their mistakes will have formal consequences beyond the face-to-face accountability that has historically characterized professional modes of interaction in the medical setting.

Takeover

It may seem puzzling that this rise in mission-led community health care took place at a time when hospitals throughout the country were passing from the control of missions to the government. By 1975, considerable progress had been made in establishing a community health system at Bethesda, but many other mission hospitals had already been taken over. At Hlabisa Hospital – a former American Lutheran Mission hospital situated in the same northern region of KwaZulu as Bethesda and Manguzi – the takeover and consequent turnover of staff, in line with government policy of replacing white with African staff, was 'forced through' rapidly by the government (Sweet 2009: 353). Subsequently, in the KwaZulu homeland as a whole, 'the last mission nurse sponsored by the American Lutheran Church left in 1978 and the last doctor in 1981 so that by 1980 all Lutheran hospitals had been handed over to the South African government' (ibid.).

Similarly, at the Charles Johnson Memorial Hospital, at Nqutu, also in KwaZulu, run by an Anglican mission and the site at which renowned mission doctor Anthony Barker and his wife Maggie Barker had worked for some thirty years, was taken over speedily in 1973. The Barkers left soon after, returning to their home country of England, having been forced out following the government's refusal to renew Anthony's permit (Henderson 1993/1994). It seems that in this case, the status of Barker as a non-South African, in contrast to Hackland's citizenship status, made it easier for the government to force through this change. The government was probably also particularly eager to ensure Barker's removal because of his unusually outspoken opposition to the apartheid system (e.g. Barker 1959).

Why was Bethesda Hospital the last mission hospital in South Africa to be taken over by the government? This was likely due to a number of reasons. Firstly, the Methodist Church and its missionary branch were more resistant to takeover than many other denominations such as the Anglicans, who accepted the process more readily. This led to greater efforts on the part of the Methodist Church to enter into negotiations with the government on behalf of its hospitals (Gelfand 1984: 315). Secondly, at the time when Hackland was recruited in 1970, of all the hospitals in KwaZulu, Bethesda and Manguzi were the ones in most dire need of additional staff. Hackland, who was not a Methodist, took up the post to fill one of these vacant positions, rather than because of denominational allegiance. The government may have been more reliant on the mission's services than it was in other areas. Thirdly, the degree of influence established during these years between the doctors of the two Methodist hospitals and the homeland government meant that their status was strongly established. As I will explain, many of the doctors working during this period, including Hackland himself, went on to have considerable influence over the health policy of the KwaZulu government. The relationship was strengthened by the proactive engagement of individuals such as Daryl and Priscilla Hackland, and Dr Prozesky at Manguzi, whose strategies at improving health in the region involved liaising with

government. The timing of the Hacklands' arrival was also significant, as it encouraged renewed impetus at just the moment when
doubts and fears over impending takeover were undermining the
efforts of long-standing missionaries elsewhere.

Nevertheless, at Bethesda and Maguzi, like elsewhere, fears
of impending takeover grew. This is expressed in the archival
data through a resurgence of religious language that focused on
an integration of the missionary language of spiritual salvation
with that of community health and the idioms of an emerging,
international field of primary health care, partly driven through
NGO funding.[21] These newly emerging associations between mission and medicine at Bethesda echoed the outlook of the wider
Christian mission approach to medicine at the time. The Christian
Medical Commission, for example, emphasized the links between
Christian faith, community well-being and individual health. It is,
argued one of its members, only 'when the Christian community
serves the sick person in its midst [that] it becomes itself healed
and whole' (quoted in Litsios 2004: 1887). Both the missionary
and medical paradigms rejected the role of health care as a service
purely to cure disease, and viewed medical treatment as part of
a wider social and educational context that valued a more holistic understanding of health and personhood. So, while one was
rooted in a religious outlook and the other in a social and policy-
driven paradigm, nonetheless these similarities – and their shared
rejection of a narrow curative approach to medicine – rendered
them compatible. At Bethesda and Manguzi, the widespread shift
towards a primary health care approach enabled a rejuvenation
of missionary ideology through a synthesis of these two ways of
thinking:

> The Manguzi Community Programme is one of the ways in
> which this new concept of Community Health has found
> practical expression. It aims to provide those components of a
> whole-man type of ministry not fully catered for, at this stage, by
> Government Health Services.[22]

This synthesis was not only semantic but achieved practically
through the activities themselves, of going forth to communities,
implied in Bethesda's title of 'Go Ye in Christ'; of taking the religious message into people's homes, thus evoking the journeying

that was central to the missionizing process.[23] The Bethesda report of December 1977 states:

> Two Health Educators joined our staff from the 3rd of January and this has assisted in a more in-depth approach to Preventative Health. Mr. Mhlanga has taken over immunisations, Tuberculosis and school work, and is involved in teaching in the wards, O.P.D. and Clinics. He will penetrate into the individual Kraals and as a committed Christian is happy to be involved with personal and Christian councelling [sic]... School soup kitchens run by 'School Health Evangelists' with World Vision's help with salaries is also a possibility.[24]

A strong sense prevailed that God's 'calling' was fulfilled, in particular, through outreach work, as in the following quote from a Bethesda report of August 1980:

> We believe that those involved with this aspect of our work are being called by God to support actively an *outreach* programme. Many lives recently have been touched by the Work and been lead by the Spirit into commitment. [Emphasis in the original][25]

At Manguzi, nurses and doctors were pursuing similar programmes, despite the KwaZulu health department's stalling on the financing of clinics. Dr Draper and Dr Prozesky were responsible for pushing forward many of the initiatives, and in particular, for encouraging 'community involvement' through project committees consisting of local residents rather than hospital staff, in order to 'decrease reliance on senior hospital personnel',[26] in addition to the training of lay community health workers. At a meeting of the hospital board in August 1980, Hackland commended Drs Prozesky and Draper for their work which, he pointed out, 'was now well known through the country'.[27]

Yet, during the development of these strategies in the 1970s, the work of the hospital was continually restricted by funding problems, and while clinics did receive some financial support, they struggled, at times, against the government's prioritizing of curative, hospital-based treatment. This was particularly evident in the case of the new Manguzi Hospital that was developed immediately prior to the takeover referred to above.

The biggest concern for missionaries at both Bethesda and Manguzi at this time, once government takeover had become inevitable, was a fear of the discontinuation of spiritual 'witness'. This was expressed by a doctor at Manguzi immediately after the takeover:

> On a recent visit to a KwaZulu hospital, where the mission had decided to withdraw completely, I was struck by the total change in the place now run by SADF [South African Defence Force] doctors, totally secularized, having major staff problems, I felt a sickness to the depths of my soul to think of Manguzi similarly changed in a few years' time.[28]

Indeed, such concerns had first appeared several years earlier, when suggestions of a takeover were beginning to surface. In 1970, the staff at both hospitals requested that chapels be built on the hospital site. This was around the same time – perhaps not coincidentally – that the possibility of a takeover began realistically to be spoken about. Both requests were met promptly and enthusiastically by the church and the chapels were completed at Bethesda in 1975 and at Manguzi in 1976, symbolizing a reassertion of Christian 'witness' and spiritual presence in a place under siege by external and secular forces. At Bethesda, a Spiritual Affairs Committee was set up 'to look after the Chapel', also giving a degree of official status to this aspect of the hospital's work.[29]

In 1981, with takeover imminent, a Christian Work Committee was set up with the aim of furthering the spiritual work of the hospital by drawing on a wider interdenominational group. In the same year a Caring Committee was established at each hospital and several months later combined to form a single committee overseeing both hospitals. Its main functions were to 'provide spiritual support' to the staff, as well as to assist in seeking Christian doctors and nurses to fill vacant posts.[30]

Finally, the Christian Work Committee deemed the pursuit of its programme of community health essential to furthering the spiritual work of the mission, and aimed to

> channel donations of cash and kind to enable the Staff to continue its response to the needs of the whole Community [and

to] guide in establishing ways and means of bringing total health to all – for health is harmony of body, mind and spirit.[31]

This quote demonstrates, once again, the way in which deep-rooted mission theology of physical and spiritual healing is combined with the contemporary language of primary health care, evoking the WHO's widely publicized key goal emerging from the Alma-Ata Declaration of 'Health for All'.

This renewed spiritual emphasis, and the way in which the approach of community health fit so easily with holistic missionary conceptions of healing, meant that the contest between hospital-based and community-based approaches to health-care delivery took on a new religious significance. It came to signify for the religious staff of the hospital a struggle between secularism and faith, and between the treatment of physical disease and the attainment of spiritual well-being. So it was through maintaining a focus on community health that the mission could really leave its imprint.

Archival material documenting the lead-up to the takeover of the hospital in 1982 hint at a more complex relationship that nurses had with the hospital's leadership and Christian ethos than is suggested by nurses' rose-tinted recollections. There are suggestions from the committee reports that during the period of takeover, some nurses rebelled against the mission. At Manguzi, there were complaints that the staff no longer considered their 'Christian responsibilities and responses' as important.[32] At Bethesda, a report described 'a general feeling of antagonism between some of the staff and white families', as well as a 'great concern' that the nurses no longer wished to participate in Hospital Christian Fellowship.[33] Such comments hint at an institutional setting in which nurses had for a long time been forced to take part in religious activities. This ambivalence is evident in the comments of some nurses, who spoke of how they were required to attend prayers. This reveals a more negative experience that is often excluded from the nostalgic recollections frequently dominating nurses' accounts. Despite this, the nurses working at Bethesda during my research on the whole recalled the hospital's mission days in positive and nostalgic terms, and took pride in their Christian roots. The 'mission-trained nurse', more than anything, emerged as the enduring self-proclaimed identity of that period.

KwaZulu government support in the pursuit of primary health care

In this section, I argue that in the decade following the takeover of mission hospitals by the state, the mission period and the doctors associated with mission work did not, as was feared, lose their influence or autonomy. Instead, their work enjoyed a new period of expansion and influence. The superintendent of Bethesda from 1980 to 1989, Dr Stephen Knight, did not recall the takeover as having had any great impact on the way things were done. They continued as they had done previously, with the mission still largely in control, in practice, if not officially. Not only did the hospital receive continued support from the Methodist Church, but mission doctors also had considerable influence over the KwaZulu government. Dr Hackland himself became the head of health services for the KwaZulu Department of Health. He explained that he took this position in order to exert influence, despite his personal opposition to the IFP. He and other doctors working in the KwaZulu homeland at that time had considerable influence over the policies and expenditure of the government in the 1980s. Dr Prozesky of Manguzi Hospital, for example, was involved in the research and drafting of the Buthelezi Commission report of 1982 which proposed a programme of Total Community Development based on the 'Prozesky Model' that incorporated the work of Manguzi Hospital as a model for future health-care delivery in KwaZulu:

> There [at Manguzi] community workers are being utilised as educators and as the first line of provision for simple medical services, and the screening of patients for referral to specialist attention. Tied in with the provision of primary health care is the provision of safe water, and the hygienic disposal of human and other wastes. This in turn links in with the broader issues of community development and rural development. (Buthelezi Commission 1982: 420)

Importantly, it criticized the apartheid government's prioritizing of curative, hospital-based care, stating that 'whenever there are financial cutbacks ... the outlying clinics providing primary health care

are first affected, and the hospitals are kept running as far as possible without cutbacks' (ibid.: 393).

This is only a fragment of the Buthelezi Commission report and is not intended to negate broader criticisms of the document and what it represented (Maré and Hamilton 1987: 163–69; Pretorius 1981;Southall 1983). But it does identify one aspect of the document, and of the KwaZulu government more broadly, which has been overlooked: the influence of the community health model in determining health policy and spending. Prozesky's plans became far more feasible under the KwaZulu government than they had been under mission control, because the financial constraints suffered by the church were more severe, and the later government was forthcoming about his proposals. As Knight explained, Prozesky 'actually convinced the main financial officer of the KwaZulu government to support community health'.

While in terms of South Africa's political economy as a whole, homelands suffered fiercely from uneven distribution, the KwaZulu government's willingness to support and to fund the work of the two former Methodist mission hospitals did create a space in which doctors and nurses felt enabled to pursue their own health-care agenda.[34] Knight thus claimed that, despite the divisive and oppressive features of both the KwaZulu government and the homeland system as a whole that have tended to dominate discussions about this period, the KwaZulu government nonetheless had 'an incredibly innovative group of people working within it' that meant they could effectively implement important changes.

During the 1980s, building on the foundations set by Daryl Hackland and his colleagues in the previous decade, considerable advances in primary health care were made, including the development and implementation of the nurse training course, considerable increase in numbers of vaccinations provided, advancements in clinic-based antenatal care and a much expanded TB treatment programme.[35] The Bethesda primary health-care model was taken up elsewhere, and Knight was invited to meetings both with SANC and with the Department of Health in Pretoria, in which he was able to advance these initiatives at the national level. He described it as 'an incredibly exciting time to be working at Bethesda', arguing that this depth of influence achieved by a small group of progressive health workers would simply not be possible now. Reflecting on the managerial restructuring that occurred with the change of government a decade later in 1994, in which the role of hospital administration was separated from that of the medical superintendent, he claimed this had a massive effect on the extent of influence that doctors and other front-line workers could have over the planning of health-care delivery. For instance, when new hospital service managers arrived, they challenged the role of various community health initiatives, arguing that these fell outside of the health department's mandate. Knight added:

> They really took up the apartheid approach. It was supposed to be the end of apartheid, but they adopted this new device of legislation. Before then the whole thing was doctor-based. At that time, I was superintendent, financial administrator, and I controlled the clinics.

Thus the wider restructuring of health-care services and the reintegration of the separate departments of health into one caused a degree of fragmentation of health care at the local level, which was felt by those working on the front line to be extremely intrusive.[36]

According to Knight, another source of disagreement and fragmentation during this period was the transfer of primary health care training to SANC, thus making primary health care the sole responsibility of nurses, and excluding doctors from the process. Charlotte Searle, the most influential educator and scholar of nursing in South Africa, was extremely adverse to the idea of training nurses within health centres like Pholela. As an advocate of professionalization, she was determined that SANC maintain control.[37] Yet, this approach later had the effect of 'excluding other health-care workers from the mainstream of primary care and perpetuating the idea that doctors in the public sector should work in hospitals while nurses provide clinic-based care' (Kautzky and Tollman 2008: 22). Knight also expressed this view, suggesting that it impacted negatively on PHC at Bethesda Hospital, alienating doctors and fragmenting existing practice. Many have highlighted that since 1994, PHC has been sidelined in favour of other approaches and the potential for innovative community health that was established in the previous decade largely abandoned.

While some suggest that the establishment of PHC in South Africa was 'explicitly born of the struggle against apartheid' (Kautzky and Tollman 2008: 22), others argue that it had a depoliticizing effect. De Beer claims, for example, that the 'community health' approach

> remains trapped within the victim blaming mode of thought … The assumption that people need health education re-inforces the belief that illness arises out of ignorance. Further, the desire to use community development techniques to 'help people to solve their problems' rests on a belief that people are unable to solve their problems for themselves, and suggests that the problems are of their own making … But this line of argument ignores the truth that poverty is itself a symptom of a history of dispossession, exploitation and oppression. (De Beer 1984: 74)

The idea of radical progress in health-care delivery during the period of homeland control perhaps seems redundant in the context of an institutional and political framework so profoundly unequal in its distribution of resources. Yet, for doctors and nurses working at that time, the level of command that they had over hospital strategies and health-care policies generated a powerful sense of control and creativity at the level of implementation. This is to do with a politics of scale, in which the issues facing a small rural hospital, at times, conflict with the problems characterizing a wider political economy. For the staff working at Bethesda, the KwaZulu homeland provided a certain degree of autonomy that was swept away with the change of government in 1994.[38]

The democratic transition

In 1994, the newly elected ANC embarked on a plan to integrate the previously fragmented health-care system across the country. The homelands were dismantled and the borders of nine new provinces drawn up, which included KwaZulu-Natal. The fourteen separate departments of health – including ten that had been controlled by the homeland governments – were integrated into a single, unified health infrastructure. As the new three-tier District Health System (DHS) slowly came into being, financial investments in Bethesda Hospital were palpable. The number of staff grew quickly, and new buildings were erected. Despite these improvements, the transition from one management system to another was unsettling for many staff. Under the mission, and to a large extent following the takeover up to the change of government in 1994, the hospital was centred on the patrimonial leadership of the medical superintendent who, despite being accountable first to the Methodist mission and then, after 1982, to the KwaZulu homeland government, had considerable control over the administrative running of the hospital. After 1994, the demise of apartheid and the dismantling of the homelands accompanied a rapid bureaucratization and integration of health services. At the national level, this process focused upon *decentralization* as a key imperative, substantiated in the form of the three-tier system of government in which the local district was to have considerable decision-making power. Despite the injection of resources and the official emphasis on decentralization, many clinical staff experienced this transitional period as a suffocating encroachment of government demands. It felt as though control had been swiftly removed and relocated in a distant place. Over time, the creation of an additional local layer of government has led to the decentralization of responsibility without a corresponding decentralization of power and resources. As a former doctor expressed with frustration:

> Around about 1994, we had these meetings about the district health system. And this was the new big thing, you know, this was going to change everything. And I remember standing up at a meeting and saying it would only make sense if it was another level of management and not just another level of bureaucracy. In other words, if the budgets were still held at the provincial level, then a district office was just going to be another irritating level of bureaucracy. So this district health system only made sense if they devolved managerial decision-making, including authority to spend resources, to district level. And I mean, it's true, they've basically become … irritating levels of bureaucracy rather than a budget-holding authority.

Charged with responsibilities but with little in the way of resources, Gillian Hart argues that local government has become the key site of contradictions and tensions in contemporary South Africa:

> [L]ocal government has become the impossible terrain of official efforts to manage poverty and deprivation in a racially inflected

capitalist society marked by massive inequalities and increasingly precarious livelihoods for the large majority of the population. Ironically, attempts to render technical that which is inherently political are feeding into and amplifying the proliferation of populist politics. (Hart 2013: 5)

This became apparent at Bethesda in mid-2014, when angry protesters descended on Gedleza Clinic over faulty water infrastructure that, the protesters believed, had been intentionally turned off by the local government. Tyres were burnt, and the road was shut down. Several people were arrested and the clinic was temporarily closed. Such scenes are increasingly common across South Africa.

For the staff at Bethesda, decentralization meant the detachment of administrative from medical functions, a gap which was mediated increasingly by paperwork. I interviewed Jonathan Pons – the medical manager of Bethesda Hospital at the time – in his home in Swaziland. He had moved there after leaving Bethesda, partly to escape what he considered to be the encroaching dysfunctional authoritarianism of the South African government. Like many of the doctors who had worked at Bethesda Hospital during the period of homeland rule, Dr Pons had become exasperated with the ways in which the hospital was changing. Like Steve Knight, he also recalled nostalgically the freedom that he and his colleagues had experienced prior to the transition to ANC rule. This was partly the consequence of what he called 'bad governance' by the KwaZulu Department of Health, whose corruption and 'incompetence' meant that the staff were left virtually to their own devices. Despite the freedom this 'absentee state' – as he called it – inadvertently bestowed, it came with endless frustrations. Pons described his relationship with the KwaZulu Department of Health in the following way:

> I couldn't bear phoning them, because they didn't answer phone calls. I would phone and ask for the person in charge of issuing capital items. The person would tell me he wasn't there, and I would ask, 'Where is he?' They would tell me, 'I don't know, but his jacket is on the chair'. His jacket was always on the chair.

His account implied that bureaucratic problems of a different sort began to increase after 1994. He described what happened when the hospital began to use a fax machine in 1995. At first:

> The secretary would come running to me with it, because it was like a telegram! But after some time, it was just grinding all day. We received circulars by fax all the time. They'd be all over the ground.

The documents dealt with all kinds of issues, he explained, from changing services benefits, to housing related tax issues: 'endless administrative issues', he said with a dismissive wave of his arm. When they first started, he continued, the wastepaper basked was filled every two weeks. By the time he left, it was filled every day. His disparaging tone suggested a comic dismissal of superfluous administrative tasks. This reflected a deep despondency toward the bureaucratic intrusions of government that, by the time Dr Pons left Bethesda, he argued, had 'taken over' the running of the hospital.

In Chapter Five, we will see that paperwork has become a node of contention for nurses as well, though given their positions and roles, they are not able to dismiss it so flippantly. For nurses, another crucial signifier of the bureaucratic transition is a perceived decline of religion at the hospital. These concerns came to the fore in 2006, when the hospital manager declared that the hospital chapel would no longer be used for prayer meetings and services, arguing that the space was needed for conferences and board meetings. Since then, the only religious services that took place in the chapel were those that marked special or important occasions, such as memorial services for a member of staff who had died. The change carried a symbolic weight that became clear in conversations with nurses, during which complaints about the chapel's closure were usually aired in the context of criticisms of hospital management.

During these conversations, the event seemed to signify and remind nurses of the changes associated with the end of mission medicine and the subsequent bureaucratization of health-care delivery. A chaplain, who regularly visited the hospital, discussed with me this significant change of recent years. Before the closure of the chapel she used to give regular 'public addresses'. The patients would hear these via large speaker systems in the wards. She would also show religious videos to patients. Her activities were now restricted to individual bedside visits. She explained: 'With this new democracy, you are not allowed to preach your faith to people. It is against the law. They think it is like brain washing or something.' She explained that individual bedside visits enabled patient choice about whether or not to participate in religion, whereas the previous activities precluded individual consent. Her explanation revealed clearly the feeling that a Christian ethic was being undermined by new kinds of practices falling under the remit of state authority.

The creation of the chapel at Bethesda is recorded in the archived minutes of the hospital's meetings. It was opened in 1975, when the hospital was run by the mission branch of the Methodist Church of South Africa. This was a moment during which government takeover was virtually inevitable. The notes from this period are full of foreboding, with doctors expressing fears about the secular forces beyond their control. Therefore, though nurses spoke of the chapel as a symbol of an earlier period of institutionalized religion, the chapel was in fact established in reaction to fears of secularization. Even the opening of the hospital itself in 1937 had occurred during a period in which mission activity was in global decline (Hardiman 2009). Despite nurses' nostalgic reference to mission days, which implies a linear process of secularization, the religious ethos of the hospital was from the outset constituted alongside the secular. This was manifest in a perceived secular threat represented by the encroachment of government. Secularity, like state power itself, has always been present in the life of the hospital.

From the perspective of many nurses, however, there has been a shift marked by the decline of religion and in its place the insertion of liberal democratic idioms of 'democracy', 'rights', 'accountability', 'bureaucracy' and so on. One nurse who had worked at the hospital since before its takeover by the government explained the way in which Christian practices had changed:

> Going to church services is no more a straightforward thing now. You have a choice whether you go or you don't go. And some of the things that were not allowed before, they are now allowed. You can have a radio in the room – things which were not allowed. So people listen to their radios and if you want to go to church you go. If you don't want you don't want ... You know, the *rights* – things came with the rights of people to choose.

As with the reference to 'this new democracy' made by the chaplain, this statement acknowledges the increasing influence of liberal democratic notions of 'rights' and 'choice' in calling into question the previously 'straightforward' authority of Christianity and the mission. Such examples appear to fit neatly alongside a Weberian model of secularization, whereby religion has become a matter of individual belief and choice, diverted to the private sphere, and no longer upheld by the institution itself. Yet, while the chaplain complained that she is no longer permitted to preach in wards, the example of the morning prayer session suggests that mediums of communal Christian prayer and song still contribute to an institutional agenda, taking a formal and regular place in the daily schedule of wards.

Conclusion

Mission training was a contradictory experience for nurses. While they suffered the racial paternalism of mission hierarchies, a career in nursing also offered autonomy from patriarchal structures at home. Professionalism therefore offered a degree of freedom, at a time when marriage was the only option available to many women. By the 1980s, when the hospital was nominally controlled by the KwaZulu homeland government, paternalism had softened and the hospital achieved a degree of autonomy not shared by its counterparts in the cities. This was achieved inadvertently, in a context where the homeland government was unable or unwilling to intervene. This created an opportunity for nurses and doctors, who recall the period as an exciting and creative moment for rural health care.

The experience of mission medicine, which from the perspective of nurses continued until 1994, is crucial for understanding why nurses recall with nostalgia a period regarded by many as having been highly oppressive. The subsequent separation of administrative from clinical functions at the hospital, closely related to the Weberian transition from patrimonial to bureaucratic modes of administration – though not entirely explained it – created a feeling that professional autonomy was being eroded. In Chapter Five, I discuss the reproduction of nostalgia and how nurses use recollections of the past to construct temporal narratives about the erosion of professionalism. For now, we turn to an exploration of how nurses navigate projects of care and professional ethics in the contemporary work setting.

CHAPTER FOUR

Accountability, Hierarchy and Care

During my fieldwork at Bethesda Hospital, many of the activities I observed indicated the deeply socialized and stratified roles that have been described in medical settings around the world (e.g. Andersen 2004; Gamarnikow 1978; Latimer 2000). Shaped by habitual routine and the repetition of medical vocabulary, they suggested an institutional culture with a longue durée. Part of my time was spent in the TB ward, located in a small building at the far end of the hospital, separated from other wards by a small courtyard. It was one of the busiest wards in the hospital owing to the high prevalence of TB in the area. In 2006, when I began research, there was a prevalence rate of 20 per cent of the catchment population and a cure rate of 42 per cent.[1] The rapid increase in the prevalence of HIV/AIDS in the area had caused a resurgence of TB, including new drug-resistant strains.

The main male TB ward contained fourteen beds, but several other rooms had been converted to cater for the overspill. The ward was bright during the day, with large windows looking out onto the small paved courtyard outside. Two large ceiling fans spun constantly and a television provided a continual hum of background noise, although no one ever seemed to be watching it. The walls were a pale yellow colour, and decorated with various posters produced by the Department of Health, covering topics such as sanitation, breastfeeding and patients' rights. The beds formed two lines along either side of the room. The patients wore light blue cotton pyjamas provided by the hospital. At the end of each bed was a tall, metal stand upon which rested a large red folder, the patient file, containing information of the corresponding patient. The ward held some of the sickest patients, many of who were below the age of forty. While some would return home, many would not recover.

Nurses' work entailed intimate, daily encounters with pain, discomfort and death. The masks that some used to cover their mouths were a reminder of the fragile boundary between them and their patients. Some nurses working here spoke of their fear of contracting TB, especially because of increasing rates of multi- and extra-resistant strains of the disease. Several described the risk as a mental strain, but were not in a position to negotiate their ward allocation. Nurses were visibly demarcated from patients and visitors by their uniform, on which were differently coloured epaulettes attached to the shoulder to signify their level of training. This was an important marker of status at the hospital.

In a situation where there were many patients and too few hands, the work of the nurse was as much about finding solutions to problems and constraints, one unpredictable situation at a time, as it was about following routines or conforming strictly to protocol. One nursing manager described this as a 'game' – you have to 'keep playing that game', he would tell me. There is daily creativity involved in solving problems: negotiating with other ward managers to move nurses temporarily from one department to another; assessing a child's condition to judge whether it is safe for her to share a bed, and so on. In the absence of a doctor, experienced nurses could provisionally diagnose certain conditions and order X-rays and blood tests to reduce the work of the doctor when they arrived. Sometimes, problems could be resolved by negotiating, but at other times one would have to 'fight' and 'make noise'. 'When a case is severe, you need to be aggressive,' one manager explained, 'because if a patient dies, you will also be partially responsible.'

All spoke about treading a fine line between resolving problems as they arose and the need to conform to protocol. Any divergence from protocol, nurses repeatedly explained, exposed one to potential accusations of wrongdoing. This tension can be characterized in terms of Jean-Pierre Olivier de Sardan's distinction between 'official norms' – those that state actors are supposed to follow, which are laid out in the regulatory arena of policy documents, protocols and scope of practice – and 'practical norms' – those they pursue in their daily work: 'Formal bureaucratic norms and informal practical norms form the two end points of a continuum, within which social actors' strategies are played out' (Olivier de Sardan 2014: 409). There is always, inevitably, a discrepancy between the two.[2] A tension exists because the purpose of accountability is to expose the discrepancy; but in the context of resources shortages, the gap is inevitable, and could even be productive. Nurses use a combination of ingenuity, negotiation and work to navigate the gap successfully.

In the normative arena of policy documents, media narratives and wider public discourse, 'accountability' – like 'rights' – has become a quintessential idiom through which democracy is envisaged. Practical experiences of accountability take many different forms, both formal and informal (Olivier de Sardan 2014: 425). Many of the interactions I observed suggested that different and sometimes conflicting kinds of accountability were mobilized at different points, implying a more muted terrain of contestation than the 'breakdown' of order and liminal anarchy described by von Holdt (2005). Like the softer, everyday forms of resistance that James Scott (1985) identifies, they were nonetheless persistent, daily and, for some nurses, produced ongoing feelings of anxiety and uncertainty.

Two modes of accountability

One morning I was observing a ward round in the TB ward – part of the daily routine in which a doctor, accompanied by a member of the senior nursing staff, visited each patient, assessing, diagnosing and carrying out minor procedures. 'Look at this guy,' the doctor said, smiling as he approached one patient. 'He's doing so well. I'm so pleased with his progress.' He turned to look at the nurse who was accompanying him, asking 'Can he walk?' The nurse said nothing, looking at him with an expression of uncertainty. 'Has he been walking when I'm not here,' the doctor persisted, 'or just lying down?'

'He has not been walking,' the nurse finally declared. 'Well, he's got to start walking more,' the doctor retorted. 'It's the only way he's going to get better. Tell him that the more he walks, the sooner he'll be able to go home.' Before the nurse had a chance to convey this message in Zulu, the doctor was passing the metal frame to the patient, encouraging him to stand up and walk, and congratulating him enthusiastically as he did so, commenting repeatedly on how much he was improving. 'I don't know whether to send him home now,' he paused, looking at the patient indecisively, as he struggled to push himself up onto the frame. 'Because if I do, he might stop walking, but he's doing so well now!' The cause for the doctor's indecision was conveyed in his repeated asides about whether the nursing manager, to whom they referred as 'Matron', would allow him to delay the patient's departure. 'I think we'll keep him here a bit longer,' he said tentatively. He paused thoughtfully again, while the nurse helped the patient to walk a few steps, then, in a more decisive tone, said, 'The matron's going to kill me, but a couple more days. He's doing so well.'

During this exchange between a nurse, doctor and patient, some of the predominant themes of hospital sociality were at work. With the nurse serving the role of principal interlocutor, the two worked together as professional colleagues. Despite this, the nurse's subordination to the doctor was evident, conveyed by the latter's assertiveness and the nurse's deferential behaviour towards him, and by the direction in which accountability flowed between the two. It was the nurse who responded to the doctor's questions, partly because her work was contained within the TB ward, so she had a more intimate understanding of the patient's condition than did the doctor, whose visits to the ward were intermittent and brief. But the flow of accountability in this direction also reflected a historically entrenched subordination of nursing to the medical profession. As a white, English-speaking, male doctor and a black, Zulu-speaking, female nurse, their relationship mirrored familiar hierarchies of race and gender that historically have shaped medical settings in the region.

This face-to-face accountability between nurse and doctor, emerging in the course of daily interactions on wards, was nothing new: it was a manifestation of the way in which nurses have been socialized since the earliest days of mission training to be subservient towards doctors (Kumwenda 2005; Marks 1994). The doctor's expression of concern about going against the wishes of the matron was, in addition, an indication of another type of accountability at work. This was one that has emerged in a recent period of post-apartheid transition to a new style of management. In this form of managerialism, channels of accountability existed less between front-line workers themselves than between two separate spheres of clinical and managerial practice, dealing with distinct and often contradictory priorities that formerly were subsumed under the remit of the medical superintendent, outlined in Chapter Three. The tension between the doctor's concern for individual patients, and the concerns of the matron, who was under pressure to reduce the hospital's statistics for 'average length of stay', is one that arises in the context of resource shortages. At the time of my research, the average length of stay (ALOS) for hospitals belonging to Umkhayakude District Municipality was considerably higher than the national average, which meant that managers faced additional pressure to reduce it (Day et al. 2009: 168). In this instance, the doctor's comments demonstrated his accountability to a senior managerial representative, who was absent from the ward.

The doctor's deliberations, in this example, show how different logics intervene in the moment-to-moment exchanges between him and other staff, producing tension. In this scene, and many other daily encounters, new forms of audit and accountability combine with existing idioms in ways that defy any strict teleology or distinct replacement of one type of accountability with another. The doctor chose to keep the patient in longer, even though he was concerned about what the matron would say. His decision, although conflicting with official aims to keep to a minimum the patient's length of stay, obeyed the 'spirit' of the institution's overall aim (Olivier de Sardan 2014: 409).

While this kind of division between administration and clinical work at Bethesda is relatively new, it has long characterized healthcare delivery in other settings, in South Africa and beyond. In the United Kingdom, Joanna Latimer argues that the tension between institutional management and patient care represents 'two competing moral discourses: a utilitarian discourse, which demands that more people are treated, and a professional discourse of care for the individual' (2000: 28). Ethnography from Bethesda's wards suggests these two moral discourses do not carry equivalent weight, but that the narrative of individual care tends to assume a moral high ground, while the utilitarian discourse is negatively associated with 'bureaucracy'. Some doctors approach work with a clinical bias: bureaucracy is the object of complaint, the perpetual obstacle to achieving patient care. Unlike the majority of nurses, doctors were outspoken in their criticism. As one junior doctor said, during a focus group discussion:

> We [doctors] are in contact with the patients every day. You know, you see how things on paper either negatively affect patients or things that are supposed to enhance patient care actually have no effect whatsoever, you know, and that never gets to the top… because they sit in little glass offices up there. But I think sometimes it looks beautiful on paper, but [they] actually have no idea how to implement it, have no idea if it's actually going to be workable, and have absolutely no clue how it's going to affect the patients at the end of the day.

Nurses were frequently more reserved in their criticisms, partly because unlike medicine, the historical trajectory of nursing was one of only partial professional autonomy. Doctors, in contrast, inherit from the history of their profession a powerfully autonomous field of operation. Nurses' exposure to, and fears of, audit were consequently more pronounced, while doctors tended to speak their mind. But nurses, doctors and administrators did not consistently adopt one perspective over another. As we saw in the example from the TB ward, daily work involves navigating between the two. Everyone was involved in the ethical work of traversing the gap between official and practical norms, rather than the two approaches being embodied in different actors.

Much of the normal conflict that arose from day-to-day had to do with these kinds of strategies, at times with unexpected outcomes. One hot day in January 2007, I took a three-year-old child from the surrounding area to the hospital with an ear infection. She had tested positive for HIV several months earlier, and a friend had asked me to help, explaining that the child was an orphan and that none of the people caring for her were in possession of any documentation that could identify her. This had made it difficult for her to access treatment, because they had been told by one of the HIV counsellors that she needed identification in order to be eligible. The child sat silently on my lap while we waited for two hours to see the doctor. A smelly liquid emanated from her ear, a common symptom associated with the progression of HIV to AIDS. When we finally saw the doctor, the appointment was brief. 'This is going to sound harsh,' the doctor told me, 'but this country is in the middle of a pandemic. To be honest, when people come and they don't have all the criteria, I don't think twice about sending them away.' Eventually, after several conversations with sympathetic nurses, one of them managed to arrange treatment for the child.

I had been taken aback by the incident, perhaps partly because it ran counter to the strong ethic of individual care I had encountered among doctors in general. Many nurses and doctors agonized over decisions caused by administrative or resource constraints that might hamper individual care. This was an unusual moment, in which the language chosen seemed to assume a moral consensus based on utilitarian logic. It showed that tangible consequences can arise depending on whether utilitarian or caring discourses are mobilized.

Nurses and doctors manage and move between different modes of accountability. The patrimonial-style authority of doctors that was so characteristic of the colonial period remains significant, and can either operate alongside or in tension with bureaucratic modes of accountability. These are not separate fields, one superimposed on another, but instead are reconstituted and negotiated in quotidian daily practices. I turn now to the ways in which these differing modes of accountability affected the nursing ethos and professional ethic.

Inscribing accountability

Early in my field work, I was leaning against a wall in the shade, writing notes from a ward visit, when a nurse spotted me and came over. 'I've seen you around here all day,' she said in a friendly, curious tone. 'What are you doing?' I explained my research, about which she expressed passing interest before proceeding to tell me that she had her own research project and that, perhaps, I could help her with it. She was studying a course at the University of KwaZulu-Natal while working at Bethesda. She wanted to do her project on HIV/AIDS among pregnant women, but didn't have the experience of doing research and wasn't sure about what kind of information she needed to collect. She invited me to visit her at work one day, and I gladly agreed. 'I think God has brought you to me,' she said smiling.

When I did make the trip, it had taken a couple of visits to find a time when she wasn't too busy to see me. We discussed both of our research projects, and she asked if I could help her with something else. She was making an application to the Department of Health for funding to support her studies, and needed help to write the covering letter. I agreed, and we soon sat down to write it together. A few days later on a second visit, she told me that the nursing manager was impressed with the letter, and had written her a good supporting statement. 'It's amazing,' she said, 'because I knew I was late with it and I had to do it, and you came along at exactly the right time.' Her comment reminded me of the serendipitous nature of fieldwork and how unexpected events – the experience simply of being in the right place at the right time – can often form the substance of meaningful ethnographic encounters. For Cecilia, the fortuitous encounter was explained by God's presence and, as I would come to learn, its immanence in all aspects of life.

Cecilia and I gradually became friends over the months that I did research at Bethesda. Some forty years older than me, she sometimes affectionately referred to herself as my grandmother: 'Come to visit *gogo* (granny)?' she would say, when I dropped by to see her at work. Our relationship was, from the outset, based partly on reciprocal assistance. She helped me with my research, and I assisted her with a variety of written tasks. Gradually, other nurses would seek my help as well. It was partly in assisting the nurses to write that I got to know them and came to learn about the bureaucratic workings of the hospital.

It also helped me to develop a deeper sense of commensurability between their work and mine. Both they and I converted our observations into text, a process entailing particular epistemological and ethical challenges. Some written tasks of the nurses were similar to those of ethnographers, especially the need to immerse oneself in the memories of specific events and to recall and transform into text what was previously an intuitive, embodied knowledge. As I entered the office one day, Cecilia was scribbling away in a book, with a textbook open in front of her. She told me to come and sit down. She explained that she had been given a case study to complete. She was presented with a set of symptoms and had to describe what she would do to diagnose the condition, and why. When she read it, she explained, her immediate feeling was one of dread, provoked by the thought that she did not know what to write. After some moments she recalled that she had seen a patient earlier that week with the same symptoms. When she remembered what she had done for the patient, she was able to complete the written task: 'It is second nature what to do. I just know what to do and do it … but for some reason, having to write it down and explain it is difficult.' As an ethnographer, I could relate to this challenge of translation.

Cecilia grew up in a small mining town in the province of Mpumalanga, and came to Edendale Hospital in KwaZulu-Natal to train as a nurse. She loved her training, and was full of praise for how meticulous it was. She explained how they would clean the beds every day, as well as the mattresses, the posts and the windows: '[We cleaned] everything properly. The cleaners only did the floors. We did everything else. And it was professional, we did a professional job on it … and I really liked that.' During such conversations, I learnt that Cecilia rejected the elitist separation of menial work from professional nursing that had long featured in the occupation's ideological drive for status. Instead, she spoke of a love for the simple tasks: 'I really like wounds,' she would tell me. 'I love to wrap them up all neatly, and then I love seeing them heal.' She explained, in quasi-religious language: 'It's amazing to watch the patients being brought back to life.'

Cecilia was an example of what Jean-Pierre Olivier de Sardan calls a 'reformer', an employee who seeks to improve delivery by whatever means in a given situation, as opposed to a 'conservative' who is 'content with the current situation and the rents they derive from it' (Olivier de Sardan 2014: 426). In any workplace, he argues, both kinds of employees exist. At Bethesda, doctors praised Cecilia's attention to detail. Her interaction with other nurses was assertive but warm. Outside of working hours, people would approach her for advice. She also sometimes assumed the role of a religious counsellor. One evening we were together in Cecilia's room, and a friend who was a staff nurse came to speak about the job she had applied for, nervously seeking support to allay her concerns that the application might not have been successful: 'It is just those matrons that are a problem,' said the nurse, fearful that negative personal relationships with seniors might hold her back. 'No, they are not,' Cecilia said to her, 'because it is not up to them. It is up to God … God can do what he likes to those matrons. As long as you are walking with God, he will be faithful to you.' I sensed a slight frustration in the junior nurse, not to have received more practical advice. But as a born-again Christian, religion was the lens through which Cecilia interpreted every situation. It offered clarity and left no room for uncertainty.

Spending time with Cecilia and other nurses at work, I began to see how work consisted of multiple daily struggles and inter-actions, involving compromise and considerable emotional energy. Staff and resource shortages were not simply a background con-text or preexisting state, but were dynamic realities that re-created from moment to moment the constraints of each new situation in which a decision had to be reached. Her actions suggested a stra-tegic engagement, as she balanced the demands of the institution against the day-to-day challenges of work. But despite her reform-ist outlook, she also understood the need to acquiesce to certain kinds of bureaucratic stipulations. Unlike doctors who were openly critical of arbitrary and time-consuming bureaucracy, she tended in conversation – like most nurses – to defend the purpose of these requirements. Conformism was a strategy that was used by reform-ers and conservatives alike.

As I suggested earlier, the perceived separation of clinical from managerial concerns means that the two are mediated differently, not necessarily via face-to-face interactions in the wards but by new procedures of audit often involving considerable paperwork. Concepts of 'accountability' and 'audit' have entered the vernacular as popularized idioms, though in practice new forms of account-ability merge with existing ones, rather than taking their place. In a context in which accountability has become a key trope of institutional bureaucracy, nurses attempted to conform to the nor-mative moral yardstick imposed by ideas of accountability, while also expressing a sense of moral uncertainty and discomfort with these. Such feelings were a result, in part, of a contradiction felt by many, that administrative tasks fulfilling the extensive bureaucratic requirements of the hospital are given priority over and above clini-cal care itself, even or especially in a context of severe staff and resource shortages. In the process of research, I attempted to make sense of this apparent incongruity, exploring the ways in which staff engage with and try to overcome the moral ambiguities and chal-lenges posed by their work.

In the rest of the chapter, I propose several things. First, certain paperwork practices intended to improve accountability do not make nurses more accountable, but instead promote conformism. Second, the intense fears that nurses harbour in relation to audit and accountability must be understood in the light of South Africa's precarious labour economy. In this context, the managerial authority imposed on nurses constitutes an implicit threat of dismissal, which undergirds and motivates their behaviour. A focus on documents is useful for elucidating the strands of continuity with South African 'paper regimes' (Dhupelia-Mesthrie 2014) past and present. In the next section, I briefly outline this wider context of documents and their roles in state bureaucratic systems in a way that links these historical strands.

The file as a technology of audit

The patient file has long structured and channelled the transmission of knowledge in hospitals. Some thirty years ago, Colin Rees (1981) provided a detailed excavation of the role of the patient file. Files, he argued, are not simply the products of their environments, but they also shape those environments. The meaning of a document's content is indeterminate, its interpretation is contingent on existing bodies of knowledge, and it means different things to different people. The file, he argued, is not simply a description of the work of nurses and doctors, aiding the 'real' work of patient care, but is a constitutive feature of the work. This early sociological approach challenged Max Weber's original conception of the file as a tool of rational organization, and was followed more recently by a growing anthropological literature that extends ethnographic attention to the ambiguous and paradoxical, material and social complexities of paperwork in bureaucratic settings (M. Hull 2012; Gupta 2012).

What is the relationship between paperwork and the precarious experience of work in post-apartheid South Africa? Documents have been important tools for policing the boundaries of citizenship everywhere. Paperwork has been described as a key mechanism used by governments to document and control populations (Scott 1999). Recent literature attempts to understand its specific role in the South African context. Following the arguments of James Scott, who saw documentation as a way of simplifying and enumerating information about populations in order to make them knowable and therefore governable, the focus in the South African literature has been mostly on registration and border control. Key among these is Keith Breckenridge's work on the apartheid government's extensive system of population registration, which brought into being four racial categories as administratively distinct groups conferring varying entitlements (Breckenridge 2014). The identity document was integral; by inscribing racial classifications often based on a single ad hoc decision by a government official, it set individuals on radically different life trajectories. The arbitrary yet consequential character of documentation is jarringly exposed in this literature. Individuals could be banned from re-entry to South Africa simply because of losing a document, diverting the course of their life forever (Dhupelia-Mesthrie 2014). Building on Scott's work, several studies have usefully shown that a focus on paper trails exposes not just the excesses but also the limits of state power, either because its administrative capacities could not keep up with the desire for total governance (Breckenridge 2014; MacDonald 2014), or because the need to render populations knowable was offset by the reluctance to confer rights that is entailed in documentary processes of registration (Szreter and Breckenridge 2012; Amit and Krige 2014).

Documents assist the management of national borders and the boundaries of citizenship, rendering knowable and countable South Africa's population, while criminalizing, deporting and refusing entry to those deemed ineligible, illegal or 'undesirable' (Hyslop 2014; MacDonald 2014). This literature highlights the relationship between paperwork and labour management. Tensions have arisen, for instance, between reluctance to allow entry at the border and the need to supply the needs of a burgeoning labour market.[3] Obtaining documents of entry to South Africa, whether temporary or permanent, was a right of passage into the workforce and formed an implicit commitment to work as a condition of entry. In the case of population registration, ring-fencing access to jobs was a device used to compel registration, for instance by making it a condition of entry into nurse training courses (Breckenridge 2014: 231).

To extend this argument, the graduation certificate might be seen as one kind of border control, with professions utilizing state-sanctioned systems of accreditation to control access. Here, I suggest that documentary regimes in state institutions such as hospitals also manage the borders of citizenship, particularly given the work–citizenship nexus that characterizes contemporary experiences of belonging in South Africa (Barchiesi 2011). Serving as a tool of managerial authority, paperwork renders workers accountable and creates feelings of contingency in relation to work. Instead of making populations countable, these practices make citizens *accountable*.

In nursing, a focus on the production of text intensified following the emergence of the nursing process, which placed writing at the core of nurses' work. Introduced in the United States in the 1960s, its implementers describe the nursing process as a systematic, scientific framework to enable the provision of 'individualized, total patient care' (Uys 2005: 126). It is characterized by the separation of nursing into four phases: assessment; planning; implementation and evaluation. It emphasizes rigorous documentation at each stage. Originally intended as an educational tool for experienced nurses, it was quickly transformed into a standardized model for nursing care. By the mid-1970s, it was introduced in the United Kingdom, with South Africa and other countries following shortly after that.

Institutions such as hospitals tend to mimic each other. As DiMaggio and Powell (1983) show, they do this for a variety of reasons, whether due to political pressure, expected efficiency gains or as a response to uncertainty. In the case of the nursing process, its implementation globally derived both from a desire for improved efficiency via institutional comparability and standardization, and from the drive for professionalism. It emerged at a time in America, when nursing status and autonomy was more under threat than ever, offering experienced nurses a contained set of specialized tools which enabled enhanced control over of their work. Similarly elsewhere, it was popular among nursing elites because it could be used to carve out a sphere of professional autonomy, governed by its own internal systems (Lindsay and Hartrick 1996: 107). It emphasized intellectual skill and could 'impose an institutional ideal' on all new nursing entrants (Dingwall, Rafferty and Webster 1988: 213). Ironically in these contexts, it is now widely observed that the nursing process has exposed nurses to more, not less, external control. Intended to facilitate the standardization of care giving in line with the idea of nursing as a rational, academic exercise, it also became open to external interference as each step within the process became legible, quantifiable and therefore conducive to auditing. It thus became a tool of management, in some cases exacerbating the tensions between managerial and professional interpretations of nursing.

In South Africa, many suggest that the implementation of the nursing process has been disappointing, generating unnecessary paperwork in a context in which staff shortages are often critical (Marks 1994: 211; Uys 2005: 130–32). Even as early as the 1980s, critics in South Africa were describing it as merely 'a compulsory form-filling exercise' (Rispel and Schneider 1991: 117), resembling bureaucratic tendencies everywhere. When nurses at Bethesda spoke of the nursing process, they generally did so in the context of speaking about paperwork and workload, and emphasized their role as a producer of written knowledge. When asked about it, most nurses at Bethesda would respond with a mantra I heard many times over during the course of fieldwork: 'If you haven't written it down, it has not been done.' An intense fear often accompanied this mandate, as nurses felt that their written outputs were both a source of protection from, and exposure to, accusations of misconduct. Paperwork was a means of documenting staff competency and containing it within material format, giving it a permanency and objectivity it would not otherwise have. Patient files and other kinds of documentation, among the other purposes they served, were additionally an ongoing audit mechanism for assessing staff.

From the perspective of many clinical staff at the hospital, the completion of administrative procedures had taken priority over other nursing duties. As one senior nurse working on the TB ward put it:

> You write until you are tired. If you didn't write, it seems as if you didn't take care of the patient. Even if you have bathed, fed and treated the patient, if you have not written, it is as if you have not done it ... And if you leave the patient, and do the writing, they say you are very excellent ... Nurses write, but they don't finish the job.

This statement alludes to the frustration felt by many nurses, that their work in the wards was unappreciated by management. The comment also expresses the feeling of intense pressure frequently experienced by nurses as a result partly of the time-consuming nature of administrative duties – especially in the context of severe staff shortage. The comments hint at what David Mosse (2005) has suggested in relation to policy documentation on a development project in India: that written documents are constructed independently of the practical activities they purport to describe. They are there, Mosse suggests, to communicate 'success', rather than to accurately resemble reality.

This type of comment is such a typical feature of health-care delivery around the world as to have become virtually anodyne, reflecting the ubiquitous character of bureaucracy as a 'face-saving' activity. But given the particular constraints of the rural South African context, the consequences could be severe. One ward sister described this during a research interview in her office. She explained that a managerial requirement of the ward is to monitor and record the basic information on patients at half-hourly intervals, but argued that this is unachievable given the extent of staff shortage currently experienced on the ward. 'If you have six patients,' she said, 'it is not possible to carry out this task for all those patients with only one nurse.' Despite this reality of ongoing resource limitations however, she regularly finds that 'the chart is nicely plotted every half hour'. She explained that it is impossible then to rely on any of the information at all, because she cannot tell what has been entered correctly, and what has been 'made up': 'I don't mind if I see gaps,' she said, 'as long as you write what you did.' She went on to say that 'It cannot be like this ... What do you interpret this writing as?'

In this example, the file became meaningful only in its reified form as a physical marker of professional capability and institutional accountability: but one whose usefulness is ultimately called into question. This exemplifies Ben Kafka's (2012) argument that paperwork can unravel the state's own objectives. Several nurses expressed a fear of being implicated in patient death as a consequence of overwork and time constraints. The tone of the ward sister changed, gaining urgency and frustration, as she raised this central moral issue. She finally drew a comparison with an earlier period: 'There was shortage before, but we were managing . . .'

This moral challenge faced by nurses exists partly because of the severe shortage of staff, making half-hourly monitoring unfeasible, but the comments of the ward sister suggested that she had excluded staff shortage as the key factor. The nostalgic reference to 'before' was indicative of a wider commentary about a perceived process of deterioration and fragmentation in nursing standards. She acknowledged that shortages existed prior to the restructuring of management systems in 1994, yet claimed that work was manageable then. Rather, her comments reflect on new pressures experienced by nurses, due to requirements placed upon them in the current setting. Her comment is explained in part by the fact that, up until restructuring in the mid-1990s, lines of authority were carried out in a more direct and face-to-face manner in wards. The separation of managerial practice from medical work (creating a 'gap' filled by audit procedures) has sometimes resulted in what she described as a 'breakdown' of communication, where the administrative demands placed on front-line workers do not match with the day-to-day needs and constraints of daily work. Audit fears at times come to take precedence.

Patient files have been central to nursing for decades, and are not themselves the product of recent changes. It is the use of the file as a way of auditing staff that appears to be changing, given the increased absence of doctors and managers from wards, owing in part to resource shortages and in part to new managerial structures. In the final example, I describe a type of documentation and its use that is the result of new managerialism. It makes explicit an implication contained in the chapter so far, that because paperwork is often quite separate from the clinical work process, it seems almost to have taken on a life of its own, coming to be understood as an end itself. But before this, let me first situate these practices within the wider, global context.

A model on the move?

The global rise of audit regimes have accompanied public sector reform from the late 1980s. Following the failure both of centrally planned systems in the 1970s and of the rigorous privatization of the 1980s, governments turned their attention to a renewed examination and a subsequent reconfiguration of the role of the state in the economy and in relation to service delivery. An emerging consensus rested on the belief that the private sector was best able to provide efficient and cost-saving services, yet the flawed experiments of privatization in previous years signalled the necessity for careful state regulation, marking the inception of a 'second wave of neoliberalism' (Smith 2004: 375). Led at the helm by Margaret Thatcher's Conservative Government, the role of the state became increasingly that of facilitator. Public services – though remaining under state regulation – began to model themselves on the principles of the private sector. The accompanying administrative model for public sector reform – called New Public Management (NPM) – was designed to introduce entrepreneurialism and other private sector values into the public sector. Organizations such as the World Bank promoted NPM as one element under the wider banner of 'good governance', which countries seeking aid or loans were encouraged to implement.

Driven by an ethos of private management, the subsequent restructuring of public institutions included a shift to output measurement rather than input control, the devolution of management, the introduction of performance-related rewards and systems for ensuring the accountability of individuals and institutions. This has produced a vast infrastructure of accountability mechanisms, including practice criteria, policy targets, performance indicators, and a myriad of surveillance, assessment, and evaluation techniques through which the increasingly 'consumer'-, 'user'- or patient-centred concerns for transparency, confidentiality, and 'good practice' ostensibly are realized. Since the late 1980s, such rhetoric and its associated practices have been limited neither to specific types of institutions nor to particular locales, but have become pervasive features of a whole spectrum of public institutions and private companies globally, a phenomenon described by Michael Power (1997) in the UK context as an 'audit explosion'. The UK National Health Service is one such example of this kind of reform, in which outcome orientated assessment corresponds closely with a host of policies aimed at improving efficiency and lowering costs (Lacey 1997).

The subject has been taken up in anthropology, notably by Marilyn Strathern, who argues that new accountability regimes signal not only the practical restructuring of institutions but, more fundamentally, the emergence of a cultural form on a global scale: 'That there is culture on the make here is evident from the concomitant emergence, and dominance, of what are deemed acceptable forms' (2000a: 1). The diverse practices that make up audit culture are cultural in the sense both that they are ubiquitous, giving rise to a moral consensus about the aims and roles of organizations, and that they legitimize organizations and the state itself 'through the twin passage points of economic efficiency and good practice' (ibid.: 1).

In South Africa, the former director-general of the Department of Public Service and Administration describes the intended shift among public service workers 'from a personnel administration approach which essentially implies the policing of adherence to regulations to a human resource management approach which focuses on creating an enabling work environment in which the creative energies of public servants can be harnessed and actualized' (Ncholo 2000: 91). This statement conveys Marilyn Strathern's observation that 'the accompanying rhetoric [of audit culture] is likely to be that of helping (monitoring) people help (monitor) themselves, including helping people get used to this new "culture"' (2000a: 4).

Its critics highlight the structural and pragmatic obstacles that prevent the realization of this transition in public sector culture. Despite what many viewed as a largely successful initial stage of transition in restructuring and decentralizing the health system, South Africa's public institutions tend overall to suffer from low bureaucratic capacity that continues to undermine effective health-care provision (Bateman 2006). Chronic shortage of staff is one of the most serious obstacles. In the mid-1990s, the government increased nurse and doctor salaries in order to attract and retain staff, but this had the effect of shrinking public health sector employment by 8 per cent in order to stay within budget (McIntyre et al. 2006: 439). This shrinkage was exacerbated by the government's policy of cost containment, which generated further incentives for contracting out services to the private sector. Thus, some authors argue, policies focusing on cost efficiency have led to the 'stagnation' of public health-care financing (McIntyre et al. 2006: 436). Others suggest that 'staying within budget became and remains the key preoccupation of managers, implicitly relegating equity and other dimensions of institutional change to secondary goals' (Schneider, Barron and Fonn 2007: 297). Given such constraints, health workers inevitably find it more difficult to meet the requirements of their job. It is under such conditions that mistakes are more likely to happen and that fears of accountability are heightened.

The production of documentation as audit culture

The production, control and exchange of information was a central feature of the hospital's bureaucracy, and took the form of policy documents, audit reports, research findings, patient files, hospital memos and so on. One requirement of the KwaZulu-Natal Department of Health was that each member of clinical staff produce a quarterly document of five 'Key Result Areas' (KRA). This strategy, introduced by the head of the department for the KwaZulu-Natal Department of Health, enabled a system for informing management of individual work plans and constituted an additional means of monitoring and assessing staff (see Figure 4.1).

On the one hand, this initiative could be seen as part of an ongoing effort to decentralize decision-making and to minimize the so-called gap between policy and implementation, particularly in response to a proliferation of research that explained the widespread problem of low staff morale partly as a result of a failure of management to involve front-line workers in policy decisions (McIntyre and Klugman 2003). It was one attempt, therefore, at reorienting staff to the values and principles of NPM (Ncholo 2000). Other measures included the formal recognition of individual achievement, promoting career mobility and providing performance awards. On the other hand, it indicated an intensification of procedures of audit, providing another means for generating a sense of individual professional responsibility.

On one occasion during fieldwork, Cecilia asked me to assist her in writing her KRAs. She was extremely anxious, explaining that the deadline was in a few days, and that she didn't have the time, in addition to all her other work, to complete this document as well. I explained that I was happy to help, but that given my lack of training in nursing, and my insufficient knowledge of her specific job requirements or the particular short-term needs and financial capacity of the department she was working for, I was not sure that I could be of much assistance. That I had neither the knowledge nor the experience effectively to offer suggestions was a concern that she dismissed immediately as irrelevant. She explained that what was important was that I was able to write, to synthesize points, to use a computer, to type quickly, and to express sentences and display them in a way that would be acceptable to the management. That evening, after her shift had finished, we sat down at the computer to write them, together with another nurse from the TB ward, Sister Jali, who had also since requested my help.

NAME:
RANK:
POST:
PERSAL No.:
Period of Assessment:

KRA 1
To decrease HIV related morbidity and mortality
OUTPUTS: Less HIV/AIDS related deaths by 20 per cent

Key Activities	Performance Standard		Resource Requirements		Enabling Conditions
	Indicators	TIME(completed by)	Human Resources	Financial Resources	
1. Promote VCT 100% 2. Conduct at least two health promotion campaigns and surveys 3. Provide condoms and femidoms in all facilities 4. Appoint and train staff in order to sustain decentralization of ART distribution points 5. Establish ART defaulter Tracer team	Target of 80% attending [　] Hospital will know their status Increased uptake of VCT & PMTCT services, target 80% Increase of condom & femidom uptake by 20% Increase ART uptake to 3500 registered patients Increase adherence to ART	Ongoing	PHC Manager Doctors, Nurses, Counsellors, Community PHC Manager Dietician, Doctors, Nurses, Social Worker, Counsellors, Community	Normal HIV & AIDS Budget	Full compliment of Human Resources and other resources

FIGURE 4.1 *Key Result Area (KRA) document.*

The emotional effort and concern given over to the success-ful completion of this document was evident in the conversation between us as we worked. Sister Jali expressed her relief that we were managing to complete the task, telling me in a serious tone how much she had worried about doing it, that she had feared she would have been unable to think of the correct points, or to use a computer, and had lost sleep with worry about it. She thanked me repeatedly, saying that 'the spirit of God chose someone to help relieve the trouble in my soul ... I would have sat for hours staring at this work. The spirit of God has looked upon you'. I explained that I was happy to help her, especially as she had given up her time to help me with my work. She continued in the same manner of elated relief however, in between the completion of pieces of our work: 'I will sleep well tonight ... I must pray to God because I don't know why he has chosen me ... Why is God doing this? I must have been near to hell because God has sent someone to help me.' Cecilia was sitting quietly, focusing on the task in hand. On hearing these exclamations, she interrupted: 'I heard a voice from God, sending me to you. I knew that you needed help and I came.'

I was taken aback by the nurses' use of such intense religious speech in relation to an activity as apparently banal as filling a form. I could see that my willingness to help was, for them, fortuitous. The use of religious language might have been motivated in part by a strategic incentive. The nurses were concerned to demonstrate their gratitude to me, and wanted to justify their need for my assis-tance. Perhaps my surprise derived from my own ingrained assump-tion of a separation of religious and secular idioms, giving rise to an awkward juxtaposition that was absent for them. For many of the nurses whom I came to know, especially but not exclusively those who identified as 'born-again', the sacred was woven into many aspects of life. One friend told me, in tears, that during her long and difficult labour, she was taken to the small theatre room for a caesarian section. Three doctors tried for a long time and with grave difficulty to remove the baby. At one point, all seven of the nurses in the theatre stopped what they were doing and began to pray. How do we understand the pervasive presence of religion in an institutional setting that has undergone such a major transition away from its missionary past? What should we make of the use of religious language paired so seamlessly alongside secular modes of rational bureaucracy, those governed by new liberal democratic idioms of 'accountability', 'rights' and the like? These are questions to which I turn directly in the next chapter. For now, it is sufficient to note that the degree of emotional exertion invested in the process of creating the KRA document, and the concern with submitting it in time for the deadline, was an indication of the importance that they attributed to the activity. This was conveyed primarily with the use of religious language.

As we worked, it became quickly apparent to me that the nurses' major preoccupation was with the correct visual layout of the document, which contrasted with their virtually indifferent attitude to its content. We used examples from previous years as templates, not only to guide the structure of our document, but also using much of the content from these earlier KRAs. We transferred some of the points into the current version where possible, because many of them were generic in their broad applicability and could be inserted directly without requiring any amendments. Others needed to be adjusted slightly, so that they became relevant to the particular department that we were focusing on. There were no discussions or comments among the nurses about the feasibility of the various initiatives that they were including, how these would be financed or by whom they would be undertaken, even though some would clearly require significant planning and additional financial and human resources for their practical implementation, certainly beyond those currently available. The table did include columns entitled 'Human Resources' and 'Financial Resources', under the heading of 'Resource Requirement', but the same generic information was copied for each point without queries, doubts or comments being raised (see Figure 4.1). As we worked, I contemplated the already extremely large workload of both of these nurses, and the inadequacy of the facilities and the staff shortages currently experienced by their respective departments. At one point, I asked Cecilia tentatively if she thought she would be able to carry out all of these initiatives in the foreseeable future. 'Oh yes,' she told me, 'we will have to implement all of these.'

I recognize that the production of formatted and formulaic documents, increasingly with the use of computers, is ubiquitous in a broad spectrum of public life, both worldwide and in South Africa. Here, I do not intend to address their efficacy in general terms, nor to assess the feasibility or effectiveness of various policy initiatives. Rather, I wish to draw attention to the processes surrounding the production and exchange of such documents in local settings, and the value ascribed to these activities. What emerges from this example is that the production of the KRA document is an end in itself, serving three main purposes. First, it is a surreptitious method of placating staff and their concerns about their lack of involvement in decision-making processes by creating an illusion that they have greater responsibility and autonomy than in fact they do. This creates an implicit logic whereby the responsibility for any apparent 'failure' to fulfil these and other initiatives falls on individual nurses. Secondly, it is a means of auditing staff or, rather, of generating a culture and expectation of audit, even though the *implementation* of KRAs is not monitored. This was expressed clearly in the emotional labour given over to the production of this document, and the nurses' fears of missing the deadline. Thirdly, it is a way to create and maintain a representation of institutional order. The documents could be shown to external auditors from the provincial Department of Health.

The final statement made by Cecilia, that she intended to implement all the initiatives, is an indication of this, an example of the way in which nurses attempt to maintain the legitimacy of both themselves and the institution by claiming an effective link between policy and implementation. Her comment surprised me because, in other respects, she could be very critical of aspects of work that she deemed unhelpful or unnecessarily time-consuming. The comment suggested that when it came to certain bureaucratic requirements, she was willing to adopt the route of least resistance, which sometimes meant uncritically endorsing them.

Thus KRAs share with patient files this ambiguous lack of fit between paperwork and implementation. The case of the KRA document is more explicit though because, unlike patient files that are crucial for the treatment of patients, its practical role at the level of implementation is largely absent. The visual uniformity of the KRA document is a material expression of the conformism and rote learning that characterizes many nurse training courses. But the aesthetic of a document can also reveal much about the systems of surveillance governing their production. This becomes apparent when compared with Mirco Gopfert's (2013) description of the writing practices of the Nigerien gendarmerie. In his account, the production of written descriptions of incidents for use in court involves a similar focus on the aesthetic of the document rather than on its content, which is frequently inaccurate or fabricated. But the outcome is extremely different. There is no preoccupation with producing the 'correct' aesthetic that will be deemed acceptable and authentic by seniors – as in the case of nurses – thus producing a current of conformity. On the contrary, creativity and individuality of expression is emphasized. Among the gendarmerie, then, the aesthetic production of a document becomes a vehicle for the creation of individual identities and social status. The key difference is that policing in the Niger occurs in an environment of impunity where writing is not subject to scrutiny by seniors. Rather than being a technique of discipline, paperwork becomes a mode for the building of status.

The KRA document signifies a wide range of possible outcomes beyond the instance of its production. It involves the exchange and passage of documents – from front-line workers, to departmental managers, to hospital management, and sometimes to representatives of the provincial Department of Health – tracing and mapping out the lines of hierarchy, and therefore the relational statuses between people. Relationships of seniority and rank are played out and constructed by the passage of such items from one person to the next. The transformation of knowledge into the written form is fundamentally a social process, then, and one that carries with it certain risks. As Matthew Hull points out, 'the physical perdurance of files beyond the circumstances of their creation situates them within a horizon of uncertainty' (2003: 290). It is the uncertainty produced by the document, rather than the clarity, that affects nurses beyond the moment of production.

This is significant in a bureaucratic context, because it helps to account for the enormous significance attributed to the consolidation and containment of ideas and strategies 'on paper', even in a context in which basic needs of patients are often not being met. The KRA initiative represents a shift in the form taken by accountability, from one played out through daily interactions between staff in the workplace, to one based on the production of paperwork intended to mediate the gap between clinicians and management, in the context of decentralised managerialism.

The nurses became increasingly frustrated with the performance-related pay system that was linked to the KRA process. When I returned in 2013, I found that nurses were required to grade their own performance on a scale from one to five, with one being the poorest performance and five the best. The grade would be discussed and decided by a nurse together with the registered nurse in charge. If a four or a five was agreed on, the registered nurse would be required to write a supporting statement on their behalf which, if accepted, could form the basis for a salary increase. Nurses explained that they were encouraged to submit number three, explaining that the nurses in charge did not want to do the paperwork involved in writing a motivation. Mixing English and Zulu, one nurse said to me of her seniors, '*bayesaba i*-challenge' ('they are scared of a challenge'). She went on to express how the process, quite contrary to its intentions, produced mediocrity and conformity: 'This is depressing us because we end up in one level.' Such an outcome allows the neo-liberalized institution to sustain a stable image of success while managing and disciplining the workforce in ways that render them, in line with the new order of 'flexible accumulation', as just another pair of hands among many.

Conclusion

A few weeks after helping the nurses to write their KRAs, I was sitting with Sister Jali during her morning tea break. We were talking about the public servant strike that had taken place several months earlier. She began explaining to me the problems as she saw them that the hospital suffered from, saying 'there is no transparency in this hospital'. She reminded me of the KRA documents that I had been helping her with, and said that she recently discovered that all the documents were now missing. I was taken aback, and asked what had happened. She repeated several times and with obvious frustration that they were all missing: 'They are saying that they did not receive them. So we are having to do them again! That is what I mean that there is no transparency … We do not know where these documents went.' As she finished these words, she began to look agitated, sitting forward on the edge of her chair and looking down at her hands, and before I had the chance to inquire any further about what had happened to them, she stood up abruptly, saying that she only had ten minutes of tea break and that she must get back to the ward, and with a brief 'goodbye', rushed off down the corridor.

The disappearance of the KRA document symbolized for this nurse a failure on the part of management and highlighted a feeling of distrust in her relationship with managerial representatives, a feeling which was given moral authority through reference to the normative discourse of 'accountability', indicated here by her use of the idea of 'transparency', and the way in which she turned this idea back upon management. Yet, her frustrations were rooted in a perception that management was ultimately exempt from the structures of accountability to which she felt the nurses themselves were subjected. The lost documents are another example of the contingency or indeterminacy of paperwork, the unexpected consequences that may arise from the production of documents, and that may lead to the emergence of particular interpretations that go beyond the remit of the document's content.

Fears of accountability are reflected in – and exacerbated by – the image of management as distant and invisible. This 'othering' of management is evident in the example just given in which the nurse refers to management in terms of a separation between 'us' and 'them'. The distinction that emerged between managerial and clinical spheres after 1994 produced a tension whereby senior managerial staff were criticized for rarely attending the wards or observing the daily provision of medical care, and were perceived to be overly concerned with bureaucratic matters.

The doctors' explicit criticisms of management contrasted with the more cautious approach of many nurses. This was evident from the nervous display by the nurse as she rushed back to the ward and Cecilia's earlier comments suggesting acquiescence to bureaucratic logics. Unusually outspoken in her criticism of hospital management, the nurse perhaps became sensitive to the possibility of having disclosed too much, an example of the way in which a culture of accountability serves as a check on the actions and utterances of employees. Her unease was enhanced by the context of our discussion, and particularly given my role within the hospital as a researcher. At that moment I may have represented a potential threat, implied by the collection of information in a context in which systems of accountability are increasingly rigorous. This was one of many uncomfortable moments when my own positionality was implicated in the structures of power and knowledge production nurses feared. It highlighted the similarities between the KRA document and the ethnographic document, both potentially items of audit, both travelling into an uncertain future – one lost, the other not yet written – both lying beyond Sister Jali's control.

I do not wish to exaggerate the role of paperwork as merely a technique of audit, or to suggest that there is no relationship between some accountability mechanisms and patient care. For example, many nurses and doctors insist that the incident form, which members of staff complete following an error, is essential for ensuring and improving quality of care. What I have done, instead, is to describe the wider context in which nurses' subjective fears of these processes are formed, as subtle expressions of workplace insecurity. Unlike most doctors, some nurses resent having to complete the incident form. This resentment does not derive from an uncaring attitude towards patients. Rather, what my data suggest is that a lack of control by nurses over their work (it is often doctors who request the completion of the form) underpins this insecurity. This should be understood in relation to the more limited professional autonomy experienced by nurses vis-à-vis doctors, which is rooted in the history of the profession.

But how do nurses themselves explain what is happening? In the next chapter, I explore how nurses' views are informed by longer histories of mission, Christianity and changing governance.

CHAPTER FIVE

The Sickness of Democracy and Healing Religion

In October 2013, the *Mail & Guardian* newspaper published an article about Chris Hani Baragwanath Hospital in Soweto.[1] The article was a response to 'a desperate bid' by eight doctors to expose the poor working conditions and to force a response from what they perceived to be an indifferent and ineffective management. The article consisted of a set of images, each displaying a uniformed doctor standing or sitting in an empty operating theatre or hospital corridor. Each held up a handwritten signboard covering the face, dramatizing their anonymity for fear of punitive action for speaking out. The signs displayed messages about unsustainable workload, poor care, inadequate stock and broken equipment:

'Mother delivered baby on toilet floor: told to "wait her turn" in crowded labour ward'.

'Antipsychotic tablet stock out – unstable patients discharged without proper prescription'.

'Patient in need of simple operation discharged (theatre lists too long). He died a few weeks later'.

The images were intended not only to communicate written messages about the poor conditions of the hospital, but also to make known a culture of impunity among senior management and the fear and deference expected of clinical staff. The voices of nurses were absent, even though their alleged behaviour – such as absenteeism or cruelty towards patients – was also the object of criticism in the article's text. Rather, it was the moral authority of the doctor, representing the 'real' work of patient care – in opposition to the inept but all-powerful machinery of state bureaucracy – that found a voice. These were the images of South Africa's fragmented society two decades after the inception of democracy, of hidden 'ivory towers' on the one hand, and a 'languishing' majority on the other, in the words of one angry article respondent.

Academic accounts of South Africa's public hospitals emphasize a 'breakdown' of discipline at all levels of staff (von Holdt and Maserumule 2005; von Holdt and Murphy 2007). Drawing much of his data from Baragwanath, Karl von Holdt suggests that the authoritarian order that became entrenched in hospitals under apartheid was reliant on a racialized rationale in which nurses observed obedience towards their white seniors, both doctors and matrons (2010: 252). Nurses were prevented by anti-union and anti-strike legislation from developing collective bargaining power to improve their conditions. Ultimately, this workplace regime crumbled in the face of growing dissent, culminating in widespread public sector strikes in 1992, during which twelve people were killed. This has left the health sector, von Holdt argues, in a state of liminal disorder. The eradication of existing hierarchies has failed to give way to an alternative system of organizational discipline. Many members of staff at Baragwanath respond to the current situation with 'nostalgia for the time when Baragwanath functioned effectively as a hospital, a time when supervisors knew how to supervise and discipline was discipline' (von Holdt and Maserumule 2005: 439).[2] The inception of democracy shattered the racialized ideology that preceded it and in so doing, shook the foundations of the workplace order.

Von Holdt (2010) argues that a culture of impunity has since taken hold whereby respect for ward-based skills and discipline has been decentred in favour of a focus on career progression, fuelling the entrenchment of a black middle class. Attempts to preserve newly won African sovereignty, he argues, gave rise to excessive preoccupation with 'face' – an outward facade of institutional success despite the realities on the ground. We can see hints of this in the comments of one Baragwanath doctor in the newspaper article mentioned above. Speaking of the anticipated response by the hospital to the article, she said that the 'management will probably put more energy into finding out who the culprits are rather than improving service delivery'.[3] Such 'colonial legacies', argues von Holdt, mean that the health-care setting is crippled with dysfunction.

Others have emphasized stasis instead of breakdown, suggesting that new models of governance have failed to transform health care in the post-1994 period because of the intransigence of apartheid era management models. For instance, Philip Wenzel writes, 'If there is a dominant reality in the practice of public administration, it is the persistence and endurance of the traditional model of governance, its hierarchy and rules, and its preoccupation with organogrammes and statutory mandates and with superiors' permissions' (2007: 50). Ultimately, both the focus on breakdown and the emphasis on continuity imply the inability of new models to transform existing, entrenched practices. In health care, as in other parts of South African society, these accounts suggest, transformation is held back by the country's stubborn and ever-present past.

While reading these explanations, I was struck by the incongruity between the arguments made in the literature and those that prevailed in the narratives of the nurses with whom I did research at Bethesda Hospital. Nurses frequently discussed the problems that they encountered at work as a sickness of democracy itself. For them, it was the new, not the old system, that was generating tensions in the workplace. Their perspectives resonated with a point made by Michael Burawoy and Katherine Verdery, that what appears as a stubborn clinging to old practices, and a resistance to embracing the 'new', may in fact be 'direct *responses* to the new market initiatives, produced *by* them, rather than remnants of an older mentality' (1999: 2, italics in the original). Nurses are frustrated with the layering of new legislation, in a context where the resources are insufficient to implement them, and they fear new regimes of audit and accountability.[4]

At Bethesda, ethnographic research over time allowed me to step back from these arguments about either the persistence or the loss of the past, and to explore how quotidian events, actions and embodied emotions reproduced – or created anew – different workplace ethics. Doing this enabled insight into the tensions created in these daily interactions. In the previous chapter, I described how workers experience varying modes of governance in the workplace. These have changed, but have not completely transformed, in the post-apartheid period. Hierarchy remains entrenched in the nursing profession. Deference towards seniors is still a dominant mode of sociality on the wards, while at the same time being challenged and undermined by new bureaucratic modes of governance.

In this chapter, I turn to the nurses' own commentaries about these processes. One consequence of the challenge to workplace hierarchy is that the nurses perceive that there is less 'discipline' in the wards. In attempting to explain this, one nurse repeated a familiar line: 'It is something to do with this democracy, this human rights.' Not able to elucidate the connection, yet spoken in a tone that implied that what she was saying was almost self-evident, she drew upon a wider ideological framework associated with liberal democratic values as an explanation for the changes felt locally.

Generational tensions often emerged as a central theme in these conversations, as older nurses treated the perceived attitudes of their juniors as indicative of this decline. This was revealed in a conversation between two older nurses and me, as we sat in the small kitchen of the Gateway Clinic.[5] We were discussing the changes that they had witnessed at Bethesda over the years. One of them said, 'Before, we had a calling for nursing, unlike today [when] you come for money … People just want to get paid. Because you get paid even to do the training now.' I took her up on this point, reminding them that nursing students received payment for missionary training under an apprenticeship scheme. She agreed, but declared that it was far less than what it was now, shouting out, 'Peanuts! You hardly got a thing!' At this point, the other nurse interjected: 'When I started I remember I only got 87 Rand a month!' They both proceeded to laugh and joke about this for a while, repeating the amount with exaggerated astonishment and regaling me with the names of small food items that could be bought today for the same amount. 'How are the wages for nurses now?' I asked. 'The wages are good,' said the second nurse, 'they are getting a lot of money now . . .'

Here, the older nurses distinguished themselves from their younger counterparts who, they claimed, were entering nursing for the financial incentive it provided, rather than out of a sense of duty or 'calling'. This contrast was further exaggerated by the comparison they drew between the amount of wages then and now. However, many of the older nurses, in numerous other conversations, have emphasized the importance of salaries as an incentive for having entered nursing, because of the need to earn money to support their parents and siblings. In many cases, the nurses were the only working members of their household, supporting other family members and even distant kin or neighbours. As I explained in Chapter Three, nursing also gave women a valuable route to financial independence. This indicates that the financial incentive was as much a factor then as it is now, and certainly implies a more complex and heterogeneous set of influences acting on women as they chose to enter nursing. Earlier in the same conversation, the nurses had complained about the salaries they received now in comparison to those earned by migrant nurses overseas, suggesting that money was as much a concern for them as it was for their junior counterparts.

In this chapter, I contextualize these generational dynamics within a wider set of narratives among nurses about democracy and its ills. A growing body of literature from across the African continent has unearthed negative discourses about 'democracy', much of it alleging the untranslatability of democratic idioms into fraught post-colonial situations. Traditionalist narratives are often interpreted as the source of these perspectives; implying that if these places were not struggling under the yoke of past legacies and cultural dogmas, democratic principles would take effect with greater efficacy. Jean-François Bayart (2000) mounts a powerful critique of this line of reasoning, showing how Africans selectively draw upon global idioms to serve situated material and political interests, a process he calls 'extraversion'. As I have suggested in the previous chapter, and will expand upon in this chapter and the next, new kinds of religiosity refract these debates in a variety of ways, throwing up multiple interpretations. I turn to this issue in the second half of this chapter. For now, it is necessary to explore in further detail the nurses' own narratives and explanations in relation to their work.

Generational tensions at work

One day I was sitting and drinking tea with a tutor from the nursing school. We were discussing the problem, as he saw it, of a lack of motivation among the students that he taught. At one point he exclaimed, 'It is because of this democracy, this thing of human rights!' I prompted him to explain further and he said, 'They know they are free. They have got their rights now, so they don't care.' He told me about his experiences of growing up on a farm owned by white farmers near to Pongola, a town situated about forty kilometres from the hospital. He had struggled for his education, because the farmer for whom his family worked wanted him to stay and work on the farm. Each day, he had to sneak away to school when everyone else was gathered in the morning to begin the day's work. Describing himself as 'a product of the old regime', he claimed that his childhood had taught him the values and rewards of working hard. Today, in contrast, students do not have the same motivations to drive them: 'Now they have their rights, but they are not making use of them,' he exclaimed. Referring to young people in general, he described how he sees them at the side of the road as he drives home from work, drinking beer and dancing. They expect to be admitted into nursing school, he told me, but are not willing to put the effort into their studies in order to 'improve themselves'.

After this, the tutor returned again to a description of his students' behaviour in hospital. They are often late, he told me, or cannot be found. They don't make the effort to learn or to concentrate, so he finds himself teaching the same things many times over: 'They don't care. They don't like the patients. They don't like the profession. They like' – he paused here for dramatic effect, as if trying hard to think of anything his students liked – 'nothing! They like nothing!' At this point he was laughing loudly. 'But if they want to ruin their lives, then it is not my *indaba* (concern).[6] It is their *indaba* ... But it will affect the patients. That is the problem.' I asked why they would pursue nursing if they disliked it so much. He said, 'It is the money. They do it for the money, nothing else.'

These comments reminded me of those made by Mr Oram, a former senior tutor and matron, who worked at Bethesda during the mission period. Oram spoke of his students having a particular 'attitude to life' that he deemed as not being conducive to nursing (see Chapter Three). Both comments carried the same air of condemnation, and the attribution of a single, static motivation to students' behaviour. A paternalistic outlook pervaded both of these narratives.

But, whereas Mr Oram's attitude was infused with a logic of racial difference, the nursing tutor's remarks instead evoked the rationale of the post-apartheid worker–citizen (Barchiesi 2011) – the idea that freedom is synonymous with the right to work. They also resonate with more recent accounts of generational conflict. Jean and John Comaroff speak about a wider 'burgeoning experience of intergenerational disarticulation', especially in the context of HIV/AIDS, which has produced a crisis of social reproduction (J. L. and J. Comaroff 2004: 337). At Bethesda, a perceived moral decline is often associated with, and thought to be driven by, young people. Frequently, they are blamed for the stripping away of the Christian ethos in nursing and are held responsible for a moral decline of the profession. The older nurses' condemnation of juniors speaks to this wider feeling of uncertainty about the future, where moral and professional anxieties generate a rift between the old and young: 'New discrepancies open up between the genders and the generations, striking hardest against those most responsible for building a future' (ibid.: 340). This anxiety was expressed clearly by a senior nurse when she said, 'I always think of my siblings and my children. Older nurses will die. I will die. What will this next generation be?'

But the nurses who criticized the younger staff for being driven by a desire for money often failed to acknowledge the wage discrepancies that separated their junior counterparts from them. Unsurprisingly, the junior nurses had a different perspective. One staff nurse, for example, raised the issue that only fully registered nurses receive the Rural Allowance, saying 'so even when it [the hospital] is short staffed, we are getting nothing. Sometimes there are 20 patients and only three staff, but we still do not get a rural allowance for working here …'[7] For many junior nurses, their concerns focused on poor working conditions and a feeling of their work being unnoticed and unappreciated by senior staff and by management. One staff nurse told me in an interview:

> We have to work under stress. Sometimes there are only 3 nurses, with 27 or 22 patients. And all the work is supposed to be done … The matrons don't say 'thanks'. They are always scolding us. They are *always* scolding us!

Younger nurses complained of frequent chastisement by their seniors. This frustration was palpable when speaking to younger nurses; many felt that their seniors treated them with disdain and did not appreciate their work.

Switching between English and Zulu, another junior nurse spoke about her seniors, to whom she referred as '*laba abaphezulu*' ('those at the top'):

> They put a lot of pressure on us. You don't feel comfortable if they are next to you. If you see one of them coming, you can even just hide, because you know that you are not going to be well treated. The doctors too, they shout at us nurses, even in front of patients. So you can feel under-valued. But this is wrong because *sonke siyadingana* (we all need each other).

Later in the conversation, she described a feeling of paralysis, an inability to act, provoked by these feelings:

> You are afraid even to touch anything, because you don't know whether what you are doing is right or wrong. You'd rather not do something, because you don't know whether it is right and don't want to be shouted at.

The stereotype of the young, indifferent nurse is pervasive. But many junior nurses spoke with compassion and concern about the effects that the difficult hospital conditions were having on patients. The same nurse spoke about how her fears of seniors stifled her ability to provide the kind of patient care that she felt was needed:

> When you're working with people, it is important to be caring, and to show the patients that you are caring about them. Many patients do not need treatment, but they need to be treated kindly. You have to talk to them. They know from the way that you are touching them whether you are treating them kindly or not. They can feel. Also the way that you talk, they know whether you are acting with love or not. You must be open and kind. You must talk to them a lot. The patients need this, not just treatment, because many of them are not only physically but psychologically ill. If you are not satisfied at work, it becomes hard (to do this).

Despite the diversity of opinions and experiences among the junior staff, their seniors could often explain their complaints in terms of a moral defect linked to an attitude of ungratefulness among the profession's lower ranks. Another told me how things had changed since 1994: 'Before, I rarely found a nurse sitting on the ward … Things are relaxed now … They'll tell you of rights; that is how it is now, but I'm not used to that.' She continued, linking this to a lack of discipline that she felt had become the prevailing norm in contrast to the strict training she had received: 'They are lazy. Even the epaulettes people don't want to wear anymore. They have them under their jerseys or not at all. But that is not right because as a nurse you must be well identified.' Given that the epaulettes that nurses wear on their shoulders are the quintessential symbol of professionalism, the comment suggested that professionalism itself was under threat, together with the values of hierarchy and discipline that are seen as having characterized an earlier era of nursing.

Generational tensions also reflected the insecurities held by some older nurses about their grasp on new bodies of knowledge. Though rarely expressed, I came to realize that some nurses felt that their juniors, who were often adept at navigating new structures and protocols – especially those who had been trained in the city – would climb the rungs of the professional ladder, leaving them behind. This emerged in the following conversation with a senior nurse, who received her nursing certificate from McCord's mission hospital in Durban in 1984. Nursing was very stressful, she explained to me, wiping the sweat from her brow as we sat under a canvas tent erected in the grounds of the hospital for World AIDS Day. 'The problem is that there are always new things to take on board.' The rapidly changing disease landscape of the last thirty years has introduced major challenges for nurses. To do the job properly, she explained, it was necessary to learn thoroughly about HIV, about all its associated diseases, and about the treatment and its side effects, and so on: 'The old school of nurses like myself did not learn those things in training because HIV wasn't a problem then.'

To do the job correctly, she explained, you have to be constantly reading, learning and applying what you've learnt. This is difficult without support or the opportunity for further training. With each different job or promotion comes a new set of tasks to learn. Yet you do not receive training for these tasks when you enter the new job. 'You have to take it from the air,' she added, with a theatrical hand gesture as though plucking a feather with two fingers from the air. 'So how can they expect us to do it properly? There is not enough support.' I remarked that her senior position indicated that she had been successful in her career. 'I am only an assistant nursing manager. I've only got one,' she said, smiling and pointing to the epaulette appended to her shoulder. The epaulette was green, indicating that she was trained in midwifery. 'Chief Professional Nurses are the good positions. But you need a degree these days. You need a degree, but I am old.'

The fear of deskilling and therefore of losing one's professional credibility is a real threat in the context of rapidly changing fields of knowledge. This helps partly to explain the importance of memories of the past as a source of identity. Older nurses seek recourse to alternative representations of professionalism, especially by evoking the past while denigrating the liberal values associated with the contemporary workplace.

Rights, democracy and professionalism

The liberal democratic ideas of 'rights' and 'accountability' are common signifiers in the post-apartheid period. Human rights were enshrined as the foundation of South Africa's radical Constitution and Bill of Rights (1996). Other liberal concepts such as democracy and citizenship have become key tropes of public moral debate in South Africa since the demise of apartheid (Chipkin 2003; 2007). Richard Wilson suggests that 'human rights talk has become *the* central language of nation-building in democratizing countries such as South Africa' (2002: 210). During the years preceding the transfer of power to the ANC, human rights was a counterpoint to apartheid's emphasis on group categories and so-called separate development. The 1996 Bill of Rights and the institutions of the Constitutional Court and the Truth and Reconciliation Commission (TRC) consolidated the idea of rights as a defining political concept associated with post-apartheid transition and with the nation-building project. The notion of rights, Wilson argues, enabled the politicization of constitutionalism, linking it with a wider pan-Africanist and anti-apartheid struggle. This legitimized the new state project and set of legal institutions accompanying it (ibid.: 211). The idea of rights has consolidated the image of the country's distinct and redemptive break with its past: 'Where the previous state had been authoritarian, repressive and oligarchic in nature, the new state is intended to be democratic, developmental and committed to a culture of human rights' (Cameron and Tapscott 2000: 81).[8]

Similar themes emerged in the 'Submission on Nursing' to the TRC, by the Democratic Nursing Organisation of South Africa (DENOSA) in which it is stated that apartheid legislation 'constituted gross violations to the rights of nurses' (1997: 5). The document as a whole is oriented towards a vision of 'establishing a human rights culture in the health sector' (ibid.: 4). The discourse has permeated the language of health-care delivery, linked closely with the tropes of 'accountability' and 'good governance'. The *Batho Pele* programme ('People First' in Sesotho) is a set of principles for health providers and users based on 'the right to access public services in an equitable, convenient and cost-effective manner'[9] as enshrined in the 1996 Constitution and Bill of Rights. Its eight principles are intended to guide managers and health-care workers in correct practice, laying out an agenda for the reformulation of service delivery that is oriented towards customer choice. They emphasize the right of patients to hold public servants accountable.[10] Human rights rhetoric sits alongside increased emphasis upon performance management, accountability and commercialisation – all strategies implied in the *Batho Pele* programme and motivated by the GEAR-led priority of fiscal control. Rights-based narratives are therefore also linked to an economic agenda focused on the reduction of expensive state administration.

It is tempting to argue that nurses' suspicions of rights discourse derives from the persistent gap between the progressive claims of official narratives and everyday realities, both at the hospital and in the communities where they live. Since 1994, unemployment has deepened and expectations of material improvement in basic living conditions have, for many, remained unmet (Marais 2011; Robins 2005). Nursing itself has experienced a similar contradiction: despite increasing emphasis on employment rights, workplace equity and transparency it is overburdened by high workloads, severe staff shortage, poor pay, and labour fragmentation, leading some authors to describe the nursing sector nationally as having reached a state of 'general crisis' (von Holdt and Murphy 2007: 330). By 2015, nurses and researchers were calling for action to quickly address what Laetitia Rispel and Judith Bruce described as a 'profession in peril' (Rispel and Bruce 2015: 117).

Two decades after the dramatic transition to democratic rule, the reasons given by Rispel and Bruce for this climacteric moment in nursing bear resemblance to those that, in the 1980s, led Patricia Owens and Howard Glennerster to describe nursing as having 'reached a crossroads'. Crippled with staff shortage and low morale, they suggested, nursing was facing 'a crisis of professional identity' (quoted in Marks 1994: 194). While today's South Africa is marked by more protracted political tensions than the emergency situation of the late 1980s, increasingly it shares with that period a growing pressure, and a deepening sense that things cannot continue as they are. With high levels of unemployment and a crippling AIDS epidemic, hopes of a better life for many have been dashed. The ANC is facing unprecedented challenges to its legitimacy, with rising numbers of strikes and protests taking place around the country. The Marikana shootings and the intermittent outbursts of xenophobic violence signal darker, more deadly tensions. State institutions are increasingly targeted as the focus of protest. In 2015, the area around Bethesda Hospital was in the midst of a prolonged drought; cattle died and people waited through the night at boreholes to fill bottles with intermittent trickles of water. Eventually, residents took to the streets to demand government assistance, focusing their protest on the hospital: the most visible and prominent state institution in the area. In October, Bethesda Hospital was forced to shut down for several days as local residents blocked the roads with stones and burning tires. This is a pattern replicated across impoverished municipalities throughout the country.

Nurses have experienced the worst of these crises, both in their everyday work and in their homes and communities. While hospitals often become the physical targets of community vitriol, nurses themselves continue to shoulder the blame for all manner of social problems. Public moral discourses about the alleged cruelty of nurses remain commonplace, often drawing on stereotypes rather than reality. In *Native Nostalgia*, Jacob Dlamini pits nurse cruelty alongside corruption as among the worst of South Africa's social ills. He writes that township residents burn down government property 'especially if its shelves are forever empty because some state official has pocketed the money intended for essential medicines and the nurses on duty are surly sisters more adept at insulting patients than at providing primary care' (2009: 20). In a context of intensifying focus on accountability, such stereotypes can perpetuate a fearful workplace atmosphere and cause resentment among staff.

We might expect, under such circumstances, that rights would become the object of criticism. As others have suggested, the danger of rights discourse is the presence of an ever widening 'gap between the rhetoric of rights and the economic and socio-cultural realities' (Robins 2005: 2). 'Rights' emerges as a vacuous concept, and is appropriated as an expression of a wider disillusionment.

In this chapter, I suggest that the emphasis on rights as a negative discourse also signals a more specific experience of erosion of professionalism, indicative of an underlying feeling of contingency in relation to work. Consider the following excerpt from a research interview with an enrolled nurse:

> **Nurse:** There is a lot of paperwork. But that was caused by the government. [It is necessary] to write down everything that you have said because of the communities that are suing the hospital.
>
> **Me:** What type of thing do you write down?
>
> **Nurse:** Everything. What is the patient's time of arrival; what you did at this time and that; everything.
>
> **Me:** And what would happen if you failed to write it down?
>
> **Nurse:** When the case comes and the relatives want to sue the hospital, you are informed, you have to write the incident, you have to go to SANC [South African Nursing Council] for a hearing. Nurses are scared. We are doing it, but we have to be sure of what we are doing.
>
> **Me:** You have to make sure because you can be blamed individually?
>
> **Nurse:** Not even blamed; they can tear off your certificate because of that. We are doing it, but there are a lot of challenges, or a lot of rights for the patient. They don't care about your rights as a nurse.

This conversation brings together several of the themes from earlier chapters: the preoccupation with paperwork as a condensed medium of accountability; the empowerment of patients at the expense of the nurses themselves; and the fear of dismissal. The discussion is concluded with a reference to rights, which are ostensibly enjoyed by patients but not the nurses themselves. Nurses are aware that the unambiguous position of authority that they previously held in relation to their patients is challenged by the new democratic principles of accountability and patient rights. The *Batho Pele* principles, with which all health-care workers are expected to become conversant, serves as a code of practice that locates the patient as a rights-bearing consumer. Nurses frequently declared that their own rights were sidelined in favour of those granted to the patient. According to this perspective, one's right is another's threat, and the citizenship entitlements granted to one undermine those granted to another. Underlying these concerns is the fear of erosions of autonomy: rights are associated with declining control over professional knowledge.

The ideology of professionalism historically has served a purpose similar to that of citizenship today, in dampening legitimate grievances and workplace inequalities by insisting on unity. As Barchiesi says, '*virtuous* citizenship resides in hardworking individuals, loath to complain and ready to sacrifice for the well-being of the nation' (2011: 4, italics in the original). Similarly, as Shula Marks (1994) explains, the well-being, cohesion and status of the nursing profession had to be prioritized above the individual quibbles of its members, whose striking and other protestations were seen to bring the profession into disrepute. We might therefore expect the two ideas – professionalism and citizenship – to operate in tandem, reinforcing each other. But what the nurses' commentaries reveal is a tension between them. In the post-apartheid work order, duty to the nation as the worker-citizen displaces duty to the profession. Through discourses of accountability and rights, the professional is rendered subordinate to the citizen. The liberal ideology of citizenship has displaced that of professionalism, transferring control of professional knowledge, via accountability mechanisms, to a wider citizenry and blurring the status boundaries between nurses and patients.

Recent studies have argued that South Africans' rejection of liberal democratic principles is based on a belief that egalitarian individualism flattens the hierarchies of age and gender that are imagined as necessary to an idealized social order. People crave the reinstatement of hierarchies based on the cultural logics of the rural homestead (Hickel 2015), or of the stratified workplace (Barchiesi 2011). At Bethesda, the nurses' suspicions of democratic principles must be understood in relation to the decline of religion at the hospital, especially designated by its transfer from mission to state control. This is intimately connected with nurse professionalism and status, as imagined in relation to an earlier mission period. As Belinda Bozzoli writes, education and Christianity were to the missionary 'not merely a fact of self-justification, but the symbol and apex of a social order' (1981: 57). Religious markers of prestige that fuelled professional aspiration are still apparent today, and conflict with the levelling effects of neo-liberal managerialism. However, I argue that nurses' discontent with new health-care practices must be taken seriously on their own terms, without assuming necessarily that this has to do either with apartheid legacy or with the cultural untranslatability of liberal democratic discourse.

The 'secular' has not featured in post-apartheid processes of state building to the extent that other liberal values such as 'rights' have. However, attentiveness to it is necessary for a fuller understanding of the nostalgia that appears widely to be felt across South Africa. Specifically at Bethesda, it is crucial for understanding the significance of the older nurses' recourse to the idea of 'calling' as an attempt to preserve professional integrity.

To introduce this theme, I begin with how religious and secular values emerge at a national level in the controversies surrounding the new termination of pregnancy (TOP) legislation. These debates led to a confrontation between government and the professions, and thus highlight the importance of religion as a field of signification in relation to questions of professional autonomy, power and citizenship.

Termination of Pregnancy Legislation: professionalism under threat

On 1 February 1997, the Choice on Termination of Pregnancy Act (Act 92 of 1996) came into effect. This legislation broadened what had previously been a highly restrictive set of conditions under which legal abortions were permitted, as legislated by the Abortion and Sterilisation Act of 1975.[11] It entitled women of any age to have access to safe and free abortions at a public facility. I discussed this during an interview with the then superintendent at Bethesda Hospital – a devout Christian, with an outlook partially inherited from mission ethos. He described a feeling of 'alarm' upon hearing about the passing of the Act. As we spoke, it became quickly apparent that he viewed the new legislation as an affront. It was an unwarranted imposition of state power on the ethical and professional autonomy of nurses and doctors: 'The government simply instructed us to be ready [to perform abortions],' he told me angrily. After the act was passed, the hospital staff went to several clinics and spoke to members of the community. All were alarmed. He reported the *izinduna* (senior members of traditional authority) saying: 'We'll come and get you if you have an abortion', and 'We'll get that nurse or doctor [who carries out the procedure]'.

I responded with a question: 'They threatened health workers?'

'No,' he quickly retorted, 'but they simply disagreed. They were saying that they did not want their children aborted. They wanted them brought into the world.'

His views, strongly informed by his religious outlook, are replicated among health workers across South Africa. In a survey conducted in KwaZulu-Natal, 6 per cent of nurses supported abortion on demand (Harrison et al. 2000). By early 2000, only 32 per cent of the 292 public health facilities designated to provide the service were actually functioning as such (Vincent 2011: 265). What the figures suggested is a widespread adherence to conservative Christian values, and a suspicion of the secular, liberal ideas that informed the 1996 TOP legislation. Moreover, these moral concerns are closely twinned to questions of professional identity. As events unfolded, it became clear that the autonomy of the professions vis-à-vis the encroaching power of a centralized state administration undergirded the divisive issue.

In an attempt to persuade health workers to accept a different perspective, the Department of Health introduced a course rather euphemistically named, Values Clarification Workshop. Nurses, doctors and other health-care providers were required to attend the one-day course. It aimed to challenge the anti-abortion position that was widespread and was hampering the capacity of public hospitals to provide the service. At Bethesda, the superintendent wrote to the Department of Health in protest about the course. Demonstrating his continued clout as a senior doctor, his intervention led to the discontinuation of nurses from Bethesda Hospital being sent to do the course.

The defiance of the medical manager was reflected nationally in a legal battle between an organization called Doctors for Life and the Speaker of the National Assembly, which was representing the South African government. Doctors for Life brought a case against the government, challenging the legislation drawn up to increase women's access to abortions. The National Council of Provinces (NCOP) was challenged in court on the grounds that it had failed to engage adequately in public consultation.[12] The court upheld the challenge because, it argued, the failure on the part of most provinces to hold public hearings or to invite written submissions was unreasonable in the light of the NCOP's constitutional obligation. This was especially the case, they determined, considering the level of public interest attracted by the Choice on Termination of Pregnancy Act. Consequently, the legislation was declared invalid. But the victory for Doctors for Life was short lived. The legislation was later passed when brought once again before the court, following a series of public hearings held by NCOP to fulfil its constitutional mandate.

Similar disquiet about the Act was expressed in the senior ranks of the nursing profession. In a study of the attitudes of nurses to the new TOP legislation, Mokgethi, Ehlers and van der Merwe concluded that:

> Some professional nurses experienced guilt, depression, anxiety and religious conflicts as a result of providing TOP services. Despite the legislation of TOPs, these services remained stigmatised. Professional nurses did not want to work in these services and also did not want to be associated with them. (2006: 32)

Despite the formalism of new bureaucratic systems many hospitals in South Africa were, and remain, hostile if not prohibitive environments for nurses and doctors wishing to assist with abortions or for patients seeking them (Potgieter 2004; Taitz 2000). At Bethesda, a collective taboo makes compliance with state legislation socially challenging for nurses, who can face opprobrium from their co-workers. The matter continues to be a source of tension at Bethesda, frequently provoking discussion about so-called interference by government. In 2013, only two nurses and one doctor performed abortions at Bethesda Hospital and its surrounding clinics.

A tension between managerial and professional power underpins these hostile sentiments. For instance, in another study, nurses declared that they would leave the profession altogether should they be forced to conform to the new legislation (Poggenpoel, Myburgh and Gmeiner 1998: 4). The controversy surrounding abortion brings clearly into view concerns about the perceived imposition of bureaucratic forces on the moral and professional autonomy of nurses. It also points to religion as a crucial field of signification, and of secularization as a symbol of the perceived deterioration of workplace ethics.

Locating the secular

For many nurses, religious and secular values occupied points along a timeline. As I have suggested, this came to be envisaged in terms of the generational differences between the perceived attitudes of younger and older nurses. The nurses at Bethesda did not use the term 'secular' or 'secularization'. However, they did link the decline of religion with the rise of 'democracy' and 'rights', implying a perceived teleological process resembling Weber's secularization thesis. Understanding this perspective is important in helping us to make sense of the ambivalence that nurses feel towards their work. The dualistic separation of religious and secular values feeds into a temporal and moral framing of work and the practices of distinction that reproduce the category of professionalism.

In his influential writings on religion, Talal Asad characterizes secularism as integral to the 'project of modernity', which he suggests, 'aims at institutionalizing a number of (sometimes conflicting, often evolving) principles: constitutionalism, moral autonomy, democracy, human rights, civil equality, industry, consumerism, freedom of the market – and secularism' (Asad 2003: 13). The language of secularism is featured in South Africa's democratic transition, but never centrally. In his book *Protecting Human Rights in a New South Africa*, Albie Sachs (1990) presents a vision of the role he thought religion should play in the new process of nation building. Sachs was a prominent figure in the ANC and was appointed by Nelson Mandela as judge to the Constitutional Court of South Africa in 1994. Emulating familiar values of liberal democracy, he advocated a 'tolerant' secularism. He viewed this in terms of a nation-building process that was inclusive and in which the separation of state and religion would be mediated actively by dialogue and cooperation:

> The state should be neither theocratic nor atheist, but secular, tolerant, and accepting of the deep importance religion has for millions of South Africans. Religious communities, for their part, should be free to organize their worship as they please, and encouraged to take part in the life of the nation. (Sachs 1990: 44)

In 1993, just before the first democratic elections, religious leaders produced a document called 'The Declaration on Religious Rights and Responsibilities'. Like Sachs's contribution, it rejected the idea of a religious state, but argued that the relationship between religion and the nation be guided by principles of responsibility, dialogue and freedom. In these documents, secularism was conceived of as necessary and desirable.

Moving from the prescriptive to the descriptive, however, the secular plays a much less prominent role in discussions about the relationship between the state and religion in South Africa. Instead, this literature highlights the ways in which state building draws heavily on religious imagery, and how religion continues to occupy a central place in governance and nation building. For instance, in an analysis of the TRC, Ebrahim Moosa highlights the centrality of Christian symbols and concepts. Describing the proceedings as a 'secular Eucharist', he points out the TRC is in fact perhaps closer to the religious than the secular. It required, he suggests, 'a faith in the *mysterium* of the event, a faith in the rite of reconciliation, a belief in the rituals of confession, rather than an expectation in the outcome of the process' (2000: 117–18, italics in the original). This was a quasi-religious performance on a national stage, a 'simulacrum', conjuring the ritual symbolism of the Eucharist for the achievement of spiritual reconciliation.

Moosa's descriptions exemplify a recent observation by Matthew Engelke that 'As a principle of statecraft, secularism simply isn't part of the core vocabulary of African modernities' (2015: 89). However, if we widen the lens beyond contemporary discourses of statehood to the emergence and decline of the missions, and to the history of nursing in South Africa, we find that narratives of secularization have featured explicitly. Secularization has served as a symbolic threat to professionalism, and has signified class-based struggle. As Engelke points out, such narratives in African contexts have been overlooked in debates about the secular, due in part to long-standing association of Africa with superstition and the occult, as well as with widespread adherence across the continent to Christianity, Islam and other religions. I argue here that a focus on the secular is necessary because the nurses themselves – albeit not using the term 'secular' – associated processes of democratization closely with the decline of religion.

At Bethesda, this process has been indexed by events such as the closure of the chapel and its reuse as a meeting space (see Chapter Three). Many bemoaned the decline of religious influence and blamed it for the problems that they experienced at work. Despite remembering the draconian discipline to which they were subjected in the past, they recalled with nostalgia a period contrasting sharply with the dystopian future that lay ahead.

Called to nursing

Sister Kheswa, now a chief professional nurse working at Bethesda Hospital, was raised with her two sisters and three brothers in an Anglican mission. Strongly influenced by her grandfather, who was a prominent Anglican preacher, she described her life as having been 'spent in the ministry'. She began her nurse training in Manguzi Hospital in 1978, in the last few years of its control by the Methodist Church. Since then, she has worked in hospitals in Nelspruit, Pretoria and Nongoma, before finally coming to Bethesda in 1997.

Sister Kheswa explained that by 1977, she had decided to become a teacher. Yet, her plan was interrupted by a vision from God:

> I saw that vision in 1977. God said, there will be a time in the future when there will be sick people who won't [be able to] help themselves. He showed me that vision. I didn't know that there will be this HIV and AIDS.

She realized that God had 'called her' to become a nurse. Years later, when she came to Bethesda, she was first given the job of treating patients with HIV in one of the nearby clinics. She explained: 'I realised that this was the vision I saw in 1977 … I saw that I was really called for these people.' Her Christian faith continued to provide an ongoing source of motivation at work:

> You keep on reminding yourself that there is somebody who is looking at you, while you are busy operating, while you are busy talking, or advising the patient … You are accountable to God as well as to the hospital, in a way. So in my life I just take my patients as God, not as patients as such, but as God. Fear him, respect him, try to do everything according to God.

For Sister Kheswa, then, talking about God offers a way of expressing a deep moral concern about her patients. The idea of being 'accountable' to God implies a strong sense of purpose in relation to work, and is expressed by using the current, workplace language of accountability. The comment hints at the centrality of religion for a revitalized understanding of accountability among nurses, which as we see in the next chapter draws upon theocratic principles, instead of secular, democratic ones.

This was the most literal account of a 'calling' from God that I heard among the nurses. But many of them drew on the concept of a 'calling' to explain their chosen career. Sister Kheswa's reframing of her experience in terms of the current crisis of HIV and AIDS demonstrates how representations of the past reformulate and exist in dialogue with present concerns. Religious idioms associated with the past are constructed in ways that intersect with contemporary workplace debates.

The idea of vocational 'calling' resonates deeply with the history of nursing. For Charlotte Searle – South African nursing academic and educator – the moral and practical well-being and advancement of the profession relied upon 'a philosophy, deeply rooted in the Christian faith, which leads one into nursing and keeps one there' (Searle [1968] 1980: 17). In *The Protestant Ethic and the Spirit of Capitalism*, Max Weber ([1930] 2005) traced historically the idea of the 'calling'. During the Reformation, the term emerged to denote a link between religious moral purpose and one's duty in worldly affairs, in contrast to the Catholic vision of a secluded, monastic life. The idea gained further traction under Calvinism, Methodism and other puritan sects. They broadened its use to imply a religious pursuit in work and disciplined labour of various kinds. This provided a moral basis, argued Weber, for the emergence of capitalism.

Here, we find an important link in Weber's work between religion and professionalism, one that emerges prominently in the history of nursing.

The close alliance of nursing with religious institutions until well into the twentieth century has ensured the salience and continued reassertion of religion in the present.[13] The connections apparent in older nurses' comments between Christianity, morality, status and professionalism resonate with the history of nursing in South Africa, where Christian faith, 'Western' etiquette and mission education were all indicators of upward social mobility. These were some of the alluring appeals of nurse training that was as much an instruction in lifestyle as it was in occupational skill (see Chapter Three). As one of the nurses at Bethesda said, 'we used to be institutionalised ... We were taught everything, how to behave, even outside the hospital'. She used the word 'institutionalised' to refer to a process of acculturation during nurse training that she viewed as having penetrated every aspect of life. Through the prism of religion and the 'respectability' associated with it, professionalism extended beyond the workplace and into one's social and moral worlds.

The idea of being 'called' to nursing carried with it connotations of benign and quintessentially female goodness – important qualities of professional status in nursing historically. In contrast, at Bethesda the pursuit of nursing ostensibly for financial gain is perceived as a newer kind of aspiration. One nurse explained:

> That aspect of nursing as a calling has diminished. That was important for the old nurses of my time ... [Nowadays] if it is time to go off, even if there's a patient who needs service, he'll go. [Whereas] *we* were able to sacrifice.

The concept of 'calling' here introduces a temporal framework. Younger nurses are portrayed as lazy and uncaring, in contrast to those associated with the earlier period, who exemplify greater willingness to work and, in this instance, to do overtime. The motivation for this rests on the concept of the 'calling', deemed to be lacking in those entering nursing today. It is evident here that older nurses' professional ethic is located in a deep history of mission medicine and Christianity.

However, nurses have long been represented, on the one hand, as Christian, caring, compassionate and beneficent and, on the other, as unskilled workers motivated primarily by financial concerns. Far from being a new source of conflict, the perceived threat from secularism in nursing has a long history. This division has often signified class differentiation. The two contrasting images of nursing as an elite profession and as a menial hands-on job have been imagined through the lens of a religious/secular dichotomy. Such ideas were reinforced and perpetuated by key figures in the profession such as Charlotte Searle. For much of the twentieth century, and particularly during the apartheid era, Searle was the most prominent educator and scholar of nursing, and the most influential nurse in the country. She wrote extensively about her profession and contributed immensely in shaping it. She was a leading proponent of professionalization. She wrote of the earliest 'secular nurses' in post-Reformation Europe:

> They lacked the strict disciplinary control to which the members of the religious orders had been subjected, and they also lacked the cultural refinement of the religious sisters. The monks and nuns had worked in the hospitals for religious reasons and on humanitarian grounds, but the new type of nurse came into hospitals for economic reasons. (Searle 1965: 134–35)

This quote hints at a dichotomous representation that found cultural footing initially in the early missionary context in Africa. Yet the concerns expressed here, about the lack of discipline and of the primacy of the financial incentive, bear remarkable resemblance to the contemporary narratives at Bethesda. The quote is laden with Searle's own assumptions about the relationships between class ('cultural refinement'), religious calling and her idea of proper nursing, drawing on the perceived moral and status differences that separated 'religious' from 'secular' nurses. For her, the prospect of secularism in nursing undermined its integrity and moral standing. It posed a threat to its status as a profession.

Throughout the twentieth century, ideas of Christian duty were thus twinned to a search for professional prestige, accompanied by a moral condescension towards those who appeared to be doing the job for personal gain. The latter was most often associated with the lower rank and file of nursing who were denigrated for undermining the reputation of the profession, by going on strike for example, regardless of the enormous disparities that separated its different levels (Marks 1994: 196). Questions of religion and secularism were, therefore, intimately bound up with the ongoing struggle for professionalization within a framework of intense stratification.

As nursing developed through the twentieth century, pressures intensified. The technological advancements of medicine and health care provided nursing with an opportunity to fashion itself as a 'science', equivalent to that of medicine. Yet, it also presented a perceived threat, seemingly undermining the implicitly gendered and religious associations of nursing that had fashioned its identity as one guided by womanly ideas of moral duty, care and compassion. Religion and technical prowess would now compete with one another as signifiers of professionalism.

In an address to the Department of Nursing Science at the University of Pretoria in 1968, Charlotte Searle tackled the tension between these two competing visions:

> If the nurse is a mere 'paid' worker, she will fail man in his moment of greatest need; if she is merely 'charitable' and unable to contribute to his therapy, she is a danger, and if she is a mere 'scientist', the support needed by those who are vulnerable will be lacking. Scientific developments in medicine present a great challenge to nurses, not merely at the level of the acquisition of knowledge, but also at the level of interpersonal relationships and ethical values. ([1968] 1980: 3)

Her comment expressed the seemingly contradictory ideas of nursing as a morally imbued and compassionate, caring pursuit, and as a scientific occupation akin to that of the medical doctor. She expressed this sentiment more explicitly later in the address, outlining the dangers of the latter approach:

> The mass of medical material, the emphasis on cause and effect in a scientific study such as medicine, burden the nurse with a sense of guilt because she permitted the demands of science to smother her humanitarian role and in this way to desert her patient. Since we nurses are aware of this, we want to take up the challenge of this scientific age. We realise that our greatest challenge is

to ensure a balance between the demands of science and the demands of the individual. Nurses realise that the greatest threat of this technological age is that medicine may be deprived of its humaneness. (ibid.: 14)

Here she outlined a careful compromise, willing to forego neither the Christian underpinnings of nursing consolidated during the mission era, nor the scientific reputation accessible to nurses in a new 'technological age'. The moral side of nursing, the 'humane' approach offered exclusively by the nurse, was closely twinned to the Christian moral ethos described above in which nurses were 'to moralise and save the sick, not simply nurse them' (Marks 1994: 208). Indeed, it was this that earlier set nurses apart as an elite social category. The bureaucratization of health services thus fed into discourses about the perceived moral decline of the profession and simultaneously challenged the status gains made by nursing thus far. It threatened to swamp nursing with government demands and standardizing procedures, thus transforming it into a set of technical procedures dictated by the state. Nursing was at risk of becoming an unremarkable and functional branch of an increasingly centralized health system:

> The impersonal nature of a government-organised service dominated by bureaucratic ways of thinking... has been responsible for periods of decline in the quality of nursing. The bureaucrat views the nurse as a mere pair of hands that daily have to perform the prescribed stereotyped procedures. To him – be he doctor or layman – the uniqueness of the sick person and the personal support required by him have no meaning. (Searle [1968] 1980: 7)

Bureaucratic demands threatened, fundamentally, the class status of nurses. Although Charlotte Searle represented the highest echelons of the nursing profession, separated from the vast majority of her colleagues both by race and by class, her comments nevertheless reflected and reinforced deep-seated concerns that have reverberated across the nursing spectrum in South Africa, and re-emerge in the contemporary context of Bethesda Hospital. In 1968, Searle had anticipated a crisis caused by encroaching bureaucratic control in nursing, which she interpreted as an attack on both ideologies on which the professional status of the nurse has rested: religious and academic. Both the religious and the intellectual connotations of professionalism were threatened by the demands of government.

Religion and autonomy

If the idea of vocational 'calling' is evoked to suggest a feeling of moral purpose in relation to work, it also provides a metaphor for speaking about professional autonomy. Nurses seek ways of establishing and maintaining a sense of professional identity in the face of increasing fragmentation, high workload, and poor pay and working conditions that have made the high burdens of illness all the more difficult to address from day to day on the wards. The association emerges in Mazo Buthelezi's biographical discussion of Thembani Grace Mashaba, a 'nurse pioneer' from KwaZulu-Natal. As a matron at Ngwelezane Hospital, Mashaba

> discovered that her professional calling could not be contained, compressed and compromised into the job descriptions. Her visibility, accessibility and presence throughout the initial stages were in such demand that she found herself now and then going on duty in the evenings and on weekends as well as doing hospital rounds at night. (Buthelezi 2004: n.p.).

The concept of 'calling' here refashions hard work as a personal moral project.

At Bethesda, a linear temporal logic accompanies this outlook, which bears resemblance to Weber's secularization thesis. With its moral overtones of Christian duty and responsibility, the idea of being 'called' to nursing signifies a period in the history of Bethesda Hospital prior to its takeover by the government. Consequently, the nurses' perceptions of the hospital's missionary past and the subsequent secularization of the institution play heavily into contemporary issues concerning workplace hierarchy, status and morality. They link a moral commentary about a lack of care within their profession to the demise of mission medicine. Older nurses, in particular, perceive that their own religious motivations are no longer relevant to those entering the profession today. This has enabled them to draw upon long-standing associations between nursing and the respectability of their own mission education in attempting to maintain the status signifiers that separate them from their junior counterparts.

Yet, it would be misleading to see this commentary as purely instrumental on the part of older nurses. For them, talking about the deterioration of nursing and in particular, their loss of authority over junior nurses, is a way of articulating important shifts in the organisation of power at Bethesda. Here, we find spatial as well as temporal logics playing out. James Ferguson and Akhil Gupta (2002) have suggested that one of the defining features of the state as an imagined entity is its perceived spatial separation from, and position 'above', local contexts. What looks from a macro-scale like an integration and decentralization of power may be experienced by those who work within government institutions such as Bethesda as a stripping of authority and agency. Imagined in terms of a spatial metaphor, the loss of control felt by staff at Bethesda had to do with the detachment of administrative from medical functions. The roles of the hospital manager and medical superintendent became distinct, no longer embodied by one individual. As I have shown in earlier chapters, this had a considerable impact upon the structural organization of the hospital: a change that is felt strongly today. Both the temporal and spatial configurations of power in the contemporary workplace are experienced as antithetical to the preservation of professional autonomy. This creates feelings of insecurity, and a sense of being 'left out', as one senior nurse put it.

As I showed in Chapter One, it is important to emphasize that the experience of distantly located governmental powers did not begin in 1994. Since its inception, the mission hospital and various government officials and departments struggled for influence and control. During the period of homeland rule, the hospital was reliant on funds and equipment from Ulundi. Communication could be so unreliable and intermittent, that power could feel elusive and distant. But while resources had to be fought for, decision-making was localized. As I showed in Chapter Three, nurses and doctors were to a large extent left to their own devices. Autonomy was therefore achieved somewhat inadvertently.

But certain patterns and tendencies of homeland rule have remained influential in the post-apartheid era. Counterposed to this, we find religion once again emerging as a significant metaphor of professional autonomy. Consider one senior nurse in a managerial role, now seeking opportunities to acquire land for farming along-side looking for further career progression opportunities in nursing. I asked whether she would like to become a hospital manager, and she paused and smiled, revealing that this thought was on her mind: 'But the problem is, I am not political. You have to affiliate to get these higher posts; you have to be card carrying'. She was referring euphemistically to ANC membership. To her, the systems of patronage that are widely recognized as undergirding access to senior state employment, was antithetical to her religiously informed position which was non-partisan.

This time, religion signifies autonomy from party politics; and specifically the neo-patrimonial form of politics incubated during the homeland period, that persists today. One Zulu-speaking doctor stated this another way:

> In politics, people are behaving badly; they cause problems. There are many people suffering here, suffering badly, because of politics. I do not like to involve myself in politics. I was raised as a Christian, and have faith in God only. We cannot trust in a particular political system, because it always breaks down eventually. But God will find a way. Those are my beliefs.[14]

Here we are reminded of the story of the bus crash in Chapter One, which demonstrated how nurses evoked a professional ethic tied to mission training, in contrast to local political allegiences. Whether claiming autonomy from secularism or from political processes, religion serves as an avenue through which nurses and other health workers assert a professional ethic of autonomy and care in contrast to these.

Conclusion

The nostalgic narratives of some nurses seem to support the idea that they remain wedded to hierarchical models of the past, unable to adapt to newer democratic processes. Many of these sentiments echo the concerns of elite members of the profession in previous decades, represented by prominent nurse educator, Charlotte Searle, for whom secularization was a threat to the profession. The desire for reinstatement of hierarchies is in part the reproduction of a struggle for professional status that has long characterized nursing in South Africa. In perceiving a decline of religious influence at the hospital, however, nurses are also engaged in a critique of democracy in the terms of its own language and suppositions. They speak from a position that accepts a partial decline in religion, notes the emergence of alternative paradigms such as 'patient rights', and condemns the bureaucratic changes accompanying these paradigms on the grounds that they do a disservice to nurses and in some cases to patients. It is important to take seriously the nurses' criticisms of new health-care practices, without assuming necessarily that their failures are a consequence either of apartheid legacy or of the cultural untranslatability of neo-liberal modes of governance.

In South Africa, dominant narratives about the role of the ANC government as the key economic and political benefactor to the middle and upper classes underpins an assumption of a strong relationship between the professions and the state. The middle classes are taken to be the key beneficiaries of the corporate–state nexus in South Africa. Consequently, the professions are seen as carefully protected and nurtured. In this chapter, I have described a counter-tendency to this dominant narrative. In this rural hospital, nurses experience the contradictory processes of decentralization and centralization of power that is characteristic of post-colonial state building in Africa (Wunsch 2014). In a climate of audit and difficult working conditions, nurses seek ways of reclaiming autonomy. Both professionalism and religion serve as important discourses of autonomy, the latter being drawn upon in the creation of particular temporal and spatial conceptualizations. These reproduce professional identity in specific configurations that are localized, but that also signify at a wider scale a changing relationship between the state and the professions.

Professionalism is not only a matter of class mobility and social status; it is also about how to pursue projects of care during uncertain and resource constrained times. Religiosity at Bethesda is the expression of a yearning for a world that is known, rather than one in which power operates elusively. The reassertion of religious values alongside the admonishment of 'rights' is part of this longing for stable truth in an uncertain time.

CHAPTER SIX

Aspiration Beyond Professionalism

For much of the twentieth century, nursing represented one of the few avenues to high status for black women, offering access to the privileged position that set them apart from the greater black population. The hierarchies of the nursing profession, mirroring those of society at large were racialized, so that to be aspirational meant to traverse these boundaries and adorn the symbols of racial otherness. One missionary stated that civilization could be achieved not through conversion alone, but only if 'you lived in such homes as Englishmen live in, dress, and walk, and use knives and forks like Englishmen' (quoted in Ross 1999: 339). As Deborah Posel (2010) has explained, the freedom not only to be wealthy but also to consume the outward symbols of wealth and success became indelibly linked to whiteness; in contrast, blackness was a sign of restricted entitlement to an inferior mode of consumption and lifestyle.[1]

The mission education received by nurses was one avenue for acquiring the desired modes of dress, style and language that enabled – though never absolutely – a transgression of this boundary. In the post-apartheid period, the 'respectable' styles once embraced by nurses now seem anachronistic, bringing forth recollections of mission-era paternalism. In her perceptive analysis of South Africa's current political crisis, Gillian Hart suggests that there are two types of middle classes in South Africa today: one which was nurtured under the homelands, and another which sees its advancement stemming from the opportunities of the post-apartheid period. Nurses have typically been associated with the former; they are now engaging in various ways with the latter, as new avenues to income creation, prestige and moral purpose become visible.

In this chapter, I describe the ways in which nurses are generating new subjectivities that challenge the borders of the formal economy, national boundaries or secular liberal values. In what follows, I describe two sets of practices that assert different kinds of values: supranational and theocratic. These offer alternative possibilities beyond the restricted regimes of the workplace. As such, they hint at the limits of democratic discourses and the fragility of South Africa's state-building project. Gillian Hart (2013) warns against conceiving of counter-hegemonic tendencies as lying *beyond* the state, in a segmented and ill-defined sphere of civil society. Drawing on Antonio Gramsci, she suggests that hegemony is not stable but processual, producing contestation and confrontation more than simply passive consent. State hegemonic discourses encompass the processes frequently attributed to a separate sphere of civil society. According to this interpretation, it is the work of democratic narratives and ideas, such as accountability and rights, to contain and pacify popular antagonisms. Increasingly, as Hart and others show, these efforts are proving inadequate in the face of growing dissatisfaction (Hart 2013; N. Smith 2015). The practices I describe in this chapter do not altogether reject neo-liberal discourses of democracy, but rather reappropriate them in different guises, and combine them with other values, thus 'strengthening the capacity to aspire' (Appadurai 2007: 29). They produce a language that helps to reshape the terrain of citizenship – specifically, one not confined to the post-apartheid workplace. These emerge not as direct claims – as the literature on biological citizenship describes – but as more subtle ways of affirming belonging.

International migration

Since the mid-1990s, international migration has offered an exciting and lucrative career option for nurses in South Africa. At least fourteen nurses left Bethesda Hospital to work in England between 1998 and 2002. These fourteen were highly experienced and well-qualified nurses, several with degree level qualifications, and all working in senior positions. The impact of their departure on the human resource capacity at the hospital was severe, particularly in a context of the existing shortage of specialist skills. A small number have applied since then but have been unsuccessful, probably due to the changes in British immigration policy (Hull 2010). All in all, fewer left for the United Kingdom after 2002.

Nevertheless, migration remains for many an important career aspiration. Nurses frequently raised the issue of working in England, often in response to discovering that I myself am from England, prompting a stream of questions about what it is like, in what ways it is different from South Africa, and what it would be like to work there. Almost all knew, or had heard of, at least one nurse who had moved to England to work. Many students therefore, while disgruntled about poor wages, talked with excitement about embracing the professional life and 'climbing the ladder', which many saw as synonymous with travelling overseas in search of 'greener pastures'. The professional opportunities offered in South Africa's public sector were perceived as limited, and inadequate by many. A clear sense emerged from these discussions that overseas migration presented itself as a realistic and feasible career option. Although, for most, the final choice to migrate would involve logistical obstacles, all knew that the possibility of doing so existed, and that they were in possession of internationally desirable skills. Migration held an important place in regular social discourse, as an idea, a feasible career option, and an aspiration that, for a few, might be actualized. But such opportunities were only available to some and not to all. In what follows, I show that others reverted to existing, more traditionalist stereotypes to counteract the status claims of the returned migrants and to vilify those who decided to move overseas.

Migration to and from the city formed the backbone of South Africa's labour system, during its rapid industrialization at the beginning of the twentieth century, and remains a normal part of life for many. Historically, the manipulation of gendered roles was an important part of this process. Male migration was more common in the earlier part of the twentieth century than female migration, and served ideologically to reproduce the patriarchal family structure. In contrast, the migration of women seemed rather to have been associated more with the breakdown of the family. Anne Mager describes a similar tendency in the Ciskei reserve in the 1940s and 1950s, where 'male discourse constructed women who went to town as subversive' (2001: 270). Such associations, as we shall see shortly, reappear in contemporary discourses about women's overseas travels.

Bongile grew up in an area of KwaZulu-Natal, about 100 kilometres south of Bethesda Hospital. She went to a hospital in the Mpumalanga province to pursue her nurse training, and became an enrolled nurse in 1982. She worked there for several years, later training as a fully qualified, professional nurse in 1991. In 2001, she moved to Portsmouth in England to work for two and a half years before returning to South Africa in 2003. She worked for six months in a private hospital before finally moving to Bethesda, where she was working in the mobile clinic and training in primary health care at the nursing college at Bethesda.

Bongile had decided to go to England after a friend of hers went there and encouraged her to do the same, assuring her that it was easy to arrange and extremely lucrative. She had a five-year-old daughter at home at the time, which made the decision to leave a more difficult one, but her husband strongly encouraged her to go, saying that he would take care of their daughter while she was away. While in England, she spent as much time as possible working, doing agency work in different hospitals in addition to her full-time job. Despite the often extremely long hours that this entailed, the money that she earned enabled her to build a large house in Mpumalanga, as well as to secure additional savings. Such savings, as she and many other nurses often pointed out, would have taken many more years to accumulate on the strength of a nursing salary in South Africa. She sent money to her daughter and to husband, who was then unemployed, and to other family members regularly while she was away. Like Noreen, whom we met in Chapter Two, Bongile spoke with pride about the house she had built. The construction of one's own home – *ukwakha umuzi* (home-building) – is a rite of passage and a symbol of personal achievement.[2]

She drew attention to the lucrative benefits of converting English currency into South African rand. On several occasions Bongile spoke about the ways in which she could use the money she made in England in order to generate more wealth. She was pleased, for example, when the South African rand was devalued against the pound while she was in England, enabling her to buy even more rand with her wages. 'When you convert it to South Africa, oh, you become rich!' she exclaimed. She also explained that when the pound was strong she would apply for a loan from the bank. When the exchange rate was in her favour, the bank would debit the money from her account, enabling her to benefit further from currency fluctuations. As she explained this, she told me laughing: 'You see? You must use your head!'

This ability to be savvy with money – to manipulate, invest and convert wages – was not only important for generating additional wealth, but also demonstrated to herself and to others her skills at interacting with, and benefiting from, a transnational monetary system that was inaccessible to most. Migration overseas enabled her not only to earn more money, but also to tap into a source of knowledge which was, in itself, wealth generating. Being clever, 'using your head', and having the skill to navigate this type of income source gave Bongile a language and a status from which others were excluded.

The idea of migration enabling and enhancing access to privileged knowledge related to work as well as to wealth creation. This was evident in Bongile's comments about people's reactions to her back at the hospital in Mpumalanga, following her return to South Africa. She suggested that others perceived her as more competent and trustworthy, as a result of her overseas experience:

> When you ... say 'I once worked in England', they believe in you and then they trust you. [They] say, 'This one knows everywhere because she has been ... in another country, and she managed to cope there and work and come back'.

She prided herself also in being able to assist other nurses with the knowledge that she gleaned from being in England:

> I was so popular! You know, people were coming from different wards and saying, 'Ok, we are working with the sister who has been to UK!' [They] said they couldn't believe it. Everyone was coming one by one – 'Hello, we heard that you've been to UK' – I said, 'Yes I've been to UK' – 'Tell us how is it?' ... Everybody was so interested ... [One woman] asked me how to go about making the application go faster. So I just told her 'you should get an agency that is going to place [you]' ... She was so excited. She said, '[Bongile], you know, I'm going to England!'

Bongile described similar sorts of responses from those who lived in the area where she stays. The status gained through this activity was buttressed by the material possessions she was able to accumulate, particularly her house, as well as being in a position to donate money to relatives and friends in need. She described herself as someone who gave money freely to family and friends:

> When they receive that, they will be falling, and saying, 'Really? Is this all my money? Or I should give to somebody else?' I said, 'But you did ask! That's the money you asked for.' So everybody's just, even now they just feel like saying, 'don't you feel like going back again?' I said, 'Ah! No, no, no.'

Bongile's stories, and similar ones I heard, suggested that migrating overseas offers a powerful tool for enhancing cultural capital, bringing combined associations of wealth, knowledge and professional competence to bear in a context in which these attributes were both scarce and desirable. Migration offered a means of gaining professional status, in the working context, that is not dependent upon the traditional nursing hierarchy. In this sense, it reflected an alternative claim to status, based on new mediums of wealth creation associated with the post-apartheid opening up of labour markets, and beyond the scope of that offered by the South African workplace.

Bongile's descriptions of others' reactions to her travels likely give us more insight into her desired self-image than into the experience itself. The image of international migration as the ultimately desirable career option is offset by other concerns, introduced earlier in Bongile's story. Many nurses expressed a wish to move overseas, but were unable to do so because of obligations at home, most often involving the care of their children. One senior nurse, who had trained at the hospital in 1970 and had spent most of her working life there, told me that when many of her friends recently moved to England to work, she had also considered doing so: 'People said to me, "look you've got what they're looking for, why don't you go?"' She had many years of experience and was highly qualified, with certificates in midwifery, general nursing, occupational health, a degree majoring in nursing with community, and a diploma in financial management. She explained: 'I couldn't because of family commitments. I had to look after my son. It would have been impossible to leave him, and my husband wouldn't have coped.' She said this, laughing towards the end of her explanation, which prompted me to ask further about the uneven workload at home, which she appeared to imply by her laughter. She told me that she looked after their son, or sometimes paid someone else to when she was too busy. Her husband did not help in this way, she explained, drawing on a typical representation of African masculinity to account for his behaviour: 'This is Zulu culture. This is how things are.' Without these family commitments, she admitted, she would definitely have gone to England. But she added: 'It's not just about money; family is important too.'

Another nurse began her training at Bethesda Hospital in 1973 and, in 2007, occupied a senior managerial position having spent most of her career at Bethesda. For her, there was no incentive to go elsewhere: 'There are different reasons why people stay in one place. For me there were two reasons. Firstly I stayed because I could pursue my career path easily here. The second reason was that I got married in 1981, so that tied me to this area. This area became my home.' When asked about going overseas: 'I treasure my children more than money. And my family, I love my family more than money.' She went on to explain that her financial decisions were guided by a need for frugality and a sense of priority, particularly with a view to the future quality of life of her five children:

> I forfeit most of the things that I like, so that I make the ends meet. I make my goals to be successful. The major goals in my life now is that I have a house, which I already built, I've got. And my children are at school. They have to learn. So I forfeit a nice car, because I thought having a car is still not right for me now that the children are still at school. You know what I mean? Salaries are not enough, but you have to forfeit some of the things, say no, I am not going to have this, but I would rather have this.

In this nurse's account, values of frugality accompanied a wider moral terrain of familial love.

As these examples suggest, for many who did not migrate overseas, migration symbolizes the opposite of frugality. It represents a desire for money and extravagant consumption over and above

one's family. Another nurse put it: 'I want to stay with my family …
I would rather stay at home and eat peanuts.'

I found this criticism surprising, particularly considering the
important role that migration has played in the region historically as
a source of family livelihood and social reproduction. The assumption seemed to overlook the fact that many women moved precisely because of a desire to support their families. As Mark Hunter
(2010) shows, migration became entwined in the very meanings of
love in the early part of the twentieth century, when the ability to
provide for one's family became an integral basis for love and intimacy. Similarly, among the nurses, the choice of whether or not to
migrate was not necessarily a choice between accruing wealth and
caring for one's family. In many instances where there was someone
at home to take care of children, both could be achieved. In one
instance, it was a friend and nursing colleague who took care of the
migrant's three children for a year while she worked in England.

For Bongile, the choice between family and livelihood emerged
as the result of a specific set of changing circumstances at home.
Tempted by the higher salary, Bongile wanted to stay on longer in
England. But her decision was challenged by problems that began
to occur at home in Mpumalanga. She discovered that her husband was not taking care of her daughter properly, leaving her
alone in the house while he went out. Bongile contemplated bringing her daughter to England, but decided that she would not be
able to spend enough time with her, given her long working hours.
Concerned that this would lead to her child being 'neglected', she
decided to return home. She found work immediately in a private hospital at home in Mpumalanga. But during this time her
relationship with her husband deteriorated, causing her to leave
home, move to KwaZulu-Natal and find employment at Bethesda
Hospital, bringing her daughter with her. She explained: 'I was just
hiding, I was running away.'

Bongile's husband's behaviour intercepted the existing course of
her career, to create a dilemma and to demand a choice between, as
she herself described, 'becoming richer' and her child's happiness.
In our conversations, she rarely complained about her husband's
actions but, instead, tended to focus on the moral question that it
created for her. She identified a characteristic that she associates
with men generally, implying that as a group their behaviour is to
be expected. As she said, somewhat elusively: 'I was just planning

to call her [my daughter] to come over to England but, you know, there were those things, you know how men are.' The onus of moral choice then fell on her: 'I thought that in order to become richer, my child is suffering. The priority, it should be my child. Then I will see how I will cope. Other people are coping. It's just that I wanted to achieve everything. But I did achieve most, because even now, with the money that I made in England, I built that whole house.'

Domestic relations therefore intercept nurses' career choices, and – in this particular instance – the choice of whether or not to migrate overseas, as women struggle to balance different obligations. But as Bongile's example illustrates, migration does not necessarily involve choosing between money and family. Rather, this choice is dependent on the specific dynamics of 'domestic struggles' (Bozzoli 1983) experienced by nurses and the extent of broader social networks of support.

There are multiple factors influencing a nurse's decision to migrate overseas – from the opportunities and restrictions imposed by international labour markets, to the intimate relations that determine roles and responsibilities at the familial level. Cherryl Walker has called for analytically detaching the idea of 'womanhood' from patriarchal discourse, criticizing the idea that women should be defined first and foremost as wives or mothers. Yet, these essentialized categories still feature heavily in hospital commentaries around the issue of migration. While many nurses speak enthusiastically about the possibilities of seeking work overseas, others condemn migrants for abandoning or neglecting their family in the pursuit of financial gain. They do so by drawing on fixed gender representations of Zulu masculinity on the one hand, and female domestic responsibility on the other.[3]

However, seen through the lens of professional identity, these criticisms might be interpreted as a response to the challenge that overseas migration presents to traditional forms of nursing hierarchy and the limitations of the South African workplace. Migration is a vibrant symbol of the new and attractive possibilities available for economic participation and status groupings in post-apartheid South Africa. The moral undertones of nurses' assertions that often emerge in relation to migration overseas – that it is reprehensible to prioritize financial gain over family obligations – is perhaps a means of reclaiming power in a context in which migration competes ideologically with other claims to superior status based on the prevailing, yet increasingly unstable, nursing hierarchy. As I have shown throughout the book, this existing hierarchy, rooted in earlier missionary notions of 'respectability' and cultivated by successive colonial and apartheid governments as part of a broader ideological strategy of labour management, has long been characterized by an excessive preoccupation with status differentials. This has been forged in relation to values of professionalism. But, as this hierarchy fails to garner the same social capital that it once did, tensions arise between those that seek status via alternative avenues and those that, for whatever reason, are unable to.

As I have shown in previous chapters, religion is another medium that nurses use to navigate ethics and interpersonal relations at work. Despite the secular institutional setting, religion was flourishing. I turn now to a born-again prayer group, interesting because while it takes place at the hospital, it is not contained within the formal structures dictated by the institution. It contrasts sharply with the formalism of the institutionalized morning prayers in the wards, that I described in Chapter Three. In this respect, like the nurses who travel abroad, this is an aspirational sphere that pushes beyond the remit of work-based citizenship.

Born-again Christianity at work

One evening, as I was walking through the hospital grounds on my way to the car park, I heard the sound of four or five voices singing loudly, piercing the still atmosphere that descends over the hospital in the evenings. Following the direction of the voices, I walked back along the little path that runs alongside the main buildings. Past the paediatric ward, the path opens out onto a small, grassy courtyard, across which I could see the brightly lit dining hall. Three nurses were standing in the hall, facing in different directions, with their arms outstretched above their heads, palms facing outwards. They sang almost shouting, but in harmony: *'Igama lakhe lihle, Igama lakhe lihle ...'* ['His name is great, His name is great ...']. Two others sat on chairs either staring up or with their heads resting in their hands. I hesitated outside, but as more nurses bustled into the room, and began to put out rows of white plastic chairs, I decided to join them. Cecilia, whom we met in Chapter Four, was among the singing nurses. She saw me and, momentarily surprised, welcomed me with a hug and an enormous grin. Her eyes were gleaming and she was sweating as she enthusiastically drew people into the room while singing. Dressed in brightly coloured clothes, rather than their work uniforms, the women's comportment and interactions seemed transformed.

The meeting lasted for just under an hour and consisted of singing in between individual addresses. The first was a sermon by one of the nurses, referred to as the Word of God. Participants were then asked voluntarily to come forward to give a 'testimonial'. Testimonials usually involved the telling of an event or experience that the speaker had had, that revealed the evidence of God's presence or work in their lives. These often related to work issues, but also covered topics relating to family and life beyond work. Testimonials were usually followed by two or three minutes of individuals praying together that took place spontaneously. These prayers would be initiated spontaneously by one person, after a song had died down. At the end of the meeting, everyone hugged or shook hands with one another on their way out.

One aspect that caught my attention and drew me back to the prayer group was the content of the testimonials. They gave an explicit and collective commentary about work, which was quite different from any other meeting space or forum I had experienced during my research at the hospital. Set up in 2006 by a Nigerian doctor, whom I will call Dr Abati, then employed at Bethesda, the born-again prayer group had only recently been established when I began attending during my fieldwork. The group's meetings were held on Monday and Thursday evenings, between 7 pm and 8 pm, and were usually attended by about twenty people, although the numbers varied from five to as many as fifty on one occasion, when there was a visiting speaker. Members included mainly nurses of various categories from student to registered nurse, although no senior, management level nurse or matron attended the group during the period that I was attending. It consisted mainly, therefore, of junior nurses. I attended the prayer group eighteen times in total, between February and October of 2007. The group converged around a 'Pentecostal style' of worship (Meyer 2004), even though its members did not all belong to born-again denominations.

Initiated in America, the global born-again movement has gained huge sway in Africa since the 1980s. This charismatic renewal has been accompanied by the emergence of a plethora of non-denominational institutions with a far wider, broad-based appeal than the mission and Pentecostal churches that preceded it (Maxwell 2006: 110–11). Writing in the context of West Africa, the anthropologist Charles Piot describes global Pentecostalism as 'the most successful social movement of our time' (2010: 72). Drawing on a wide-ranging web of technological, media and cultural idioms, this new movement has tapped successfully into an emergent, distinctively 'modern' set of values that stressed individualism and professional self-improvement, offering a new type of respectability to the burgeoning, post-colonial African middle classes.

Across sub-Saharan Africa, Pentecostal Christianity has been widely identified as a site for the reconfiguration of values and subjectivities. Debates in the literature have been concerned with its relationship to political and economic change, and in what sense it forms a response to the changing material realities of people's lives, or might even be able to intervene in and change them. In South Africa, Deborah James suggests that such activities 'provide a language of conscious and engaged citizenship' (2015: 203), while Jean-François Bayart argues tentatively that Pentecostal Christianity in Africa constitutes as a 'reinvention of the democratic model ... [that] could in the course of time assume political form' (2000: 266). The born-again prayer group at Bethesda Hospital is a fruitful environment to explore these issues, particularly because, instead of occupying the enclosed space of a church, this group is situated in and actively responding to the workplace itself. All of the members share in common their workplace experiences, occupy a space in the hospital's hierarchy, and are accustomed to the bureaucratic culture that dominates this working environment. These dynamics come into play more explicitly during prayer meetings than they might do otherwise. For this reason, analysis of born-again practice specifically within the workplace is conducive for exploring the dialectic between born-again discourses and this-worldly concerns.

Testimonials at the Bethesda prayer group frequently addressed work issues. They provided a moral commentary running parallel to work itself. As in the following example they often drew on stories of intimate patient encounters as a way of reasserting moral purpose in relation to work:

We work hard, we work very hard in our job. We work so hard sometimes, we don't know whether we are coming or going. It is Monday and we feel like it is Friday already, because we are working so hard. But remember that God has chosen us. We are missionaries, chosen by God. You need to touch your patient and your patient should be healed! You should touch your dying patient, and you should walk with them. I remember one time I had a patient, a young woman. I didn't continue with her treatment because I could see that she was dying anyway. So I just held onto her hand, and I said to her, 'Do you know Jesus?' and she said, 'No, I only know my ancestors'. I said, 'Would you like to know Jesus?', and she said, 'Yes'. And as she looked at me, I could see her expression, because she couldn't talk anymore, but her face was saying, 'Thank you!' … This is what God wants. It is not about the uniform, or the high heels that we like to wear … People, we've got a serious job. This is what God has asked of us, and we are going to answer!

This statement contains widely reported characteristics of Pentecostal-charismatic theology, like the rejection of so-called traditional beliefs indicated here by the mention of ancestors, and the moral condemnation of material consumption.[4] In addition, these sentiments played into a more specific commentary that related to practices of health care and nursing. The speaker encouraged a renewed focus on the needs of the patient, and spoke to the sense in which this is undermined by an emphasis on status, symbolized here by the mention of uniform. This message was conveyed through the account of the dying woman, a story that proclaims the ultimate importance of the spiritual, rather than the physical, healing, thus echoing the outlook of earlier missionary approaches to health and healing. Yet, in doing so, it also evoked the ambivalent relationship between aspirational professionalism and moral duty.

At times, work matters and problems were openly discussed, but always within the structure of prayer and testimonial. A student nurse spoke about her frustration with the Department of Health for causing an interruption in an examination, causing her to have to resit the exam, and for failing to give an explanation. She ended her account by saying: 'So we ask for your prayers in this. It has been very painful. But I love God no matter what. I love him whether or not he answers me. God has a plan for everything ... Pray for us ... Keep it up!' This conclusion was met with claps and ululations from the group. The story engendered a communal sense of outrage that the employer had treated the students unfairly. This anger was counteracted, however, by a reference to God which provided reassurance that there was a reason for what was happening. Many similar examples suggested a certain antagonism felt towards the secular hospital-based hierarchy. They appeared discursively to replace it with a theocratic hierarchy: one that generated a sense of moral purpose in relation to work. The prayer group context offered a space in which work related problems could be aired, and those experiencing them could gain support from other workers. In this sense, it offered a legitimate public space in which to critique the activities of management, wherein the profane hierarchy was demonized in favour of a sacred authority headed by God.

At times this could engender a passive acceptance of workplace power structures. One day while we were sitting in the ward, Cecilia had once been discussing her dissatisfaction with wages. She said, 'But I don't complain, because I trust in God and I know that I will receive my just reward. That's how I see it.' The tension between social critique and passive resignation echoes a key debate in relation to Pentecostal-charismatic Christianity in Africa (Maxwell 2006; Mate 2002; Marshall 1993). It is not my purpose here, however, to determine the 'success' or otherwise of born-again Christianity as a form of resistance or, as Geschiere puts it, 'to become imprisoned in a resistance-accommodation dichotomy' (1999: 219). On the contrary, as Meyer (2001) shows, it is the openness and indeterminacy of born-again theology that accounts for much of its appeal. The born-again prayer group is a space in which nurses engage with the contradictions and conflicts of work and formulate a collective and moral response to these.

Dr Abati also addressed the issue of hospital hierarchy during a sermon, using the identity of born-again Christianity to define the separation between those who care for patients and those who do not:

There is a tendency not to care for patients. But if you are Born-again you are not like that, because you experience a change of heart ... So you are not doing something to, say, please the matron. You do it because you want to do what's right.

In this statement, unlike the previous one, the issue of intent was raised. The doctor claimed that as a born-again Christian, your behaviour should be motivated by a moral duty, rather than by a desire to 'please the matron'. This statement hints at the issues raised in Chapter Four, making a reference to hospital hierarchy and the pressure on nurses to prioritize the demands made by more senior, managerial staff, sometimes at the expense of their own sense of what their patients required. I described there why the aims and demands of the management do not always correspond to the most desirable clinical practice, and how fears of excessive audit and accountability – of 'pleasing the matron' – often come to take priority over patient care. This concern with the bureaucratic procedures of accountability was underpinned by – but also conflicted with – a moral challenge centred on the welfare of patients. Notable in this statement is the assertion of a divine hierarchy, in contrast to the hospital hierarchy, as a source of motivation for work. Another nurse's statement demonstrates this well:

> Do each job that you are doing well. Don't come in in the morning and look at your boss [try to please the boss]. Do your work to the best of your ability. Don't do it for man, but for the Lord … He is pushing you up onto a different level … We serve God's will by not conforming to this world, because people are negative. Begin to speak positively.

As in the previous two statements, the profane hierarchy of the workplace is rejected and replaced with a sacred hierarchy ruled by God, bearing similarity with Ruth Marshall's observation about Pentecostal theology in Nigeria that it offers 'an alternate form of political accountability' (1993: 234). The concept of a sacred hierarchy offers a legitimate alternative to the hierarchy of 'this world' and, importantly, one in which personal promotion is possible: 'He is pushing you up onto a different level.'

The two, alternative sources of authority are once again implied in the following speech by Dr Abati. What is interesting here is the use of the file as a symbol that links the profane and sacred hierarchies:

> Maybe earlier today you did something wrong. Someone said something to you, and it made you so angry. You boiled up, and

out of anger, you said something you shouldn't have. Afterwards, you realised that you shouldn't have done that. In that situation, you say, 'Sorry God!' – because Satan has filed that sin. He doesn't miss a thing. He is filing a report. What you must do is take that report to Jesus. Hand it to Jesus, and Jesus, not Satan, will have the final say. Then you can say to Satan, 'Satan, shut up! Satan, shut up!'

As he shouted these final words, he gestured with his index finger pointing outwards dramatically and repeatedly, as though Satan was standing directly in front of him. This provoked an enraptured response of 'Hallelujah!' and 'Jesus' from the audience of nurses.

In this example, the doctor alludes to familiar channels of hospital management procedure to demonstrate the spiritual battle between Satan and Jesus. He refers to the hospital's system of accountability, in which mistakes or acts of negligence committed by nurses are documented and filed, to be dealt with by senior members of hospital management. In Chapter Four, I described the importance of paperwork for containing and documenting staff activities, an important mechanism of staff audit and a means by which relationships of authority can be mapped out and mediated. Here an institutional culture of hierarchy and accountability is imaginatively reconstituted and envisaged in terms of relationships with, and between, the figures of Jesus and Satan. While familiar hierarchies are demonized through an association with Satan, they are replaced in the story by the divine authority symbolized by Jesus, who is given the final say.

At other times, workplace hierarchy is endorsed, such as when during testimonials, Cecilia would throw in comments such as: '... and I was speaking to the matron there and she seemed to know what I meant also...' As Marshall writes, members 'inevitably incorporate many elements of the social order which they seek to overcome' (1993: 242). In this instance, Cecilia inadvertently reinstates the legitimacy of the matron, and takes for granted her superior status and knowledge.

Gendered language and imagery was also common during testimonials. Addressing a group one evening, made up exclusively of women, a female laboratory technician made the following statement amid a wider speech on the role of women:

> For homes to be blessed, it is the duty of mothers. It is their duty
> to stand in the gap for people who are ill in this place. For the
> government to come right and to do the correct thing, it is our
> job to pray. Let us take our position as females.

In certain areas of her talk, the patriarchal idea of female duty and
service was strongly imposed, expressing the sense that women
are to blame, and must therefore take responsibility for resolving
problems. As with those who criticized migrants for abandoning
their family in the pursuit of material wealth, this testimonial also
emphasized female maternal duty as the basis of ethically oriented
behaviour:

> Look at how important a woman is in front of God. We corrupted
> the world as females. Again he set the world free. God wants us
> to be the mourners. If a woman can break a home up, then again
> she can build it up.

During the Word of God, another nurse said:

> God wants women of faith. Think of Miriam. She danced in
> front of the whole army, and praised God's name there in front
> of them.[5] And they were amazed at her, not because she was
> naked, not because she was a woman, but because she was brave.
> God wants women to stand like that, women that will be able to
> stand for the truth. In our job, us nurses, there is no more truth.
> There is no more truth. We are supposed to check the BP every
> 15 minutes, but we just go and write it in the book [make it up].
> God needs us to raise up the standard! Doing God's work is like
> saying, 'I'm going to do this in the correct way, even if the whole
> ward is against me.'

Workplace competition and a loss of moral conscience in nursing are
once again raised here. Born-again Christianity is offered as a solution, providing a renewed motivation for focusing on patient care.

In a contradictory way, born-again discourses at Bethesda seem
both to confirm and to critique existing power structures that
affect nurses' daily lives. This tension has occupied recent debates
about Pentecostal-charismatic Christianity in Africa. In relation
to gender, for example, Mate (2002) argues that Pentecostalism

serves to reinforce the patriarchal norms of domestic life, while Maxwell criticizes this view, stating that 'despite the fact that female Pentecostals claim liberation through their faith, their religion is still dismissed simplistically as patriarchal' (2006: 11). Erica Bornstein demonstrates a similar dynamic in her analysis of the relationship between spirituality and development in a Christian NGO in Zimbabwe where, she suggests, 'faith was used in development as both a controlling discourse of institutional power and a discourse that offered the transformative potential for change' (2003: 65).

In the prayer group at Bethesda, nurses reimagine and reconstitute hierarchy in the process of challenging it. The two are mutually constitutive. Testimonials are necessarily infused with the shared language of hierarchy and accountability that characterize the work setting. Through the process of incorporating these values, they are given new shades of meaning, being at once reinforced and challenged. Various anthropologists have described charismatic Christianity as creating the proliferation of witchcraft imaginaries, even as it disavows them (Piot 2010: 128). Can the same be said of its relationship with democratic ideas of bureaucracy, accountability and rights?

We can address this question further by considering the relationship between these narratives and those of the older nurses in the previous chapter. What became apparent was how infrequently nurses in the prayer group referred to 'democracy' or 'rights'. This seemed an intriguing omission, given how often such terms emerged in conversation with nurses outside of the prayer group. Moreover, the testimonials contained very little reference to the past. Instead, they were often prescriptive, outlining how nurses should re-envisage their work. Unlike the narratives that drew upon the concept of a 'calling', born-again faith did not rely on nostalgic recollections of the past. The perception of a linear trajectory of decline indexed by secularization was largely absent.

It would be incorrect to interpret this as disengagement from discourses of democracy, however. Instead, while the previous narratives critiqued democracy based on the shortcomings of its own principles – secularism, human rights, democracy itself – born-again faith was grounded in an ontologically different perspective altogether. A similar argument is made by Harri Englund in his work on Christianity in Malawi. Comparing the views of the elite and lay congregations of Catholic and Pentecostal churches, Englund identifies two forms of critique based upon differing conceptions of morality. The first, espoused by elite members of the Catholic Church, criticizes liberalism on its own terms: based on the principle of 'persons as rights-bearing subjects', they condemn particular economic policies, which are taken as an abuse of democratic freedom (Englund 2000: 586–89). Lay Pentecostals, on the other hand, emphasize 'humanity and selfhood as a condition which is acquired through specific actions and experiences' associated with being born-again. Within the lay Pentecostal paradigm, Englund argues, a rejection of liberal ideas is based upon a moral conception of unity rather than of individual autonomy.

I share Englund's scepticism about accounts of born-again Christianity that emphasize its propensity towards individualization. My experience at Bethesda suggested that the shared praying and worship in the evening prayer groups was an important way of forging relatedness, in a context otherwise characterized by intense hierarchy and work-related anxiety. The group produced meaningful, collective thought about how to care in a time of audit and scarce resources.

Moreover, born-again faith was based on a different conception of time, compared to the linear secularization process envisaged by nurses in Chapter Five. The emergence of a born-again faith among some nurses did not express a preoccupation with nostalgia, but the assertion of a religious truth removed from reliance on historical narrative. In his ethnography that documents the astonishing rise of new religious movements in West Africa, Charles Piot describes Pentecostal faith as one that 'anticipates a future while closing its eyes to the past' (2010: 164). The born-again nurses at Bethesda are indifferent to the past, and to teleologies of decline. Instead, the possibility of religious experience inheres in every event, from the dramatic recovery of a sick child initiated into antiretroviral treatment, to the fortuitous assistance of a foreign visitor, to even the most banal tasks of hospital administration. Each moment offers a possible window to the sacred. Every experience has the potential to be narrativized during testimonials, to an audience of willing witnesses. The experience of retelling offers reassurance, and tames experiences that otherwise lie beyond one's conception or control. Faced with an uncertain future, it offered an experience of immediacy that removed doubt.

Negotiating citizenship beyond the workplace

Richard Werbner has recently suggested that in Botswana, tensions arise not because some have citizenship status while others are denied it, but because of the struggles over the quality and content of citizenship: the meanings and entitlements it denotes (2004: 269). Laura Bear and Nayanika Mathur make a similar observation in India: 'Precarious citizenship is not characterized by the dynamics of absolute inclusion and exclusion associated with the colonial and welfare/developmental state. Instead, it is shaped by forms of contractually delimited partial inclusion' (2015: 28). These restricted kinds of inclusion form along the lines of specific, limited contracts and procedures between government and citizen, generated by the public goods of transparency, decentralization, austerity and so on. The ethnography from Bethesda offers multiple examples of tensions that arise out of the ambiguities of citizenship status. In a context where work is unavailable to many, work as a key site of 'virtuous citizenship' (Barchiesi 2011) is undermined. In its place, people are drawn into the field of citizenship on the basis of new criteria. Public accountability and patient rights are some of the arteries along which this negotiation takes place. For nurses, it is because the field of citizenship extends beyond the workplace, beyond the state-protected sphere of professionalism – such as to patients themselves through the discourse of 'rights' – that competing tensions emerge around how one's citizenship status is defined and what this actually means.

But the Bethesda material also points to the new moral and aspirational identities that emerge from these experiences of contingency. As Andrew Nash writes: 'Dialectical thought has flourished always in the margins and interstices of society. It seeks to follow the movement of contradictions while the major social institutions are designed to resolve or obscure them' (2009: 210). This and earlier chapters have described some of the activities that fall beyond the immediate purview of dominant state institutions – from seeking aspirational opportunities overseas, to investing salaries in informal activities, to new born-again practices that abandon liberal teleologies of democratization and secularization. What does it mean for citizenship and nation building that nurses leave South Africa in search of higher salaries overseas? How should we interpret their rejection of liberal democratic principles in favour of theocratic ideas, whether these rejections are based on nostalgic recollection of the mission era or on newer born-again conceptions? And what does it mean for citizenship that nurses question the status of their formal sector jobs, and view with envy those who generate wealth beyond the structures of state employment?

Is national citizenship inevitably eroded by these activities? To what extent do they fall beyond, or operate in tension with, the hegemonic project of state building? Let us compare the South African examples to a region like West Africa, where the developmental state has been more limited in its reach. Charles Piot describes similar kinds of activities, which have attracted huge numbers of people in Togo. These range from Pentecostal Christianity, to gambling, to what Piot describes as an obsessive desire to migrate overseas. All of these activities express people's aspirations to seek lives that extend beyond the remit of the failed nation-state project. Instead, people face outwards and their participation in these activities constitute 'passionate pleas to establish their rights to inclusion in global society' (Piot 2010: 166). These outward facing activities, Piot argues compellingly, flourish in the gaps that are created by a hollowed out state, where the government has failed to provide for the majority of citizens.

For the nurses I have described in this book, I felt that something more was at stake than a desire simply to leave, or to relinquish national identity in return for global access. These practices in the South African context signal a more contradictory process of both departure from, and reinforcement of, national belonging. Bongile enthusiastically embraced the lucrative opportunities offered by work in England. But rather than viewing this as an 'exit strategy' as Piot suggests in the Togolese context (2010: 77), the value of migration for Bongile was an elevated status at home. Far from offering an escape route, migration was the very means of accruing wealth and success at home. Another example is Cecilia, whose born-again faith allowed for a revitalized effort at work. In Chapter Two, Noreen's achievements depended on making use of government-provided tenders, and the priority given by the government to women and disabled people in accessing this work. She insisted on investing her earnings in the rural area where she was from, rather than in departing for the city. As Werbner writes, cosmopolitan citizenship does not involve abandoning the rural, but in being able to 'effectively straddle town and country' (2004: 270). Like Noreen, Bongile views her own enrichment as synonymous with community upliftment. These processes evoke something akin to Hart's (2013) characterization of South Africa's political trajectory as exhibiting contradictory processes of both denationalization and renationalization. Political change at the margins may not only challenge, but also re-energize, national discourses of belonging. These activities operating beyond the disciplining structures of state employment suggest that ideas of national citizenship are being renegotiated, but not abandoned.

Conclusion

In all of these examples, professionalism recedes as a source of identification and citizenship. Even for those migrating abroad in pursuit of career advancement, the professionalism on offer is a more expansive version of what the South African workplace can provide. For others, it is escape to the private health sector that serves a similar purpose. Democratic idioms are appropriated, refashioned and reworked in ways that assert aspirations and values beyond the scope of what is offered by government employment. These are oriented around the creation of different kinds of overlapping values: supra-national and theocratic. Earlier in the book, especially in Chapter Two, the idea of economic aspirations beyond the formal sector also emerged as important. In all three cases, desires for both material improvement and individual moral recognition are intimately bound together in sets of motives that at times appear compatible and at other times provoke tension, where traditional values are reasserted alongside newer ones – as in the example of nurses' responses to migrants. The idioms and images garnered appear flexible enough to contain both conservative and subversive elements. Rather than merely indicating a desire for status, these new assertions of value involve processes of moral self-fashioning. These practices at times adopt the tools and terminologies of democratic discourse even while, simultaneously, they express its limits. They enable the reimagining of citizenship as shared sociality, rather than one structured by the usual political hierarchies and traditional modes of control. They suggest, overall, that professionalism is a necessary, but insufficient, route to middle-class status in South Africa today.

Conclusion

What does it mean to be aspirational during precarious times? My research assistant seemed to offer a cogent answer one day. 'I need to be a professional,' he said to me, staring determinedly at the road ahead of us, as we drove out of a hotel where we had stopped for a drink. He repeated this two or three times with pointed hand gestures. His comment encapsulated the continued salience of the 'professional' as a highly sought-after title. Having grown up in an impoverished area near Bethesda Hospital, he was in the process of applying for university bursaries, in the hope of a better life. As a child, his older sister who was a nurse had been a role model for him. She implanted in him the desire to read and work hard, he told me, as he wistfully recalled her reading a book during the half-mile walk to and from the borehole to fetch water. It was not just nurses, he told me, but other government employees, like teachers and policemen, who were admired by everyone. Government employment was more desirable than jobs in the private sector, he explained, because one received more protection and benefits, and would have a greater likelihood of getting a permanent position. Pausing and searching for words, he suggested that to work for the government 'means that you have earned your place in the community'. The comment revealed the continuing association between the status of 'professional' and that of 'citizen', echoing the long-standing respectability earned by those in formal employment.

In this book, I have argued that as expectations align uneasily with a fragmented reality, the seeming affinity of these two terms is loosening. While professionalism offers a degree of security and comfort of which many can only dream, difficult working conditions and lack of control at work creates uncertainty, opening up the space in which alternative visions are formed. This emerged in the story of Noreen, whom we met in Chapter Two. Having longed to become a nurse, and failing to reach her goal, she resented the superior status to which she thought nurses and teachers laid claim. Eventually, she was able to forge an alternative, lucrative career path after starting her own construction company and receiving a government tender. Later she expressed relief that her earlier aspirations had not transpired, and deemed her new circumstances to be more desirable. In relation to Noreen's distinctively post-apartheid path to material success, the traditional professions of teaching and nursing seemed anachronistic, harking back to a time when black people gained status via the beneficence of white patrons. While nursing resembled the exclusive, racialized citizenship of the apartheid era, new entrepreneurship symbolized the proverbial pot of gold in which all South Africans might partake. This contrast was reflected in Noreen's comment that, from her perspective, while nurses pursued superior social standing and an escape from rural life, her own wealth was an inclusive symbol of social upliftment, a pride which all of her neighbours could share.

This appears, however, to raise further questions. How can nursing and similar government positions still be so sought after, while at the same time they create such feelings of insecurity and contingency? Many nurses bemoan the difficult working conditions and feelings of underappreciation by management, and look around at activities that seem to confer greater control, free from the restrictions and demands placed on formal sector employees. What I suggest is that professional identity is necessary but insufficient to meet middle-class aspirations. Consequently, work remains a crucial source of value, while also being dislodged as a dominant mode of belonging. In this concluding chapter, I consider this argument in relation to the wider context of the middle classes in South Africa and globally. In the following two sections, I explore in turn two elements of professional aspiration that have featured centrally in this book: that of accumulation, in terms of income and status, a project that has become highly precarious; and that of care, which is also a fragile and at times fraught endeavour. In the end, I suggest, the two projects are intertwined.

Precarious accumulation

A dominant narrative suggests divergent paths for the middle classes globally. In the global north, the middle classes are thought to be vanishing, as class relations become ever more polarized under conditions of economic slowdown. In places like India, Nigeria and Brazil, in contrast, many have reported the rapid growth of a well-educated, well-off middle class. Increasing media attention focuses on the flashy consumption practices of these urban dwellers, whose globalized tastes are at times credited for spurring development and at other times blamed for irresponsible expenditure (James 2015) or dependency on imports (Freidberg 2003: 447).

In anthropology, more attention has been paid in recent years to the consumption practices and lifestyles of the middle classes, rather than to their working lives and professionalization strategies. The growth of consumer culture across Africa and other parts of the global south has drawn attention to what some have described as the emergence of a more inclusive, 'new' middle class. As Henrike Donner and Geert de Neve write in the Indian context, until the mid-1980s, 'being middle-class indexed almost exclusively the lifestyles of public servants and professionals' (2011: 4). Since then, new discourses on consumerism, as well as various processes of integration and affirmative action, have weakened the hegemony of the 'old' professional classes, creating new and competing forms of 'middleclassness'.

Rather than seeing them as opposites, these two contrasting representations – the disappearing middle in the global north and the consumption-oriented, 'new' rising middle in the global south – might instead be viewed as two sides of the same coin. Both emerge from a growing understanding that value creation occurs outside of the traditional workplace. In various ways, work and labour are no longer understood to be the dominant sites for identity formation. People turn, instead, to non-traditional forms of value production, including consumption practices as well as new immaterial and informal kinds of work. The formal workplace is neither the primary site of exploitation, or of class struggle; labour itself has become more diffuse. In Michael Hardt's and Antonio Negri's (2005) terms, the working class has been replaced by the 'multitude', while Jean and John Comaroff speak of the 'phantom proletariat'

(2004: 527). This has involved a decoupling of the domains of production and reproduction, with varied and volatile outcomes. The positive and negative political possibilities seem continually to reflect one another in a conversation that moves back and forth. On the one hand, neo-liberal logics are seen to capitalize on the dearth of employment by rendering the self an entrepreneurial self, further entrenching the commodification of all aspects of life, at work and beyond (J. L. Comaroff and J.Comaroff 2010). On the other hand, the weakening of the relationship between work and value, and the activities that emerge in its place, some dare to hope, reveal inchoate opportunities for the foundation of new economic alternatives (Hardt and Negri 2005; Mason 2016).

These overarching global narratives paint a stark picture, revealing the precarious basis on which the social production of middle-class status and lifestyles is based. Even in contexts where the middle classes appear to be flourishing, the 2008 crash revealed how such lifestyles were riskily propelled by borrowed credit (James 2015). Faced with unpredictability and precariousness, the burdens of trying to sustain middle-class lifestyles become even more apparent. In South Africa, contradictions revealed themselves dramatically in 2015, when student protests erupted on university campuses across the country to reject the government's proposed tuition fee hikes. In the most widespread student protest since the end of apartheid, many students insisted that further hikes would force them out of university altogether. Commentators recognized the wider context of unemployment and inequality that created fertile ground for such a protest, bringing forth the expression of a collective anger that is proving increasingly difficult to contain. Exposing the long histories of racialized injustice around which contemporary inequalities are moulded, what began as an issue relating to tuition fees quickly turned to a wider set of questions about race and privilege, reflecting resentments that ran deep. For instance, universities were accused of being too slow to reform in the post-apartheid era, and were denounced as sites for the perpetuation of white privilege. The protests were also an assertion of citizenship claims to formal education, to entrance to the formal labour market, and to the professional life that many black South Africans had been denied during apartheid. They revealed the politicized nature of education in South Africa, and the centrality of educational training as an aspiration that remains closely paired with narratives of citizenship. The protests highlighted in a radicalized form the absolute centrality that many South Africans place on formal education and professionalization, as a public good as well as a private asset.

Professionalism, I suggest, is an important avenue for understanding the multiple articulations of middle-class identity, traversing the boundaries between work and beyond. Professionalism offers an important perspective on the intersections between work, distribution, social status and consumption. Being professional also implies a stake in particular institutional configurations. Consequently, it offers a way of analysing with precision the formal and informal networks, and specific modes of governance, that make up public administrations. Due to the work entailed in producing and sustaining professional identity, it avoids assumptions about predetermined systems of medical or neo-liberal ethics, in the hospital setting, and focuses instead on how these are produced as part of a constellation of activities and networks. Given the size and scale of state bureaucracies across the global south, professionalism remains a critical feature of middle-class strategies and identities.

I have focused, in the book, on the everyday practices through which professional trajectories are forged and expressed. A theme that re-emerged in my data in various guises was that of autonomy. This has been a long-standing concern in the sociology of professionalism, referring to the institutionalized strategies of ring-fencing knowledge and access, often in tension with managerial agendas. But questions of professional autonomy also assumed a particularly localized form in this former homeland setting. Professionalism offered a form of identification that could be formed outside of, and as an alternative to, particular kinds of political ethics. A similar dynamic emerges in Rachel Spronk's research among young professionals in Nairobi. Here, the identification with formal education and professional status allowed professionals to 'take pride in taking a particular trans-ethnic position in a country that is troubled by ethnic division' (Spronk 2012: 4). To understand the implications of this kind of professional identity, it is necessary to look beyond simply dismissing it as an apolitical, 'opt-out' worldview that some of the earlier literature on the African bourgeoisie identified (Brandel-Syrier 1978). While much literature on the state and its institutions in sub-Saharan Africa tends to emphasize corruption and cultures of impunity, professionalism offers an ideological route that positions itself in opposition to these values. It therefore also offers a perspective on how employees navigate the uneasy alliance between neo-patrimonial elements of institutional governance and managerial authority centred on the global ascendancy of idioms such as accountability. As a fraught identity, relying upon both autonomy from and dependency on the state, it offers an important perspective on the character of the relationship between the ANC 'party-state' and the country's lower middle classes in South Africa.

While 'decentralization' is a term that denotes power moving from the centre outwards, a focus on professional strategies provide insight into the often contradictory character of such processes, as they are constituted piecemeal within institutional settings. They allow a focus on how, as Timothy Gibbs puts it, 'a national state [is] being assembled from regional fragments' (2014: 184). In northern KwaZulu-Natal, professional autonomy can only be understood in relation to the history of mission medicine and Christianity in the region. There are important parallels between professionalism and religion. As Weber recognized, both have served historically as vehicles of social assent. In nursing, the two are intimately intertwined. The struggle of the mission for a viable role during an era in which missionalization was in global decline runs parallel with the formation of professional autonomy. Consequently, religion and the secular have come to form important fields of signification. Secularism has long posed a threat to professional autonomy, threatening to reduce nursing to a mechanical task. In contrast, for many of the nurses at Bethesda, religion serves as a moral basis for professional autonomy. It also signals how nurses are navigating the ethical terrain of their professional lives, in a context where inequalities of care are pronounced and work is a matter of life and death.

Projects of care

Anthropological literature on the middle classes has tended to focus on upwardly aspiring identities and how these are formed, often through consumption practices but also through other modes of status pursuit. In this book, I have argued that strategies of status acquisition must be explored alongside the projects of care that professionals are engaged in.

In public moral discourse about nursing, the pursuit of status has often been associated with the *absence* of care, or even of cruelty of nurses towards patients. A condescending and superior attitude by South African nurses towards their patients has frequently been attributed to a desire for high status, sometimes resulting in abuse or neglect (Jewkes, Abrahams and Mvo 1998; Segar 1994; Walker 1996; Walker and Gilson 2004). This 'professional arrogance', it is argued, has the effect of distancing nurses from their patients and creating a communication barrier between them (Rispel and Schneider 1991:122). Describing the deeply hostile relations between nurses and patients in a hospital in the Western Cape, Jewkes and fellow authors sum up the feelings of vulnerability, bad morale, alienation from the community and overwork that nurses described as justifying their cruel behaviour towards patients: they are 'engaged in an unremitting struggle to claim a status and respect as a middle class profession within environments in which political, professional, historical and personal factors continuously undermine this claim' (Jewkes, Abrahams and Mvo 1998: 1792). Shula Marks (1994) provides a compelling and detailed excavation of the way that professional aspiration and care have existed in tension with one another at various moments in nursing's embattled history. She shows crucially how this conflict has played out not only or primarily in the behavior and attitudes of front-line workers – where the blame is most often directed – but also in the institutional and legislative arenas that dictated wider decisions about how to safeguard professionalism, sometimes at the expense of providing the best possible care.

In this book, I have used an ethnographic approach to shed light on the complexities of workplace ethics and of care practices. Official discourses demarcate the provision of care within tightly prescribed scopes of practice. Moving beyond this, an ethnographic lens enables attentiveness to the subtle negotiations and informal practices that play out in practice, as health-care workers respond to particular constraints and dilemmas (Olivier de Sardan 2014). Although I have demonstrated that conflict exists between different levels of the workplace hierarchy, the tension between managerial and professional roles – which is emphasized both by the literature on professionalism and on neo-liberal governmentality – in practice is more complex than is often suggested. Those occupying managerial roles engage in their own interpersonal approaches and care practices, and are also responding to workplace pressures and constraints. Managerial and professional agendas – while at times occupying different spatial and temporal frames that cause friction – often also overlap and form part of one another. They are also mobilized at different times by the same people, depending on circumstances.

This book has addressed some of the tensions that arise in the creation of caring practices, in a situation where ideas of public accountability are reduced to narrow techniques such as audit. Marilyn Strathern's (2000) depiction of audit as an emergent global culture is a provocation to anthropologists, who are typically trained to treat universalisms with suspicion, especially in relation to claims about 'culture'. It provides a tentative hypothesis to be tried out in contexts in which neo-liberalism may serve as the 'exception' to dominant modes of governance (Ong 2006). One response is provided by Andrew Kipnis (2008), who uses ethnographic research on audit procedures in a school in China to mount a critique of universalist claims about the neo-liberal origins of audit practices. The procedures he describes exhibit the hallmarks of neo-liberal governmentality, like reliance on numeric targets and the cultivation of individual responsibility. However, he argues that his research participants, as well as Chinese academics themselves, view these activities not as the adoption of neo-liberalism but as the product of socialist governance. Kipnis argues that the traits that writers like Nikolas Rose identify as distinctively 'neo-liberal' have in fact a more general resonance with different philosophical and political histories, such as Confucionism and Taoism (Kipnis 2008: 287).

Kipnis's argument is important, highlighting the need for rigorous historicization and rightly rejecting the naïve idea that neo-liberal modes of governance travel from one place to the next by a process of cultural 'diffusion' (ibid: 285). But the argument is insufficient for the purposes of understanding South Africa's government institutions and the specific configurations of power and authority in this context. On the one hand, some modes of workplace accountability are the outcome of long-standing habits of professional conduct or enduring subjectivities formed through processes of Christian missionization. On the other hand, more recently emerging audit procedures, such as those I described above, do derive from a quite specific set of ideas associated with the Washington Consensus of the early 1980s onwards.

But instead of attributing neo-liberalism to cultural diffusion, or one based crudely on economic determinism for that matter, a more nuanced understanding of the relationship of African institutions to global configurations of power is needed. One framing that I have adopted in this book is provided by Jean-François Bayart, who mounts a critique of the widely held view of sub-Saharan Africa as peripheral to the world system. He argues that holders of power in Africa position themselves in the world through the strategic adoption and utilization of external resources, ideas and constraints. The discourse of democracy itself, he argues, is 'no more than yet another source of economic rents', appropriated because of its adaptability to 'the spirit of the age' (Bayart 2000: 226). In South Africa, we can observe the opportunistic appropriation of neo-liberal ideas alongside the post-apartheid 'spirit of the age'. For instance, Krista Johnson points out that the former president, Thabo Mbeki, and his team – well known for presiding over South Africa's neo-liberal transition – found the neo-liberal restructuring of the state a good fit with their Leninist conception of the importance of vanguard party leadership over mass action (2003: 202).

Bayart does not deny Africa's relationship of dependency on external powers and institutions; on the contrary, he posits that 'sovereignty in Africa is exercised through the creation and management of dependence' (2000: 228). Far from 'diffusing' around the globe, a word that evokes a kind of passive osmosis rightly rejected by Kipnis, capitalism is being appropriated and managed actively 'as an application of a doctrine' (Przeworski et al. 1995: viii). In the South African context, the transition to liberal democracy is marked by a move away from the language of national struggle to the ideologically more neutral discourses of accountability, institutional capacity, service delivery and so on that resonate with global development agendas. The adoption of the language of 'good governance' is important for securing aid. But as accountability is ever more prioritized on government agendas, many have noted that channels of political accountability appear simultaneously to be in decline (Wenzel 2007). Governments throughout sub-Saharan Africa are accountable to global funders, and only secondarily or in some cases negligibly, to health-care beneficiaries (Lee et al. 2009). The procedures of audit introduced in institutions of service delivery frequently accompany a less visible withdrawal of political accountability (Herzfeld 1992; Strathern 2000a: 5).

This central contradiction that regimes of accountability exacerbate rather than diffuse centralized concentrations of power inheres in the procedures of audit itself. While audit is intended to encourage autonomy and increased responsibility, Marilyn Strathern argues, it may erode the implicit knowledge upon which trust-based relations rely (Strathern 2006: 197), replacing them with routine procedures largely detached from 'the "real" tasks of productive work' (Strathern 2000a: 1). Moreover, 'audit tries to persuade the participants of the way the world is without acknowledging its own particular perspective' (Strathern 2000b: 287). In other words, while audit mechanisms demand from organizations a greater degree of self-knowledge and self-monitoring, they rarely operate with the same degree of reflexivity.

Official narratives of 'transparency' and 'decentralization' narrow the channels along which citizenship might be claimed, producing what Bear and Mathur describe as 'contractually delimited partial inclusion' (2015: 28). Post-apartheid citizenship becomes contingent on these work-based obligations. When nurses blame 'democracy' for their disempowerment at work, they do so as a strategy to preserve and reproduce professional autonomy. But they also do so because of the ways in which new neo-liberal practices intercept and obstruct projects of care. Current forms of state governance are denounced as inimical to care, and alternative professional ethics are formed around ideas of religiosity, family or supranational aspirations that fall outside of the purview of the stratified workplace.

This suggests the need for a nuanced approach to the study of state institutions, public services and bureaucracies. Rather than to treat bureaucracies simply in their reduced forms as techniques of discipline or expressions of financialized logic, the complex emergence of professional ethics suggests the need to understand bureaucracies as sites for the production and contestation of value – whether these be articulations of care or of contingent belonging. In all of this, bureaucracy emerges not simply as a tool of governance but a moral field in which state building occurs in piecemeal ways and its legitimacy contested.

In this book, I have argued that nurses do not simply react to neo-liberalism as a singular, cohesive system of governmentality. Instead professional strategies, managerial projects, caring practices and workplace hierarchies are continually reproduced in relation to one another. These intersecting aims are created as the outcome of real dilemmas that arise in relating to others and in operating during uncertainty. Throughout the book, I have suggested that experiences of contingency alter the work of caring, creating new temporal framings. Many older nurses use the idioms of past and present to produce binary moral frameworks. This is best conveyed in the nurses' own words. Here is a final set of remarks by a senior nurse, which I quote in full because it crystallizes so clearly this outlook – drawing on conceptions of 'before' and 'now' – and aptly conveys the feelings of fear, contingency and longing that gather around such narratives:

> Before, a doctor could support you. Perhaps you were in a situation where a patient did not become stabilized; we realised that we had fought a losing battle. We could *feel* for this patient. Even the death of a patient, laying out the body, sending it to the mortuary… You felt like crying, as if it was your own relative. But now you are blamed [for such a death]. They are faultfinders. Have I done one and two? What about three and four? For what you did not do, you are at fault for that. [Before,] we were very observant. You could not find a fault. [When errors occurred] the doctor would understand why you had failed. You could even phone the doctor at any time if you had a problem. And the doctor would come right now; they would leave everything. They would leave lunch break, because you had told them to come and there is an emergency… Now, you are scared. You are going to be suspected. You are afraid. You would rather keep quiet, even if you can see it is not correct. You don't know the rules.

She describes here the alienating experience of carrying out on human bodies tasks that are heavily prescribed by normative principles and rigid protocol. Contemporary conditions of work, she suggests, suppress human emotional responses such as empathy and grief. Here, the fear of error is antithetical to an ethic of care. The contrast between the past and present is a metaphor for what James Ferguson calls a '*nonprogressive* temporalization' in contrast to a teleology of progress (2006: 190).

We might be tempted to assume from such remarks that the new 'culture' of audit (Strathern 2000a) is flattening everything in its path. The moral is reduced to the technical, just as the political is re-imagined in purely economistic terms. But what I have argued is that nurses engage in a more subtle set of practices around the reproduction of care at work. Some of these draw on new forms of religiosity. In 'born-again' approaches to work, nurses envisage a radically different temporalization. In these framings, unlike in the above quote, nostalgic sentiments are absent and the past is irrelevant. Spirituality permeates daily life, and is felt through specific actions and experiences of being born-again, offering clarity at a time of uncertainty.

Attention to individualized projects of self-advancement are important yet insufficient for understanding the strategies of the middle classes. Instead, I have argued that projects of accumulation and those of care are intertwined. For the lower middle-class South Africans that this book has described, in a world of unstable social and economic conditions and an uncertain terrain of bureaucratic demands, both of these projects are precarious. But new ideas and desires continually take shape. 'Let us possess this nursing,' one nurse said to me in our final conversation. 'It is ours. This patient is ours.' Despite the pressures they face, nurses engage continually in imagining, and in producing in small ways, a revitalized, collective accountability.

NOTES

Introduction

1 He belonged to the Congress of South African Trade Unions (COSATU), South Africa's main trade union federation.

2 In 1965, Hilda Kuper reported a similar antipathy towards nurses, noting that they received disproportionate blame for patient dissatisfaction, and arguing that 'generalizations of cruelty or neglect of patients have not been substantiated, and undue publicity has been given to isolated incidents' (1965: 223–24).

3 In 2007, 77 per cent of professional nurses and 74 per cent of associate professional nurses were members of a union (Lund and Budlender 2009: 10).

4 In her work on consumers in Durban, Sophie Chevalier (2015) makes a similar observation.

5 Weber argued that one characteristic of a transition to legal-rational authority is a 'levelling effect', whereby previously taken-for-granted hierarchies are called into question. This is because bureaucratic positions are allocated not according to personal qualities but to technical competence. Power becomes depersonalized, and resides in the office rather than the individual.

6 Krista Johnson notes the importance of educational achievement, alongside political training and political lineage, combining liberalism and Leninist vanguardism, in the formation of elite ANC leadership (2003: 202).

7 Outside of anthropology, studies of public administration do exist, but tend to be descriptive rather than analytical, lacking a discussion of the relationship of these institutions to processes of state formation, class dynamics and political economy (Chipkin and Meny-Gibert 2012).

8 For example, an insightful chapter by Rosalind Eyben (2011) highlights the informal practices of social networking and shared consumption that are necessary for the production and legitimation of professional identity.

9   Weberian sociologists, including Parsons, identified collective trust as essential for validating the 'mandate' or 'license' that legitimised the status of professionalism (Hughes 1971; Parsons 1939). As the literature developed, a focus on trust gave way to questions of autonomy and control (Abbott 1988: 5).

10   This was because the success of a hospital depended, not on the quality of care provided but on attracting the best doctors and other skilled clinicians. These highly skilled professionals chose a workplace based on the technologies, equipment and specialized services that validated the ideology of professionalism and secured their status. In this respect, Lee (1971) argues, the real 'consumers' of hospitals are not its patients but its specialized staff. Hospitals have a tendency, therefore, to emulate each other in much the same way that members of status groups do, in an attempt to achieve parity in terms of prestige. This is one reason for why, as Di Maggio and Powell (1983) argued, institutions such as hospitals come to resemble one another so closely.

11   Horwitz describes the discrepancy as 'the contradiction at the heart of apartheid medicine' (2013: 191). Given the findings of sociological literature on medical professionalism, however, Horwitz's example would seem to reflect a contradiction at the heart of medicine more widely. This literature argues that a hospital's success depends on their reputation as providers of specialized treatment rather than the efficient use of resources (Lee 1971; Starr 1982).

12   Julie Livingston's (2012) ethnography of an oncology ward in Botswana is an exemplar of this approach.

13   Other variations on this theme include the concept of 'pharmaceutical citizenship' (Ecks 2005) and 'therapeutic citizenship' (Nguyen 2005; 2010). They share a concern with how biological presuppositions undergird the duties and entitlements associated with citizenship.

14   As post-colonial scholars have argued, the notion of citizenship is the product of a state hegemonic project in which the formation of personhood takes place in relation, first and foremost, to the idea of the state.

15   In 2014, 43.7 per cent of professional nurses were over fifty years old (Rispel and Bruce 2015: 118).

16   The homelands, or 'Bantustans', were territories set aside by the apartheid government for the purpose of creating ethnically homogeneous, independent states for South Africa's black ethnic groups. Ten were created altogether, and were subsequently dismantled following the democratic elections in 1994. The homeland of KwaZulu was officially formed in 1970 and, in 1977,

was granted internal self-government. See G. Maré and G. Hamilton, *An Appetite for Power: Buthelezi's Inkatha and the Politics of 'Loyal Resistance'* (1987).

1 Geographies of Autonomy

1　Several church bodies and denominations are active in the area, notably Zionist, Lutheran, Roman Catholic, Anglican and Methodist.

2　Political turbulence has a long history in Ubombo and its surrounding area. From the thirteenth century until the late nineteenth century this area is thought to have been politically dominated by a Tsonga-speaking people known as the Thonga. This region, between Maputo in the north and Lake St Lucia in the south was thus latterly referred to as 'Thongaland'. In the late eighteenth century, the Zulu polity started to form and by 1824, had become the dominant political force in the region. 'British Amatongaland' (also referred to as 'Maputaland') was the name given to the southern part of the area when Thongaland was divided between the British and Portuguese in 1875, creating a boundary that was later to mark the border between South Africa and Mozambique. 'Amatongaland' referred to the territory north of the Mkuze river, in between the Lebombo Mountains to the west and the Indian Ocean to the east. In 1879, the British defeated the Zulu and the area known as 'Zululand', to the south of Amatongaland, was annexed by the British in 1887. Zululand existed formerly from 1887 to 1897 as a British colony. In 1895, Britain established a 'Thongaland Protectorate'. Both Zululand and Amatongaland were annexed to Natal in 1897, after which the name 'Zululand' referred colloquially to the area north of the Tugela river. Amatongaland is more commonly referred to as 'Maputaland'. From 1910 until 1994, the whole area from south of Durban to Zululand and Maputaland in the north, known as 'Natal', was one of four provinces in South Africa.

3　This information was gathered from a file kept at the Ubombo magistrate's office that contains various pieces of historical, geographical and political information about the region, recorded by successive local magistrates and officials of the department. Thanks are due to chief magistrate Mr V. Z. Mkhwanazi for kindly permitting access to this document.

4　Personal communication with former medical superintendent, Daryl Hackland.

5   This was documented by A. W. Cragg, missionary secretary of
the Zululand Mission in 'The Fifty-Ninth Annual Report of the
Missionary Society of the Methodist Church of South Africa',
December 1940. CLHR. MISC.

6   'Number of patient days' refers to the total number of days for all
patients who were treated at the hospital. For instance, if fifty people
were treated in one day, the number of patient days would be fifty. If
a patient is treated for three days, the number of patient days is three.
This number includes outpatients.

7   Given the twentieth-century dominance of Zulu ethnic nationalism,
people living in the Ubombo area now largely identify themselves as
'Zulu'. But until relatively recently, this has been a site of fluctuating
ethnic allegiance and contestation, given the historical prevalence
of Tsonga-speaking people and the oscillating political control of
Thonga and Zulu polities. As such, ethnic categories were not as
clearly demarcated as they have become in recent decades (Felgate
1982; Hamilton 1995; Vail 1989; Webster 1991).

8   Marks noted a similar difficulty, at times meeting 'a wall of silence'
when trying to find out about such issues from nurses (1994: 272,
fn.4). Prior to 1994, involvement in political or union activity
risked penalization by the South African Nursing Council (SANC).
Furthermore, in KwaZulu, not joining Inkatha potentially resulted
in violence or dismissal. While these risks are no longer relevant in
the post-apartheid period, high levels of political intimidation and
violence during the early 1990s did have a lasting effect, generating
among nurses considerable reluctance to talk openly about these
events.

9   The violence was, however, according to some local accounts, less
severe and more intermittent than in other areas, given the strength
of IFP presence and support in this region.

10   Public hospitals in South Africa are categorized by three levels –
district, regional and tertiary – according to their size and the number
of services and specialities offered.

11   These services include Trauma and Emergency, Medicine, Obstetrics
& Gynaecology, Paediatrics, Dental/Oral Health Services, Mental
Health, Medical Social Work, Eye Care & Cataract case finding,
Rehabilitation Services including Physiotherapy & Occupational
Therapy, Dietetic Services, Clinical Support Services including
Laboratory services, X-ray services and Ultrasound.

12   Technical weaknesses in governing institutions suggest likely delays
in the implementation of the legislation.

13   http://regqs.saqa.org.za/showQualification.php?id=59257 (accessed
on 31 December 2015).

14 A second change in the 2013 legislation is intended partially to
    redress this problem. Enrolled nurses will be equipped with a
    widened scope of practice, as the existing two-year training will be
    extended to a three-year diploma in nursing. The intention is for
    enrolled nurses to work more independently and provide care for
    the vast majority of uncomplicated cases without the assistance
    of a doctor (Blaauw, Ditlopo and Rispel 2014: 6). This tendency
    to extend training programmes as a mechanism of enhancing
    professional status is well known, and it may be the case that the
    discontent of the unionized lower ranks have played a part in
    the extension of the enrolled course to a three-year programme.
    However, while the expansion of training may appear on the surface
    to enhance professional status, the wider context suggests otherwise.
    It is notable that fully registered nurse training lasted for only three
    years prior to 1986, at which point it was increased to four. Now
    we have a situation in which enrolled nurse training will take the
    same length of time that registered nurse training used to take.
    These nurses will be carrying out many of the same responsibilities
    formerly undertaken by registered nurses, with the same amount
    of training, but without being granted the title or accompanying
    benefits of a registered nurse. The expansion of the scope of practice
    of enrolled nurses also does nothing to mitigate the likely decrease
    of registered nurses in rural hospitals, thus further entrenching the
    historic inequalities that have long shaped rural–urban divisions in
    South Africa.

15 In the United Kingdom, following the introduction of Project 2000,
    Davina Allen explained, policy makers envisaged that a 'small,
    highly skilled nursing core, supported by a pool of cheaper workers'
    would resolve the problem of a growing population in need of
    health care and the rising costs associated with providing this (Allen
    2000: 17). These mixed skill alterations were driven in part by a
    desire to reduce costs. However, the outcome was a higher ratio of
    low-skilled to high-skilled nurses, compromising the overall capacity
    of the system to provide high quality care. It also ensured that the
    highly skilled work would be retained for a small and exclusive
    group, implying a continuation of the long-standing drive for
    professionalism.

16 Opportunities for further training will be much more limited for
    staff nurses holding the three-year diploma. They will only be able
    to pursue additional training in the form of a one-year advanced
    diploma in midwifery. Unlike for a registered nurse, there will be
    no route to further specialisms, or to masters or PhD level study
    (Blaauw, Ditlopo and Rispel 2014: 6).

2 The Limits of Professionalism

1 See the government's statistics website 'Stats Online': http://www. statssa.gov.za (accessed on 1 October 2008).

2 Grants are provided via a non-contributory and means-tested system. They include the child support grant, the foster-child grant, the care-dependency grant, the older persons grant, the disability grant, grant-in-aid and social relief of distress.

3 This was operationalized by the Public Finance Management Act of 1999.

4 Instead of its members being elected by nurses, 'interested parties' would recommend their preferred candidate and the minister of health would appoint a member from the various nominations. If no nominations or an insufficient number of nominations were received, the minister would be free to make the appointment single-handedly.

5 Jonathan Berger, 'Blowing Up the Bridges', *Mail & Guardian*, 18 May 2008. http://thoughtleader.co.za/jonathanberger/2008/05/18/ blowing-up-the-bridges/ (accessed on 23 December 2015).

6 'Union Questions Video Footage of Nurse in Abortion Fiasco', 27 August 2002, News 24: http://www.news24.com/SouthAfrica/News/ Union-questions-video-footage-of-nurse-in-abortion-fiasco-20020827 (accessed on 7 July 2014).

7 'Stigma Hasn't Left Abortion Patients', 24 June 2002, IOL News: http://www.iol.co.za/news/south-africa/stigma-hasn-t-left-abortion-patients-1.88558#.U7paQo1dUSE (accessed on 7 July 2014).

8 A tender is a private, short-term contract for service delivery or infrastructural development.

9 Several scholars have pointed out the ambivalence felt by many South Africans about formal employment, suggesting that in many instances, casual work is preferred. Barchiesi writes that casual work 'cushioned the impact of capitalist work discipline, allowed to safeguard cultural norms, and preserved multiple networks of production and exchange across rural and urban spaces' (2011: 15).

10 This is a reference to the town of Jozini, which shares its name with the local municipality of Jozini in which it is situated.

11 The accusation of jealousy in the statement is significant. Jealousy – *umona* in Zulu – is an important concept in the classic anthropological literature on Africa (Evans-Pritchard 1937; see also Apter 1993, 116–19). More recently, Adam Ashforth (2005) returns to the concept in the post-apartheid context of Soweto, identifying it as key to understanding the relationship between rising accusations

of witchcraft and increasing economic insecurity and stagnation. He states that there is 'a presumption of malice underpinning community life', one that is expressed primarily in the form of jealousy (ibid.: 1). Jealousy is the basis of, and the incentive for, witchcraft, rendering it a profoundly dangerous aspect of social relations, particularly when high levels of material inequality pervade everyday existence and generate conditions ripe for jealousy (or accusations of jealousy) of those who achieve financial success (ibid.: 34). In Noreen's comment, the notion of jealousy is drawn upon to signify this 'malicious' side of social life, the partial breakdown of the moral economy and the threat that this poses to social regeneration.

3 Autonomy and Control from Mission to State

1 Further indication of resistance to ethnic associations is given in the Submission on Nursing to the Truth and Reconciliation Commission of 1997 that states 'nurses in Kwa-Zulu had resisted forming their own organisation on what they felt were legal grounds' but the Act was enforced 'before they could officially contest the issue'. (Democratic Nursing Organisation of South Africa [DENOSA]. 'Submission on Nursing by DENOSA to the Truth and Reconciliation Commission' [1997] 28).

2 Lauren Jarvis (2014) also describes how involvement with foreign missionaries allowed women to renegotiate domestic relationships.

3 Farren to Evard, 8 December 1952. CLHR. 197542 No.5.

4 Manguzi Hospital Report, February 1972. CLHR. MS19 099.

5 Use of the term 'Bantu' became popular in the 1920s among liberals and black intelligensia, in preference to the terms 'Native' or the extremely derogatory 'Kaffir', to refer to black South Africans. After 1948, the National Party adopted the term officially. Because of this formal usage by the apartheid regime, by the 1970s the term had become discredited and the government abandoned it in favour of the term 'Black'.

6 Bethesda Hospital Quarterly Report, June 1970. CLHR. MS19 099.

7 CL, MC, MS19 099, Minutes, Bethesda Hospital board meeting, 6 March 1981.

8 CL, MC, MS19 099, Minutes, Bethesda Hospital board meeting 15 August 1981.

9 For a detailed debate about the 1944 National Health Services Commission see: Digby 2012; Freund 2012; Marks 1997c; 2014.

10 These achievements took place and were made possible in the
    context of a wider upsurge of support for primary health care across
    South Africa, spurred by the international excitement generated
    by Alma-Ata, and the subsequent emergence of a network of
    organisations involved in the promotion of PHC nationally, the
    National Progressive Primary Health Care Network (NPPHCN).
    Related to this, numerous small-scale health projects were set up
    across the country, of which the Bethesda initiatives were one
    example. Later, the ANC would also embraced a community-based
    health care agenda, a priority that has persisted to the present day
    and is now referred to – using the phrase coined by Kark himself – as
    Community Oriented Primary Health Care. Returning to the lessons
    of South Africa's attempts at social medicine in the 1940s through
    a rediscovery of the Gluckman report of 1944, the ANC framed
    its National Health Plan based largely upon the PHC approach
    (Kautzky and Tollman 2008). Many have since argued, however, that
    this legacy has been squandered in the post-apartheid setting, with a
    failure to pursue meaningfully the primary health agenda.

11 Bethesda Hospital Quarterly Report, 30 September 1969. CLHR.
    MS19 099.

12 CL, MC, MS19 099, Bethesda Hospital Quarterly Report, 31
    March 1970.

13 CL, MC, MS19 099, Bethesda Hospital Quarterly Report, 31
    March 1971.

14 CL, MC, MS19 099, Bethesda Hospital Quarterly Report, 30
    June 1971.

15 CL, MC, MS19 099, Manguzi Hospital Report, 4 November 1976.

16 CL, MC, MS19 099, Bethesda Hospital Quarterly Report, 31
    December 1976.

17 CL, MC, MS19 099, Bethesda Hospital Annual Report, March 1978.

18 CL, MC, MS19 099, Bethesda Hospital Quarterly Report, June 1978.

19 CL, MC, MS19 099, Bethesda Hospital Quarterly Report,
    October 1978.

20 While the contribution of nurses to community health at Bethesda
    Hospital is poorly documented in the archival records, this emerged
    strongly from the interviews with nurses and doctors.

21 By this point, World Vision and Tear Fund were both active in
    the area.

22 CL, MC, MS19 099, Manguzi Hospital Annual Report, April 1979.

23 The reassertion of religious language by mission nurses and doctors
    at Bethesda – particularly in the naming of projects and official
    discourse – expressed a fear of the secular threat of government
    takeover. This was most explicit, for example, in the following

justification for a constitutional change at Manguzi Hospital in 1971: 'It was proposed at the Medical Superintendent's Meeting that in view of increasing Government pressure and identification with the hospitals the name of this hospital be changed to "Manguzi Methodist Mission Hospital".' CL, MC, MS19 099, Manguzi Hospital report, 18 May 1971.

24 CL, MC, MS19 099, Bethesda Hospital Quarterly Report, December 1977.

25 CL, MC, MS19 099, Bethesda Hospital Report, 2 August 1980.

26 CL, MC, MS19 099, Manguzi Hospital Annual Report, April 1979.

27 CL, MC, MS19 099, Minutes, Manguzi Hospital board meeting, 2 August 1980.

28 CL, MC, MS19 099, Manguzi Hospital Report, 4 December 1981.

29 CL, MC, MS19 099, Bethesda Hospital Quarterly Report, 31 December 1975.

30 CL, MC, MS19 099, Minutes, Bethesda Hospital board meeting, 4 December 1981.

31 CL, MC, MS19 099, Bethesda Hospital Quarterly Report, 30 September 1981.

32 CL, MC, MS19 099, Minutes, Manguzi Hospital Caring Committee, 5 March 1982.

33 Report from Bethesda Hospital and Mission to Total Health Care Committee, 27 May 1983. CLHR. MS19 099. Hospital Christian Fellowship was the name given to regular group worship, which nurses were expected to attend.

34 Very little has so far been written about the successes and failures of service delivery under the KwaZulu homeland government. One interesting exception is a PhD thesis by Wanda Mthembu (2005) that offers a detailed report of HIV/AIDS interventions in KwaZulu-Natal before and after democratic elections of 1994. This gives an indication of the important influence of some key individuals during the era of KwaZulu leadership, who had worked as doctors at mission hospitals.

35 Interview, Stephen Knight, 22 June 2011. For a journalistic account of the initiatives and projects taking place at Bethesda in 1988, see J. Murray and M. Murray 1988.

36 According to Knight, another source of disagreement and fragmentation during this period was the transfer of primary health care training to the SANC, thus making PHC the sole responsibility of nurses. Charlotte Searle herself was extremely adverse to the idea of training nurses within health centres like Pholela and, as an advocate of professionalization, was determined that the SANC maintain control (personal communication with Shula Marks,

29 September 2009). Yet, some argue that this had the effect of 'excluding other health care workers from the mainstream of primary care and perpetuating the idea that doctors in the public sector should work in hospitals while nurses provide clinic-based care' (Kautzky and Tollman 2008: 22). This view was also expressed by Knight as having impacted negatively on PHC at Bethesda Hospital, alienating doctors and fragmenting existing practice.

37 Personal communication with Shula Marks, 29 September 2009.

38 PHC had its own problems in terms of incorporating conservative measure. GOBI, while well intentioned, encouraged narrow medical solutions to complex social problems, further detracting from the social determinants of ill health (Sanders 1997).

4 Accountability, Hierarchy and Care

1 'Bethesda Hospital Strategy Plan 2006–2008/9'.

2 Management science recognizes similar kinds of distinctions. For instance, Shamsul Haque distinguishes between 'formal' and 'informal' accountability within an institution, formal accountability referring to official rules, regulations, codes of conduct etc. and informal accountability referring to organizational culture, peer pressure and other unofficial forms of knowledge that are generated by workers within the shared, day-to-day interactions of the workplace (2000: 606).

3 For instance, MacDonald shows that despite the ambivalence of government officials towards admitting migrants, the 'insatiable demands' of employers in mining, agriculture and manufacturing made it unavoidable, and the 'paperisation' of borders proceeded apace with the issuing of multiple documents, in some cases supported by the Native Labour Department, who set up compounds along the Mozambique border (MacDonald 2014: 167).

5 The Sickness of Democracy and Healing Religion

1 Amy Green, 25 October 2013, 'Emergency: Help Us Help Patients', *Mail & Guardian*, http://mg.co.za/data/2013-10-25-emergency-help-us-help-patients (accessed on 25 October 2013).

2 Baragwanath Hospital is an extreme example. Located in Soweto, an area of Johannesburg that was a hotbed of anti-apartheid resistance,

Baragwanath was at the epicentre of worker unrest and strike action in the 1980s and early 1990s – resulting in deep and persistent tensions between workers – that is not as visible elsewhere (see also Horwitz 2013).

3   Amy Green, 25 October 2013, 'Emergency: Help Us Help Patients', *Mail & Guardian,*: http://mg.co.za/data/2013-10-25-emergency-help-us-help-patients (accessed on 25 October 2013).

4   Recent anthropological work on bureaucracies and the workings of state institutions shows that some of the characteristics described by von Holdt are observable in contexts well beyond Africa. In a development project funded by the United Kingdom's Department of International Development (DFID) in India, David Mosse argues that the observable mismatch between policy frameworks and their implementation is a result not of the failure or ineffectiveness of the former, but of the necessity to maintain 'coherent representations regardless of events' (2005: 2). This is a quality much like the idea of 'face' which von Holdt associates with a post-colonial mindset. Like Mosse, Michael Herzfeld (1992) departs from the idea of bureaucracy as a set of rational rules to be implemented, viewing it rather as a state of mind. For him, the 'indifference' that bureaucrats demonstrate towards their clients (often understood as an undesirable gap between inefficient and smooth bureaucracy) has to do with a mindset that categorizes and excludes certain individuals. This cognitive ordering and the indifferent behaviour to which it gives rise, he suggests, is a systemic feature of how bureaucracies work. What appear as inefficiencies and gaps are in fact intrinsic to organizational systems, not shortfalls that can be eradicated through more rigorous policy. Anthropological work on bureaucracies points to the fact that dysfunctions, which scholars of Africa tend to attribute to colonial systems, may be a feature of bureaucracies everywhere.

5   Gateway Clinic is the first point of access for outpatients. Here, they are assessed by nurses and either treated or, if necessary, referred to a doctor for further consultation.

6   *Indaba* is a commonly used word that has several related meanings including 'news', 'affair', 'item of gossip', 'topic of conversation', 'law case' and 'report'. In the context of this statement it is best translated as 'affair' or 'concern'.

7   Fully trained, professional nurses received a financial bonus, known as the Rural Allowance, of 12 per cent of their income as an incentive for working in rural areas. The bonus has caused much controversy and resentment among junior nurses nationally. In January and February of 2007, hundreds of staff nurses across KwaZulu-Natal

went on strike in demand of a Rural Allowance for all categories of nurses from auxiliary upwards.

8 'Rights' is not an exclusively post-apartheid concept in South Africa. During the resurgence of African nationalism in the 1940s, for example, the ANC adopted a rights-based discourse influenced by the post-World War II Atlantic Charter (Dubow 2005: 3).

9 See http://www.dpsa.gov.za/batho-pele/history.asp.

10 The eight *Batho Pele* principles include 'consultation', 'setting service standards', 'increasing access', 'ensuring courtesy', 'providing information', 'openness and transparency', 'redress' and 'value for money'. In KwaZulu-Natal, a further three principles have been added. These are 'encouraging innovation and rewarding excellence', 'customer impact' and 'leadership and strategic direction'. It is revealing to note that in the descriptions corresponding to these latter three, the word 'customer' replaces that of 'citizen' (applicable in the eight core principles), indicating a shift in emphasis towards a business model. See http://www.kznhealth.gov.za/bathopele.htm.

11 For instance, under the former legislation a woman could only qualify legally for an abortion if two state psychiatrists would testify that she was suicidal (Davis, Rebecca, 'Abortion in South Africa: A Conspiracy of Silence', *Daily Maverick*, 30 September 2013. Accessed online: 15 August 2016).

12 The claim was based on section 72(1)(a) of the Constitution, which states that the NCOP must 'facilitate public involvement in its legislative and other processes', and on section 118(1)(a) which makes similar requirements for provincial legislatures.

13 The idea of nursing as a 'ministry' and a religious 'calling' does appear in the nursing literature (e.g. Emblem 1992; Prater and McEwan 2006; Raatikainen 1997; Widerquist & Davihizar 2006). But this work tends generally to lack historical perspective.

14 This is not an exact quotation but an approximation of what was said.

6 Aspiration Beyond Professionalism

1 The apparently excessive consumerist desires of South Africa's political and business elite today, Posel goes on to argue, are rooted in a logical imperative deriving from these ideas: that to achieve freedom from white minority rule was at the same time to acquire the modes of life which had previously defined and restricted what it meant to be black. She quotes Julius Malema's version of this freedom, which echoes remarkably the words of the missionary

quoted above: 'The ANC changes lives. It can change you from a hobo into someone very important. This ANC has taught those who are insulting it today to use fork and knife, to taste red wine, to wear expensive suits' (quoted in Posel 2010: 159).

2 This was a persistent theme throughout the twentieth century, and an important aim despite changing relationship patterns (Hunter 2010: 41).

3 Along similar lines, others have described how South African nurses' constructions of gendered identity led them to criticise their female patients, particularly in relation to abortion (Marks 1994: 209; L. Walker 1996).

4 This conflicts with an alternative emphasis in certain Pentecostal discourses on wealth fulfillment, known as 'prosperity gospel' (Maxwell 1998; Coleman 2002; Gifford 2001). At times, during testimonials, nurses celebrated receiving money from somebody, or receiving a promise from God for more money in the future. Generally, however, an attitude of asceticism and frugality occupied nurses' accounts. Therefore, while the theme of prosperity and desire for financial success does emerge in testimonials, primarily nurses were preoccupied with their shared experiences at work. This suggests that rather than prosperity theology being integral to Pentecostal faith, the predominance of this theme in so many Pentecostal settings may have to do with Pentecostalism's flexibility; that it tends to respond to and deal with whatever aspect of life seems most pressing. At Bethesda, work is the most relevant, shared experience upon which members of the group reflect during testimonials.

5 A reference to the Old Testament story of Miriam who danced to celebrate the Israelite crossing of the Red Sea (Exodus 15: 20–21).

REFERENCES

Archival sources

Cory Library for Historical Research, Grahamstown

197542 No.5	'Reports and Statements for the Year 1948'.
	Correspondence, Mission and Extension Department, Methodist Church of South Africa. 1963.
	Correspondence, Bethesda Hospital. 1952.
197542 No.6	Correspondence, Bethesda Hospital. 1943.
197542 No.7	'Kosi Bay Native Mission Hospital. General Report'. 1940.
	Quarterly Reports, Bethesda Hospital. 1940–1941.
	Correspondence, Bethesda Hospital. 1951.
MISC	'The Fifty-Sixth Annual Report of the Missionary Society of the Methodist Church of South Africa'. January 1938.
	'The Fifty-Ninth Annual Report of the Missionary Society of the Methodist Church of South Africa'. December 1940.

MS18 690	Minutes, Zululand Mission Committee. 1941–1947.
	Minutes, Zululand and Maputaland Missionary Committee. 1948.
	Bethesda Hospital Quarterly Reports. 1947–1948.
MS19 099	Minutes, Zululand Mission Committee. 1965.
	Minutes, Board of Bethesda Hospital. 1971–1981.
	Minutes, Board of Manguzi Mission Hospital. 1970–1981.
	Bethesda Hospital Reports. 1969–1981.
	Manguzi Hospital Reports. 1970–1981.
	Minutes, Manguzi/Bethesda Hospital Caring Committee. 1982.

Primary sources

Bethesda Hospital Management Organogram.
Bethesda Hospital. 'Employee Housing Policy'. July 2004.
Bethesda Hospital. 'Bethesda Hospital Strategy Plan 2006–2008/9'. 2006.
Buthelezi Commission. The Requirements for Stability and Development in KwaZulu and Natal. Durban: H + H Publications. 1982.
Democratic Nursing Organisation of South Africa (DENOSA). 'Submission on Nursing by DENOSA to the Truth and Reconciliation Commission'. December 1997.
Department of Health. 'National HIV and Syphilis Antenatal Sero-prevalence survey in South Africa'. 2004.
Oram, H. Unpublished autobiography.
Turner, L. Unpublished autobiography.

Secondary sources

Abbott, Andrew. 1988. *The System of Professions: An Essay on the Division of Expert Labor*. Chicago: University of Chicago Press.

Allen, Davina. 2000. *The Changing Shape of Nursing Practice: The Role of Nurses in the Hospital Division of Labour*. Florence, KY: Routledge.

Amit, Roni and Norma Krige. 2014. 'Making Migrants "Il-legible": The Policies and Practices of Documentation in Post-Apartheid South Africa', *Kronos* 14 (1): 269–90.

Andersen, H. M. 2004. '"Villagers": Differential Treatment in a Ghanaian Hospital', *Social Science & Medicine*, 59: 2003–2012.

Appadurai, Arjun. 2007. 'The Capacity to Aspire: Culture and the Terms of Recognition', in David Held and Henrietta L. Moore (eds), *Cultural Politics in a Global Age: Uncertainty, Solidarity and Innovation*. Oxford: Oneworld, 29–35.

Apter, A. 1993. 'Atinga Revisited: Yoruba Witchcraft and the Cocoa Economy, 1950–1951', in J. Comaroff and J. L. Comaroff (eds), *Modernity and Its Malcontents: Ritual and Power in Postcolonial Africa*. Chicago: University of Chicago Press, 111–28.

Asad, Talal. 2003. *Formations of the Secular: Christianity, Islam, Modernity*. California: Stanford University Press.

Ashforth, Adam. 2005. *Witchcraft, Violence, and Democracy in South Africa*. Chicago and London: University of Chicago Press.

Bach, S. 2003. 'International Migration of Health Workers: Labour and Social Issues'. Geneva: International Labour Office. (Unpublished Working Paper).

Barchiesi, Franco. 2011. *Precarious Liberation: Workers, the State, and Contested Social Citizenship in Postapartheid South Africa*. New York: State University of New York Press.

Barker, Anthony. 1959. *Giving and Receiving: An Adventure in African Medical Service*. London: Faith Press.

Bateman, C. 2006. 'Lack of Capacity Devitalising South Africa's Hospitals', *South African Medical Journal*, 96 (3): 168–70.

Bayart, Jean-François. 2000. 'Africa in the World: A History of Extraversion', *African Affairs*, 99: 217–67.

Bear, Laura and Nayanika Mathur. 2015. 'Remaking the Public Good: A New Anthropology of Bureaucracy', *The Cambridge Journal of Anthropology*, 33 (1): 18–34.

Blaauw, D., P. Ditlopo and L. C. Rispel. 2014. 'Nursing Education Reform in South Africa: Lessons from a Policy Analysis Study'. *Global Health Action*. 7 (1): 26401. http://dx.doi.org/10.3402/gha.v7 [Accessed on 26 April 2016].

Bond, Patrick. 2000. *Elite Transition: From Apartheid to Neoliberalism in South Africa*. Sterling, VA: Pluto Press.

Bonnin, D. 2000. 'Claiming Spaces, Changing Places: Political Violence and Women's Protests in KwaZulu-Natal', *Journal of Southern African Studies*, 26 (2): 301–16.

Bornstein, Erica. 2003. *The Spirit of Development: Protestant NGOs, Morality, and Economics in Zimbabwe*. London: Routledge.

Bozzoli, Belinda. 1981. *The Political Nature of a Ruling Class: Capital and Ideology in South Africa, 1890–1933*. London: Routledge & Kegan Paul.

Bozzoli, Belinda. 1983. 'Marxism, Feminism and South African Studies', *Journal of Southern African Studies*, 9 (2): 139–71.

Bozzoli, Belinda. 2004. *Theatres of Struggle and the End of Apartheid*. Edinburgh: Edinburgh University Press.

Brandel-Syrier, M. 1978. *'Coming Through': The Search for a New Cultural Identity*. Johannesburg: McGraw-Hill.

Breckenridge, K. 2005. 'Verwoerd's Bureau of Proof: Total Information in the Making of Apartheid', *History Workshop Journal*, 59: 83–108.

Breckenridge, Keith. 2014. 'The Book of Life: The South African Population Register and the Invention of Racial Descent, 1950–1980', *Kronos* 14 (1): 225–40.

Brett, E. A. 1963. *African Attitudes: A Study of the Social, Racial and Political Attitudes of Some Middle Class Africans*. Johannesburg: South African Institute of Race Relations.

Briggs, C. and C. Mantini Briggs. 2003. *Stories in the Time of Cholera: Racial Profiling during a Medical Nightmare*. Berkeley: University of California Press.

Brown, Hannah. 2012. 'Hospital Domestics: Care Work in a Kenyan Hospital', *Space and Culture*, 15 (1): 18–30.

Burawoy, M. 2000. 'Introduction: Reaching for the Global', in M. Burawoy, J. A. Blum, S. George, Z. Gille, T. Gowan, L. Haney, M. Klawiter, S. H. Lopez, S. Ó Riain and M. Thayer (eds), *Global Ethnography: Forces, Connections, and Imaginations in a Postmodern World*. Berkeley: University of California Press, 1–40.

Burawoy, M. and K. Verdery. 1999. 'Introduction', in M. Burawoy and K. Verdery (eds), *Uncertain Transition: Ethnographies of Change in the Postsocialist World*. Oxford: Rowman & Littlefield, 1–17.

Buthelezi, Mazo Sybil T. 2004. *African Nurse Pioneers in KwaZulu-Natal: 1920–2000*. Crewe: Trafford Publishing.

Buthelezi Commission. 1982. *The Requirements for Stability and Development in KwaZulu and Natal*. Durban: H + H Publications.

Callebert, Ralph. 2015. 'Rethinking the Underclass: Future Directions in Southern African Labor History', *International Labour and Working-Class History*, 82: 136–42.

Carstens, P. 2001. *In the Company of Diamonds: De Beers, Kleinzee, and the Control of a Town*. Athens: Ohio University Press.

Casenova, J. 1994. *Public Religions in the Modern World*. Chicago and London: University of Chicago Press.

Ceruti, Claire. 2007. 'Divisions and Dependencies among Working and Workless', *South African Labour Bulletin*, 31: 22–24.

Cheater, A. P. 1972. 'A Marginal Elite? A Study of African Registered Nurses in the Greater Durban Area'. Department of African Studies, University of Natal (Unpublished Masters Thesis).

Cheater, A. P. 1974. 'A Marginal Elite? African Registered Nurses in Durban, South Africa', *African Studies*, 33 (3): 143–58.

Chevalier, Sophie. 2015. 'Food, Malls and the Politics of Consumption: South Africa's New Middle Class', *Development Southern Africa*, 32 (1): 118–29.

Chipkin, I. 2003. '"Functional" and "Dysfunctional" Communities: The Making of National Citizens', *Journal of Southern African Studies*, 29: 63–82.

Chipkin, I. 2007. *Do South Africans Exist? Nationalism, Democracy and the Identity of the People*. Johannesburg: Wits University Press.

Chipkin, I. and S. Meny-Gibert. 2012. 'Why the Past Matters: Studying Public Administration in South Africa', *Journal of Public Administration*, 47 (1): 102–12.

Cobley, A. G. 1990. *Class and Consciousness: The Black Petty Bourgeoisie in South Africa, 1924–1950*. London: Greenwood Press.

Coburn, D. 1988. 'The Development of Canadian Nursing: Professionalization and Proletarianization', *International Journal of Health Services*, 18 (3): 437–56.

Coleman, S. 2002. 'The Faith Movement: A Global Religious Culture?', *Culture and Religion* 3: 3–19.

Cameron, R. and C. Tapscott. 2000. 'The Challenges of State Transformation in South Africa', *Public Administration and Development*, 20: 81–86.

Comaroff, Jean. 2009. 'The Politics of Conviction: Faith on the Neo-liberal Frontier', *Social Analysis*, 53 (1): 17–38.

Comaroff, Jean and John L. Comaroff. 2000. 'Millenial Capitalism: First Thoughts on a Second Coming', *Public Culture*, 12 (2): 291–34.

Comaroff, John L. and Jean Comaroff. 2004. 'Notes on Afromodernity and the Neo World Order: An Afterword', in B. Weiss (ed.), *Producing African Futures: Ritual and Reproduction in a Neoliberal Age*. Leiden: Brill, 329–49.

Comaroff, John L. and Jean Comaroff. 2010. *Ethnicity, Inc.* Chicago: University of Chicago Press.

Cueto, M. 2004. 'The Origins of Primary Health Care and Selective Primary Health Care', *Public Health Then and Now*, 94 (11): 1864–74.

Day, C., P. Barron, F. Monticelli and E. Sello. 2009. *District Health Barometer 2007/08*. Health Systems Trust. http://www.hst.org.za/publications/850 [Accessed on 28 May 2012].

De Beer, Cedric. 1984. *The South African Disease: Apartheid Health and Health Services*. Trenton: Africa World Press.

Dhupelia-Mesthrie, Uma. 2014. 'Paper Regimes', *Kronos*, 14 (1): 10–22.

Digby, Anne. 2006. *Diversity and Division in Medicine: Health Care in South Africa from the 1800s*. Oxford: Peter Lang.

Digby, Anne. 2008. '"Visions and Vested Interests": National Health Service Reform in South Africa and Britain During the 1940s and Beyond', *Social History of Medicine*, 21: 3.

Digby, Anne. 2012. 'Evidence, Encounters and Effects of South Africa's Reforming Gluckman National Health Services Commission, 1942–1944', *South African Historical Journal*, 64 (2): 187–205.

Digby, Anne and Howard Philips. 2008. *At the Heart of Healing: Groote Schuur Hospital, 1938–2008*. Johannesburg: Jacana Media.

Digby, Anne and Helen Sweet. 2002. 'Nurses as Culture Brokers in Twentieth-Century South Africa', in W. Ernst (ed.), *Plural Medicine, Tradition and Modernity, 1800–2000*. London: Routledge, 113–29.

DiMaggio, Paul J. and Walter W. Powell. 1983. 'The Iron Cage Revisited: Institutional Isomorphism and Collective Rationality in Organizational Fields', *American Sociological Review*, 48 (2): 147–60.

Dingwall, Robert. 1999. 'Professions and Social Order in a Global Society', *International Review of Sociology*, 9 (1): 131–40.

Dingwall, Robert. 2008. *Essays on Professions*. Aldershot: Ashgate.

Dingwall, Robert, Anne Marie Rafferty and Charles Webster. 1988. *An Introduction to the Social History of Nursing*. London: Routledge.

Dlamini, Jacob. 2009. *Native Nostalgia*. Auckland Park: Jacana Media.

Donner, Henrike and Geert de Neve. 2011. 'Introduction', in H. Donner (ed.), *Being Middle-Class in India: A Way of Life*. London: Routledge, 1–22.

Dreyer, L. 1989. *The Modern African Elite of South Africa*. London: Macmillan.

Dubow, S. 2005. 'Introduction: South Africa's 1940s', in S. Dubow and A. Jeeves (eds), *South Africa's 1940s: Worlds of Possibilities*. Cape Town: Double Story Books, 1–19.

Dunleavy, P. 1991. *Democracy, Bureaucracy and Public Choice: Economic Explanations in Political Science*. New York: Harvester Wheatsheaf.

Ecks, S. 2005. 'Pharmaceutical Citizenship: Antidepressant Marketing and the Promise of Demarginalization in India', *Anthropology and Medicine*, 12 (3): 239–54.

Emblem, J. 1992. 'Religion and Spirituality Defined According to Current Use in Nursing Literature', *Journal of Professional Nursing*, 8 (1): 41–47.

Engelke, Matthew. 2015. 'Secular Shadows: African, Immanent, Post-colonial', *Critical Research on Religion*, 3 (1): 86–100.

Englund, H. 2000. 'The Dead Hand of Human Rights: Contrasting Christianities in Post-Transition Malawi', *Journal of Modern African Studies*, 38 (4): 579–603.

Englund, H. 2003. 'Christian Independency and Global Membership: Pentecostal Extraversions in Malawi', *Journal of Religion in Africa*, 33: 83–111.

Englund, H. 2006. *Prisoners of Freedom: Human Rights and the African Poor*. Berkeley: University of California Press.

Evans, I. 1997. *Bureaucracy and Race: Native Administration in South Africa*. Berkeley: University of California Press.

Evans-Pritchard, E. E. 1937. *Witchcraft, Oracles and Magic among the Azande*. Oxford: Oxford University Press.

Eyben, Rosalind. 2011. 'The Sociality of International Aid and Policy Convergence', in D. Mosse (ed.), *Adventures in Aidland: The Anthropology of Professionals in International Development*. New York and Oxford: Berghahn Books, 139–60.

Felgate, Walter. 1982. 'The Tembe Thonga of Natal and Mozambique: An Ecological Approach,' ed. Eileen Jensen Krige. Department of African Studies, University of Natal, Durban, Occasional Paper No. 1.

Ferguson, J. 2006. *Global Shadows: Africa in the Neoliberal World Order*. Durham and London: Duke University Press.

Ferguson, J. 2015. *Give a Man a Fish: Reflections on the New Politics of Distribution*. Durham and London: Duke University Press.

Ferguson, J. and A. Gupta. 2002. 'Spatializing States: Toward an Ethnography of Neoliberal Governmentality', *American Ethnologist*, 29 (4): 981–1002.

Ford, Fiona. 2011. *An Inconvenient Youth: Julius Malema and the 'New' ANC*. Johannesburg: Picador Africa.

Forsyth, S. 1995. 'Historical Continuities and Constraints in the Professionalization of Nursing', *Nursing Inquiry*, 2 (3): 164–71.

Foucault, Michel. 1975. *The Birth of the Clinic*. New York: Vintage.

Freidberg, Susanne. 2003. 'French Beans for the Masses: A Modern Historical Geography of Food in Burkina Faso', *Journal of Historical Geography*, 29 (3): 445–63.

Freidson, E. 1982. 'Occupational Autonomy and Labor Market Shelters', in P. L. Stewart and M. G. Cantor (eds), *Varieties of Work*. Beverly Hills: Sage, 39–54.

Freund, Bill. 2012. 'The South African Developmental State and the First Attempt to Create a National Health System: Another Look at the Gluckman Commission of 1942–1944', *South African Historical Journal*, 64 (2): 170–86.

Fuller, C. J. and J. Harriss. 2001. 'For an Anthropology of the Modern Indian State', in C. J. Fuller and V. Bénéï (eds), *The Everyday State and Society in Modern India* . London: Hurst and Company, 1–30.

Gaitskell, D. 1979. '"Christian Compounds for Girls": Church Hostels for African Women in Johannesburg, 1907–1970', *Journal of Southern African Studies*, 6 (1): 44–69.

Gamarnikow, E. 1978. 'Sexual Division of Labour: the Case of Nursing', in A. Kuhn and A. Wolpe (eds), *Feminism and Materialism: Women and Modes of Production*. London: Routledge and Kegan Paul, 96–123.

Gelfand, M. 1984. *Christian Doctor and Nurse: The History of Medical Missions in South Africa from 1799–1976*. Sandton: Aitken.

Geschiere, P. 1999. 'Globalization and the Power of Indeterminate Meaning: Witchcraft and Spirit Cults in Africa and East Asia', in B. Meyer and P. Geschiere (eds), *Globalization and Identity: Dialectics of Flow and Closure*. Oxford: Blackwell, 211–38.

Gibbs, Timothy. 2014. *Mandela's Kinsmen: Nationalist Elites and Apartheid's First Bantustan*. Johannesburg: James Curry.

Gibson, D. 2004. 'The Gaps in the Gaze in South African Hospitals', *Social Science and Medicine*, 59 (10): 2013–24.

Gifford, P. 2001. 'The Complex Provenance of Some Elements of African Pentecostal Theology', in A. Corton and R. Marshall-Fratani (eds), *Between Babel and Pentecost: Transnational Pentecostalism in Africa and Latin America*. Bloomington: Indiana University Press, 62–79.

Goffman, E. 1961. *Asylums: Essays on the Social Situation of Mental Patients and Other Inmates*. London: Penguin Books.

Gopfert, Mirco. 2013. 'Bureaucratic Aesthetics: Report Writing in the Nigerien Gendarmerie', *American Ethnologist*, 40 (2): 324–34.

Gow, J. I. and C. Dufour. 2000. 'Is the New Public Management a Paradigm? Does It Matter?', *International Review of Administrative Sciences*, 66 (4): 573–98.

Gray, Andy and Karrisha Pillay. 2006. 'Health Legislation and Policy', *South African Health Review 2006*, Durban: Health Systems Trust, 3–18.

Gupta, Akhil. 1995. 'Blurred Boundaries: The Discourse of Corruption, the Culture of Politics, and the Imagined State', *American Ethnologist*, 22 (2): 375–402.

Gupta, Akhil. 2012. *Red Tape: Bureaucracy, Structural Violence, and Poverty in India*. Durham and London: Duke University Press.

Gupta, Akhil and Aradhana Sharma. 2006. 'Globalization and Postcolonial States', *Current Anthropology*, 47 (2): 277–307.

Guy, J. 1982. 'The Destruction and Reconstruction of Zulu Society', in S. Marks and R. Rathbone (eds), *Industrialisation and Social Change in South Africa: African Class Formation, Culture, and Consciousness, 1870–1930*. London: Longman, 180–81.

Hamilton, C. (ed.). 1995. *The Mfecane Aftermath: Reconstructive Debates in South African History*. Johannesburg: University of the Witwatersrand Press.

Haque, M. S. 2000. 'Significance of Accountability under the New Approach to Public Governance', in *International Review of Administrative Sciences* 66 (4): 599–617.

Hardiman, David. 2009. 'The Mission Hospital, 1880–1960', in M. Harrison, M. Jones and H. Sweet (eds), *From Western Medicine to Global Medicine: The Hospital Beyond the West*. New Delhi: Orient Blackswan, 198–220.

Hardt, Michael and Antonio Negri. 2005. *Multitude: War and Democracy in the Age of Empire*. London: Penguin Books.

Harper, Ian. 2014. *Development and Public Health in the Himalaya: Reflections on Healing in Contemporary Nepal*. London and New York: Routledge.

Harries, Patrick, 1993. 'History, Symbolism and Tradition in a South African Bantustan: Mangosuthu Buthelezi, Inkatha, and Zulu History', *History and Theory* 32 (4): 105–25.

Harries, Patrick, 1994. *Work, Culture and Identity: Migrant Labourers in Mozambique and South Africa, c. 1860–1910*. London: James Curry.

Harrison, A. E. Montgomery, M. Lurie and D. Wilkinson. 2000. 'Barriers to Implementing South Africa's Termination of Pregnancy Act in Rural KwaZulu/Natal', *Health Policy and Planning*, 15(4): 424–31.

Hart, Gillian. 2006. 'Denaturalising Dispossession: Critical Ethnography in the Age of Resurgent Imperialism', *Antipode*, 38 (5): 977–1004.

Hart, Gillian. 2013. *Rethinking the South African Crisis: Nationalism, Populism, Hegemony*. Athens and London: University of Georgia Press.

Haynes, Jeffrey. 2002. 'Power in Ghana from Early Colonial Times to the 1990s', *Africa*, 72 (2): 312–21.

Heimer, Carol A. 2006. 'Conceiving Children: How Documents Support Case versus Biographical Analyses', in Annelise Riles (ed.), *Documents: Artifacts of Modern Knowledge*. Ann Arbor: University of Michigan Press, 95–126.

Henderson, S. 1993/1994. 'Anthony and Maggie Barker (Died 1993): Giving and Receiving', *Natalia* 23/24 (1993/1994): 99–101. <http://natalia.org.za/Files/23–24/Natalia%20v23-24%20obituaries%20Barker.pdf> [Accessed on 13 October 2011].

Herzfeld, M. 1992. *The Social Production of Indifference: Exploring the Symbolic Roots of Western Bureaucracy*. Chicago and London: University of Chicago Press.

Hickel, Jason. 2015. *Democracy as Death: The Moral Order of Anti-Liberal Politics in South Africa*. Oakland: University of California Press.

Hope, Kempe Ronald. 2002. 'The New Public Management: A Perspective from Africa', in Kate McLaughlin, Stephen P. Osborne and Ewan Ferlie (eds), *New Public Management: Current Trends and Future Prospects*. London and New York: Routledge, 210–26.

Horwitz, Simonne. 2011. 'The Nurse in the University: A History of University Education for South African Nurses; A Case Study of the University of the Witwatersrand', *Nursing Research and Practice*, 2011, Article ID 813270, 9 pages.

Horwitz, Simonne. 2013. *Baragwanath Hospital Soweto: A History of Medical Care 1941–1990*. Johannesburg: Wits University Press.

Hughes, E. C. 1971. *The Sociological Eye*. Chicago: Aldine.

Hughes, O. E. 2003. *Public Management and Administration: An Introduction*. New York: Palgrave Macmillan.

Hull, E. 2009. 'Status, Morality and the Politics of Transformation: An Ethnographic Account of Nurses in KwaZulu-Natal, South Africa', PhD thesis, London School of Economics and Political Science, London.

Hull, E. 2010. 'International Migration, "Domestic Struggles" and Status Aspiration among Nurses in South Africa', *Journal of Southern African Studies*, 36 (4): 851–67.

Hull, E. 2012a. 'The Renewal of Community Health under the KwaZulu homeland Government', *South African Historical Journal*, 64(1): 22–40.

Hull, E. 2012b. 'Paperwork and the Contradictions of Accountability in a South African Hospital', *Journal of the Royal Anthropological Institute* 18: 613–32.

Hull, E. and D. James. 2012. 'Introduction: Popular Economies in South Africa', *Africa*, 82 (1): 1–19.

Hull, Matthew S. 2003. 'The File: Agency, Authority, and Autography in a Pakistan Bureacracy', *Language and Communication*, 23: 287–314.

Hull, Matthew S. 2012. *Government of Papers: The Materiality of Bureaucracy in Urban Pakistan*. Berkeley: University of California Press.

Hunter, Mark. 2010. *Love in the Time of AIDS: Inequality, Gender, and Rights in South Africa*. Bloomington: Indiana University Press.

Hyslop, Jonathan. 2005. 'Political Corruption: Before and after Apartheid', *Journal of Southern African Studies*, 31 (4): 773–89.

Hyslop, Jonathan. 2014. '"Undesirable Inhabitant of the Union … Supplying Liquor to Natives": D. F. Malan and the Deportation of South Africa's British and Irish Lumpen Proletarians 1924–1933', *Kronos*, 14 (1): 178–97.

Ijumba, Petrida and Ashnie Padarath. 2006. 'Preface', in Petrida Ijumba and Ashnie Padarath (eds), *South African Health Review 2006*. Durban: Health Systems Trust, vii – xii.

Inchauste G., N. Lustig, M. Maskekwa, C. Purfield and I. Woolard. 2014. 'Fiscal Policy and Redistribution in an Unequal Society: The Case of South Africa', South African Economic Update 6. World Bank Publications, https://www.inkling.com/store/book/fiscal-policy-redistribution-an-unequalsociety [Accessed on 20 January 2015]

International Labour Organisation. 2015. 'World Employment Social Outlook: Trends 2015', [Unpublished report].

James, Deborah. 2015. *Money from Nothing: Indebtedness and Aspiration in South Africa*. Stanford: Stanford University Press.

Jarvis, Lauren. 2014. 'Gender, Violence, and Home in the Nazareth Baptist Church, 1906–1939', in Meghan Elisabeth Healy and Jason Hickel (eds), *Ekhaya: The Politics of Home in KwaZulu-Natal*. Durban: University of KwaZulu-Natal Press, 107–30.

Jewkes, R., N. Abrahams and Z. Mvo. 1998. 'Why Do Nurses Abuse Patients? Reflections from South African Obstetric Services', *Social Science and Medicine*, 47 (11): 1781–95.

Jinabhai, C. C., M. H. Coovadia and S. S. Abdool-Karim. 1986. 'Socio-Medical Indicators of Health in South Africa', *International Journal of Health Services*, 16 (1): 163–76.

Johnson, Krista. 2003. 'Liberal or Liberation Framework? The Contradictions of ANC Rule in South Africa', in Henning Melber (ed.), *Limits to Liberation in Southern Africa: The Unfinished Business of Democratic Consolidation*, Cape Town: HSRC, 200–23.

Kafka, B. 2012. *The Demon of Writing: Powers and Failures of Paperwork*. New York: Zone.

Kaul, M. 1997. 'The New Public Administration: Management Innovations in Government', *Public Administration and Development*, 17: 13–26.

Kautzky, K. and S. M. Tollman. 2008. 'A Perspective on Primary Health Care in South Africa', in P. Barron and J. Roma-Reardon (eds) *South African Health Review 2008*. Durban: Health Systems Trust, 17–30.

Keane, Webb. 2005. 'Estrangement, Intimacy, and the Objects of Anthropology', in G. Steinmetz (ed.), *The Politics of Method in the Human Sciences: Positivism and its Epistemological Others*. Durham and London: Duke University Press, 59–88.

Kipnis, A. B. 2008. 'Audit Cultures: Neoliberal Governmentality, Socialist Legacy, or Technologies of Governing?', *American Ethnologist*, 35: 275–89.

Kumwenda, L. B. 2005. 'The Training of Female Medical Auxiliaries in Missionary Hospitals in Northern Rhodesia, 1928–1952', *Le Fait Missionnaire*, 16: 103–32.

Kuper, Hilda. 1965. 'Nurses', in Leo Kuper, *An African Bourgeoisie: Race, Class, and Politics in South Africa*. New Haven and London: Yale University Press, 216–33.

Kuper, L. 1965. *An African Bourgeoisie: Race, Class, and Politics in South Africa*. New Haven: Yale University Press.

Lacey, R. 1997. 'Internal Markets in the Public Sector: The Case of the British National Health Service', *Public Administration and Development*, 17: 141–59.

Larson, M. S. 1977. *The Rise of Professionalism: A Sociological Analysis*. Berkeley: University of California Press.

Latimer, J. 2000. *The Conduct of Care: Understanding Nursing Practice*. Oxford: Wiley-Blackwell.

Lee, Maw Lin. 1971. 'A Conspicuous Production Theory of Hospital Behaviour', *Southern Economic Journal*, 38: 48–58.

Lee, K., M. Koivusalo, E. Ollila, R. Labonte, C. Schuftan and D. Woodward. 2009. 'Global Governance for Health', in R. Labonte, T. Schrecker, C. Pacler and V. Runnels (eds), *Globalization and Health: Pathways, Evidence and Policy*. London: Routledge, 289–316.

Lentz, Carola. 2015. 'Elites or Middle Classes? Lessons from Transnational Research for the Study of Social Stratification in Africa', Arbeitspapiere des Instituts für Ethnologie und Afrikastudien der Johannes Gutenberg-Universität Mainz / Working Papers of the Department of Anthropology and African Studies of the Johannes Gutenberg University Mainz 161. http://www.ifeas.uni-mainz.de/Dateien/AP_161.pdf [Accessed on 17 January 2016].

Levi, M. 1980. 'Functional Redundancy and the Process of Professionalization: The Case of Registered Nurses in the United States', *Journal of Health Politics, Policy and Law*, 5 (2): 333–53.

Lewin, Simon and Judith Green. 2009. 'Ritual and the Organisation of Care in Primary Care Clinics in Cape Town, South Africa', *Social Science and Medicine*, 68 (8): 1464–71.

Lindsay, Elizabeth and Gweneth Hartrick. 1996. 'Health-Promoting Nursing Practice: The Demise of the Nursing Process?', *Journal of Advanced Nursing*, 23 (1): 106–12.

Litsios, S. 2004. 'The Christian Medical Commission and the Development of the World Health Organization's Primary Health Care Approach', *Public Health Then and Now*, 94 (11): 1884–93.

Litsios, S. 2008. *The Third Ten Years of the World Health Organization: 1968–1977*. Geneva: World Health Organization.

Littlewood, J. 1991. 'Care and Ambiguity: Towards a Concept of Nursing', in P. Holden and J. Littlewood (eds), *Anthropology and Nursing*. London: Routledge, 170–89.

Livingston, Julie. 2012. *Improvising Medicine: An African Oncology Ward in an Emerging Cancer Epidemic*. Durham and London: Duke University Press.

Lund, Francie and Debbie Budlender. 2009. 'Paid Care Providers in South Africa: Nurses, Domestic Workers and Home-Based Care Workers', Research Report for United Nations Research Institute for Social Development, Geneva.

Maxwell, D. 1998. 'Delivered from the Spirit of Poverty?: Pentecostalism, Prosperity and Modernity in Zimbabwe', *Journal of Religion in Africa*, 28: 350–73.

Maxwell, D. 2006. *African Gifts of the Spirit: Pentecostalism & the Rise of a Zimbabwean Transnational Religious Movement*. Oxford: James Curry.

MacDonald, Andrew. 2014. 'Forging the Frontiers: Travellers and Documents on the South Africa–Mozambique Border, 1890s–1940s', *Kronos*, 14 (1): 154–77.

McCord, J. B. with J. S. Douglas. 1946. *My Patients Were Zulus*. New York: Rinehart.

McIntyre, D. and B. Klugman. 2003. 'The Human Face of Decentralisation and Integration of Health Services: Experiences from South Africa', *Reproductive Health Matters*, 11 (21): 108–19.

McIntyre, D., L. Gilson, H. Wadere, M. Thiede and O. Okarafor. 2006. 'Commercialisation and Extreme Inequality in Health: The Policy Challenges in South Africa', *Journal of International Development*, 18: 435–46.

McLennan, A. 2007a. 'Editorial: The Politics of Delivery in South Africa', *Progress in Development Studies*, 7 (1): 1–4.

McLennan, A. 2007b. 'Unmasking Delivery: Revealing the Politics', *Progress in Development Studies*, 7 (1): 5–20.

Mager, A. 2001. 'Migrancy, Marriage and Family in the Ciskei Reserve of South Africa, 1945–1959', in P. Sharp (ed.), *Women, Gender and Labour Migration: Historical and Global Perspectives*. London: Routledge, 259–74.

Mamdani, Mahmood. 1996. *Citizen and Subject: Contemporary Africa and the Legacy of Late Colonialism*. Princeton: Princeton University Press.

Marais, Hein. 1998. *South Africa: Limits to Change: The Political Economy of Transformation*. London: Zed Books.

Marais, Hein. 2011. *South Africa Pushed to the Limit: The Political Economy of Change*. London and New York: Zed Books.

Maré , G. and G. Hamilton. 1987. *An Appetite for Power: Buthelezi's Inkatha and the Politics of 'Loyal Resistance'.* Johannesburg: Raven Press.

Marks, S. 1986. *The Ambiguities of Dependence in South Africa: Class, Nationalism, and the State in Twentieth-Century Natal.* London: Johns Hopkins University Press.

Marks, S. 1993. 'The Nursing Profession and the Making of Apartheid', in P. Bonner, P. Delius and D. Posel (eds), *Apartheid's Genesis 1935–1962.* Johannesburg: Witwatersrand University Press, 341–61.

Marks, S. 1994. *Divided Sisterhood: Race, Class and Gender in the South African Nursing Profession.* New York: St. Martin's Press.

Marks, S. 1997a. 'Nursing in Post-Apartheid South Africa', in A. M. Rafferty, J. Robinson and R. Elkan (eds), *Nursing History and the Politics of Welfare.* London: Routledge, 28–44.

Marks, S. 1997b. 'What Is Colonial about Colonial Medicine? And What Has Happened to Imperialism and Health?', *Social History of Medicine*, 10 (2): 205–19.

Marks, S. 1997c. 'South Africa's Early Experiment in Social Medicine: Its Pioneers and Politics', *Public Health Then and Now*, 83 (3): 452–59.

Marks, S. 2000. 'Doctors and the State: George Gale and South Africa's Experiment in Social Medicine', in S. Dubow (ed.), *Science and Society in Southern Africa.* Manchester: Manchester University Press, 188–211.

Marks, S. 2002. '"We Were Men Nursing Men": Male Nursing on the Mines in Twentieth-Century South Africa', in W. Woodward, P. Hayes and G. Minkley (eds), *Deep Histories: Gender and Colonialism in Southern Africa.* Amsterdam and New York: Rodopi, 177–204.

Marks, S. 2014. 'Reflections of the 1944 Health Services Commission: A Response to Bill Freund and Anne Digby on the Gluckman Commission', *South African Historical Journal*, 66 (1): 169–87.

Marks S. and N. Andersson. 1988. 'Diseases of Apartheid', in J. Lonsdale (ed.), *South Africa in Question.* London: James Curry, 172–99.

Marks S. and N. Andersson. [1983] 1992. 'Industrialization, Rural Health, and the 1944 National Health Services Commission in South Africa', in S. Feierman and J. M. Janzen (eds), *The Social Basis of Health and Healing.* Berkeley: University of California Press, 131–61.

Marshall, R. 1993. '"Power in the Name of Jesus": Social Transformation and Pentecostalism in Western Nigeria "Revisited"', in T. Ranger and O. Vaughan (eds), *Legitimacy and the State in Twentieth-Century Africa: Essays in Honour of A. H. M. Kirk-Greene.* Hampshire: Palgrave, 213–24.

Mashaba, T. G. 1995. *Rising to the Challenge of Change: A History of Black Nursing in South Africa*. Kenwyn: Juta.

Mason, Paul. 2016. *Postcapitalism: A Guide to Our Future*. London: Penguin Books.

Mate, R. 2002. 'Wombs as God's Laboratories: Pentecostal Discourses of Femininity in Zimbabwe', *Journal of the International African Institute*, 74 (4); 549–68.

Maxwell, D. 2006. *African Gifts of the Spirit: Pentecostalism & the Rise of a Zimbabwean Transnational Religious Movement*. Oxford: James Curry.

McIntyre, D. and B. Klugman. 2003. 'The Human Face of Decentralisation and Integration of Health Services: Experiences from South Africa', *Reproductive Health Matters*, 11 (21): 108–19.

McIntyre, D., L. Gilson, H. Wadere, M. Thiede and O. Okarafor. 2006. 'Commercialisation and Extreme Inequality in Health: The Policy Challenges in South Africa', *Journal of International Development*, 18: 435–46.

McLennan, A. 2007a. 'Editorial: The Politics of Delivery in South Africa' *Progress in Development Studies*, 7 (1): 1–4.

McLennan, A. 2007b. 'Unmasking Delivery: Revealing the Politics' *Progress in Development Studies* 7 (1): 5–20.

Mda, Zakes. 2009. *Black Diamond*. Harmondsworth, UK: Penguin.

Meyer, B. 2001. '"You Devil, Go Away From Me!" Pentecostalist African Christianity and the Powers of Good and Evil', in P. Clough and J. P. Mitchell (eds), *Powers of Good and Evil: Moralities, Commodities and Popular Belief*. New York and Oxford: Berghahn Books, 104–34.

Meyer, B. 2004. '"Praise the Lord": Popular Cinema and Pentecostalite Style in Ghana's New Public Sphere', *American Ethnologist*, 31 (1): 92–110.

Mokgethi, N. E., V. J. Ehlers and M. M. van der Merwe. 2006. 'Professional Nurses' Attitudes towards Providing Termination of Pregnancy Services in a Tertiary Hospital in the North West Province of South Africa', *Curationis*, 29 (1): 32–39.

Moodie, T. Dunbar. 1994. *Going for Gold: Men, Mines and Migration*. Berkeley and London: University of California Press.

Moore, Henrietta. 2011. *Still Life: Hopes, Desires and Satisfactions*. Cambridge: Polity Press.

Moosa, Ebrahim. 2000. 'Truth and Reconciliation as Performance: Spectres of Eucharistic Redemption', in Charles Villa-Vicencio and Wilhelm Verwoerd (eds.), *Looking Back Reaching Forward: Reflections on the Truth and Reconciliation Commission of South Africa*. London: Zed Books, 113–22.

Morolong, B. G. and M M. Chabeli. 2005. 'Competence of Newly Qualified Registered Nurses from a Nursing College', *Curationis*, (May): 38–50.

Mosse, David. 2005. *Cultivating Development: An Ethnography of Aid Policy and Practice*. London: Pluto.

Mosse, David. (ed.). 2011a. *Adventures in Aidland: The Anthropology of Professionals in International Development*. New York and Oxford: Berghahn Books.

Mosse, David. 2011b. 'Introduction', in D. Mosse (ed.), *Adventures in Aidland: The Anthropology of Professionals in International Development*. New York and Oxford: Berghahn Books, 1–32.

Mthembu, W. 2005. 'The Genesis and Progression of the HIV/AIDS Programme in KwaZulu-Natal: Implications for Learning and Intensified Action', PhD thesis, University of Zululand, KwaDlangezwa.

Murray, J. and M. Murray. 1988. 'Bethesda Healing: Will City-Oriented Bureaucrats Become More Aware of the Inequalities between Rural and Urban Services?', *Nursing RSA Verpleging* 3: 4.

Musyoka, Jason and Jennifer Houghton, 2016. 'South Africa's New Middle Class and its Entanglement with Big "P" and Little "P" Poverty', Unpublished conference paper. https://www.researchgate.net/publication/271176292_South_Africa's_New_Middle_Class_and_its_Entanglement_with_Big_'P'_and_Little_'P'_Poverty [Accessed on 1 September 2016].

Nash, Andrew. 2009. *The Dialectical Tradition in South Africa*. London: Routledge.

Nattrass, Nicoli. 2008. 'AIDS and the Scientific Governance of Medicine in Post-Apartheid South Africa', *African Affairs*, 107 (427): 157–76.

Ncholo, P. 2000. 'Reforming the Public Service in South Africa: A Policy Framework', *Public Administration and Development*, 20: 87–102.

Neocosmos, Michael. 2010. *From 'Foreign Natives' to 'Native Foreigners': Explaining Xenophobia in Post-Apartheid South Africa, Citizenship and Nationalism, Identity and Politics*. Dakar: CODESRIA.

Nguyen, V. 2005. 'Antiretroviral Globalism, Biopolitics and Therapeutic Citizenship', in A. Ong and S. Collier (eds), *Global Assemblages: Technology, Politics, and Ethics as Anthropological Problems*. Malden, Oxford and Carlton: Blackwell, 124–44.

Nguyen, V. 2010. *The Republic of Therapy: Triage and Sovereignty in West Africa's Time of AIDS*. Durham and London: Duke University Press.

Ntleko, Abegail. 2012. *Empty Hands: The Life of Sister Abegail Ntleko*. San Francisco: Storyzon LLC.

Nzimande, Blade. 1986 'Managers and the New Middle Class', *Transformations*, 1: 39–62.

Nzimande, Blade. 1990. 'Class, National Oppression and the African Petty Bourgeoisie: The Case of African Traders', in R. Cohen, Y. Muthien and A. Zegeye (eds), *Repression and Resistance: Insider Accounts of Apartheid*. London, Melbourne, Munich, New York: Hans Zell Publishers, 165–210.

Oboirien K., B. Harris, J. Eyles, M. Orgill, D. McIntyre, N. Chimbindi and J. Goudge. 2015. 'Understanding Roles, Enablers and Challenges of District Clinical Specialist Teams in Strengthening Primary Health Care in South Africa', A. Padarath, J. King and R. English (eds) *South African Health Review 2014/15*. Durban: Health Systems Trust, 45–55.

Olivier de Sardan, Jean-Pierre. 2014. 'The Delivery State in Africa: Interface Bureaucrats, Professional Cultures and the Bureaucratic Mode of Governance', in Thomas Bierschenk and Jean-Pierre Olivier de Sardan (eds), *States at Work: Dynamics of African Bureaucracies*. Leiden: Brill, 399–429.

Ong, Aihwa. 2006. *Neoliberalism as Exception: Mutations in Citizenship and Sovereignty* Durham and London: Duke University Press.

Oosthuizen, M. J. 2012. 'The Portrayal of Nursing in South African Newspapers: A Qualitative Content Analysis', *Africa Journal of Nursing and Midwifery*, 14 (1): 49–62.

Packard, R. 1989. *White Plague, Black Labour: Tuberculosis and the Political Economy of Health and Disease in South Africa*. Berkeley: University of California Press.

Parsons, Talcott. 1939. 'The Professions and Social Structure', *Social Forces*, 17 (4): 457–67.

Penn Kekana, L., D. Blaauw and H. Schneider. 2004. '"It Makes Me Want to Run Away to Saudi Arabia": Management and Implementation Challenges for Public Financing Reforms from a Maternity Ward Perspective', *Health Policy and Planning*, 19 (Suppl. 1): i71–i77.

Petryna, Adriana. 2003. *Life Exposed: Biological Citizenship After Chernobyl*. Princeton and Oxford: Princeton University Press.

Picard, Louis A. 2005. *The State of the State: Institutional Transformation, Capacity and Political Change in South Africa*. Johannesburg: Wits University Press.

Picard, Louis A. and Thomas Mogale. 2014. 'South Africa: Decentralization and the Apartheid Legacy', in J. Tyler Dickovick and James S. Wunsch (eds), *Decentralization in Africa: The Paradox of State Strength* . London: Lynne Rienner, 183–204.

Pienaar, Kiran. 2016. 'Claiming Rights, Making Citizens: HIV and the Performativity of Biological Citizenship', *Social Theory and Health*, 14 (2): 149–68.

Pillay, Yogan, Nomvula Marawa and Paula Proudlock. 2002. 'Health Legislation', *South African Health Review 2002*. Durban: Health Systems Trust, 3–12.

Piot, Charles. 2010. *Nostalgia for the Future: West African after the Cold War*. Chicago and London: University of Chicago Press.

Poggenpoel, M., C. P. Myburgh and A. C. Gmeiner. 1998. 'One Voice Regarding the Legalisation of Abortion: Nurses Who Experience Discomfort', *Curationis*, 21 (3): 2–7.

Posel, D. 1987. 'The Language of Domination, 1978–1983', in S. Marks and S. Trapido (eds), *The Politics of Race, Class and Nationalism in Twentieth-Century South Africa*. London and New York: Longman, 419–43.

Posel, Deborah. 2010. 'Races to Consume: Revisiting South Africa's History of Race, Consumption and the Struggle for Freedom', *Ethnic and Racial Studies*, 33 (2): 157–75.

Potgieter, C. A, 2004. 'Stigmatisation of Termination-of-pregnancy Providers in State Hospitals', *HSRC Review*, 2(3): 6.

Power, M. 1997. *The Audit Society: Rituals of Verification*. Oxford: Oxford University Press.

Prater, L. and M. McEwan. 2006. 'Called to Nursing', *Journal of Holistic Nursing*, 24 (1): 63–69.

Pretorius, L. 1981. 'Plans for the Reorganization of Society: The Reports of the Buthelezi Commission and the Constitutional Committee of the President's Council', *Social Dynamics*, 7 (2): 58–69.

Przeworski, A., P. Bardhan, Perceira, L. C. Bresser, L. Briszt, J. J. Choi, E. T. Comisso. 1995. *Sustainable Democracy*. Cambridge: Cambridge University Press.

Price, M. 1986. 'Health Care as an Instrument of Apartheid Policy in South Africa', *Health Policy and Planning*, 1 (2): 158–70.

Raatikainen, R. 1997. 'Nursing Care as a Calling', *Journal of Advanced Nursing*, 25: 1111–15.

Rees, Colin. 1981. 'Records and Hospital Routine', in P. Atkinson and C. Heath (eds), *Medical Work: Realities and Routines*. Farnborough: Gower, 55–70

Riles, Annelise. 2006. 'Introduction: In Response', in Annelise Riles (ed.), *Documents: Artifacts of Modern Knowledge*. Ann Arbor: University of Michigan Press, 1–38.

Rispel, Laetitia and Judith Bruce. 2015. 'A Profession in Peril? Revitalising Nursing in South Africa', *South African Health Review 2014/15*. Durban: Health Systems Trust, 117–26.

Rispel, Laetitia and Helen Schneider. 1991. 'Professionalization of South African Nursing: Who Benefits?', *International Journal of Health Services*, 21 (1): 109–26.

Robins, S. L. 2005. 'Introduction', in S. L. Robins (ed.), *Limits to Liberation After Apartheid: Citizenship, Governance & Culture.* Oxford: James Curry, 1–21.

Rolfe, Gary. 2007. 'Closing the Theory-Practice Gap: A Model of Nursing Praxis', *Journal of Clinical Nursing*, 2 (3): 173–77.

Rolston, Jessica Smith. 2014. *Mining Coal and Undermining Gender: Rhythms of Work and Family in the American West.* New Brunswick: Rutgers University Press.

Rose, Nikolas. 1999. *Powers of Freedom: Reframing Political Thought.* Cambridge: Cambridge University Press.

Rose, Nikolas and Carlos Novas. 2005. 'Biological Citizenship', in A. Ong and S. J. Collier (eds), *Global Assemblages: Technology, Politics, and Ethics as Anthropological Problems.* Oxford: Blackwell Publishing, 439–63.

Ross, R. 1999. 'Missions, Respectability and Civil Rights: The Cape Colony, 1828–1854', *Journal of Southern African Studies*, 25 (3): 333–46.

Roseberry, William. 1994. 'Hegemony and the Language of Contention', in G. Joseph and Daniel Nugent (eds), *Everyday Forms of State Formation: Revolution and the Negotiation of Rule in Modern Mexico.* Durham: Duke University Press, 355–66.

Ross, Robert. 1999. 'Missions, Respectability and Civil Rights: the Cape Colony, 1828–1854', *Journal of Southern African Studies*, 25 (3): 333–46.

Sachs, Albie. 1990. *Protecting Human Rights in a New South Africa.* Cape Town; Oxford: Oxford University Press.

Sanders, David. 1997. 'The Medicalization of Health Care and the Challenge of Health for All', http://www.phmovement.org/sites/www. phmovement.org/files/phm-pha-background3.pdf [Accessed on 5 July 2012].

Sanders, Todd and Harry G. West. 2003. 'Power Revealed and Concealed in the New World Order', in H. G. West and T. Sanders (eds), *Ethnographies of Suspicion in the New World Order.* Durham and London: Duke University Press, 1–37.

Savage, J. 1997. 'Gestures of Resistance: The Nurse's Body in Contested Space', *Nursing Inquiry*, 4: 237–45.

Schneider, H., P. Barron and S. Fonn. 2007. 'The Promise and the Practice of Transformation in South Africa's Health System', in S. Buhlungu, J. Daniel, R. Southall and J. Lutchman (eds), *State of the Nation: South Africa 2007.* Cape Town: HSRC, 289–311.

Schneider, H. and L. Gilson. 1999. 'Small Fish in a Big Pond? External Aid and the Health Sector in South Africa', *Health Policy and Planning*, 14 (3): 264–72.

Scott, James. 1985. *Weapons of the Weak: Everyday Forms of Peasant Resistance*. New Haven: Yale University Press.

Scott, James. 1999. *Seeing Like a State: How Certain Schemes to Improve the Human Condition Have Failed*. New Haven: Yale University Press.

Searle, C. 1965. *The History of the Development of Nursing in South Africa 1652–1960: A Socio-Historical Survey*. Cape Town: Struik.

Searle, C. [1968] 1980. 'A South African Nursing Credo: Address Given in Accepting the Chair in the Department of Nursing Science, University of Pretoria, Delivered on October 3, 1968'. Pretoria: South African Nursing Association.

Seekings, Jeremy. 2009. 'The Rise and Fall of the Weberian Analysis of Class in South Africa between 1949 and the Early 1970s', in *Journal of Southern African Studies*, 35 (4): 865–81.

Seekings, Jeremy and Nicoli Nattrass. 2005. *Class, Race, and Inequality in South Africa*. New Haven and London: Yale University Press.

Segar, J. 1994. 'Negotiating Illness: Disability Grants and the Treatment of Epilepsy', *Medical Anthropology Quarterly*, 8 (3): 282–98.

Smith, L. 2004. 'The Murky Waters of the Second Wave of Neoliberalism: Corporatization as a Service Delivery Model in Cape Town', *Geoforum* 35 (3): 375–93.

Smith, Nicholas Rush. 2015. 'Rejecting Rights: Vigilantism and Violence in Post-Apartheid South Africa', *African Affairs*, 114 (456): 341–60.

SATRC. 2003. Truth and Reconciliation Commission of South Africa Final Report 5(8). Cape Town, South Africa: Juta.

Southall, R. 1983. 'Consociationalism in South Africa: The Buthelezi Commission and Beyond', *Journal of Modern African Studies*, 21 (1): .77–112.

Southall, R. 2004. 'Political Change and the Black Middle Class in Democratic South Africa', *Canadian Journal of African Studies*, 38 (3): 521–42.

Southall, R. 2016. *The New Black Middle Class in South Africa*. Auckland Park: Jacana.

Spronk, Rachel. 2012. *Ambiguous Pleasures: Sexuality and Middle Class Self-Perceptions in Nairobi*. New York and Oxford: Berghahn Books.

Starr, Paul. 1982. *The Social Transformation of American Medicine*. New York: Basic Books.

Strathern, M. 1999. *Property, Substance and Effect: Anthropological Essays on Persons and Things*. London: Athlone Press.

Strathern, Marilyn. 2000a. 'Introduction: New Accountabilities: Anthropological Studies in Audit, Ethics and the Academy', in M. Strathern (ed.), *Audit Cultures: Anthropological Studies in Accountability, Ethics and the Academy*. London: Routledge, 1–18.

Strathern, Marilyn. 2000b. 'Accountability… and Ethnography,' in
M. Strathern (ed.), *Audit Cultures: Anthropological Studies in
Accountability, Ethics and the Academy*. London: Routledge,
279–304.

Strathern, Marilyn. 2006. 'Bullet-Proofing: A Tale from the United
Kingdom', in A. Riles (ed.), *Documents: Artifacts of Modern
Knowledge*. Ann Arbor: University of Michigan Press, 181–205.

Street, Alice. 2014. *Biomedicine in an Unstable Place: Infrastructure
and Personhood in a Papua New Guinean Hospital*. Durham and
London: Duke University Press.

Sullivan, Noelle. 2012. 'Enacting Spaces of Inequality: Placing Global/
State Governance Within a Tanzanian Hospital', *Space and Culture*, 15
(1): 57–67.

Sweet, H. 2009. 'Expectations, Encounters, and Ecclesiastics: Mission
Medicine in Zululand, South Africa', in M. Harrison, M. Jones and H.
Sweet (eds), *From Western Medicine to Global Medicine: The Hospital
Beyond the West*. New Delhi: Orient Blackswan, 330–59.

Szreter, S. and K. Breckenridge. , 2012. 'Introduction: Recognition
and Registration: The Infrastructure of Personhood in World
History', in K. Breckenridge and S. Szreter (eds), *Registration
and Recognition: Documenting the Person in World History*.
Oxford: Oxford University Press, 1–36.

Taitz, L. 2000. 'Medics Refuse to Perform Abortions: Backstreet
Abortions Rife as 166 Clinics Take a Moral Stand', *Sunday Times*, 4
June, p. 1.

Thompson, Grahame. 2000. 'The Limits to "Globalization": Taking
Economic Borders Seriously', http://citeseerx.ist.psu.edu/viewdoc/dow
nload?doi=10.1.1.482.5716&rep=rep1&type=pdf [Accessed on 29
January 2015].

Tsing, Anna Lowenhaupt. 2005. *Friction: An Ethnography of Global
Connection*. Princeton: Princeton University Press.

Uys, L. R. 2005. 'The Nursing Process in South Africa', in M. Habermann
and B. Parfitt (eds), *The Nursing Process: A Global Concept*.
Edinburgh: Elsevier, 123–34.

Vail, L. (ed.). 1989. *The Creation of Tribalism in Southern Africa*.
London: James Currey.

Vincent, Louise. 2011. 'South Africa's Abortion Values Clarification
Workshops – An Opportunity to Deepen Democratic Communication
Missed', *Journal of Asian and African Studies*, 46 (3): 264–77.

von Holdt, Kurt. 2005. 'Work Restructuring and the Crisis of Social
Reproduction: A Southern Perspective', in E. Webster and K. von
Holdt (eds), *Beyond the Apartheid Workplace: Studies in Transition*.
Pietermaritzburg: University of KwaZulu-Natal Press, 3–40.

von Holdt, Kurt. 2010. 'The South African Post-Apartheid Bureaucracy: Inner Workings, Contradictory Rationales and the Developmental State', in Omano Edigheji (ed.), *Constructing a Democratic Developmental State in South Africa: Potential and Challenges*. Cape Town: HSRC Press, 241–60.

von Holdt, Kurt and B. Maserumule. 2005. 'After Apartheid: Decay or Reconstruction in a Public Hospital', in E. Webster and K. von Holdt (eds), *Beyond the Apartheid Workplace: Studies in Transition*. Pietermaritzburg: University of KwaZulu-Natal Press, 435–59.

von Holdt, Kurt and M. Murphy. 2007. 'Public Hospitals in South Africa: Stressed Institutions, Disempowered Management', in S. Buhlungu, J. Daniel, R. Southall and J. Lutchman (eds), *State of the Nation: South Africa 2007*. Cape Town: HSRC, 312–41.

Walker, C. 1990. 'Gender and the Development of the Migrant Labour System c. 1850–1930: An Overview', in C. Walker (ed.), *Women and Gender in Southern Africa to 1945*. Cape Town: David Philip, 168–96.

Walker, C. 1995. 'Conceptualizing Motherhood in Twentieth Century South Africa', *Journal of Southern African Studies*, 21 (3): 417–37.

Walker, L. 1996. '"My Work Is to Help the Woman Who Wants to Have a Child, Not the Woman Who Wants to Have an Abortion": Discourses of Patriarchy and Power among African Nurses in South Africa', *African Studies*, 55 (2): 43–68.

Walker, L. and L. Gilson. 2004. '"We Are Bitter but We Are Satisfied": Nurses as Street-level Bureaucrats in South Africa', *Social Science and Medicine*, 59: 1251–61.

Webber, J. A. 2000. 'Fragmented, Frustrated and Trapped: Nurses in Post-Apartheid Transition at King Edward VIII Hospital, Durban', PhD thesis, Department of Sociology, University of Natal.

Weber, M. 1978. *Economy and Society: An Outline of Interpretive Sociology*. Berkeley: University of California Press.

Weber, M. [1930] 2005. *The Protestant Ethic and the Spirit of Capitalism*. London and New York: Routledge.

Webster, D. 1991. '*Abafazi Bathonga Bafihlakala*: Ethnicity and Gender in a KwaZulu Border Community', in A. D. Spiegel and P. A. McAllister (eds), *Tradition and Transition in Southern Africa*. Johannesburg: Witwatersrand University Press, 243–71.

Wenzel, P. 2007. 'Public Sector Transformation in South Africa: Getting the Basics Right', *Progress in Development Studies*, 7 (1): 47–64.

Werbner, Richard. 2004. 'Epilogue: The New Dialogue with Post-liberalism', in H. Englund and F. B. Nyamnjoh (eds), *Rights and the Politics of Recognition in Africa*. London: Zed Books, 261–74.

West, H. G. 2003. '"Who Rules Us Now?" Identity Tokens, Sorcery, and Other Metaphors in the 1994 Mozambican Elections', in H. G. West and T. Sanders (eds), *Ethnographies of Suspicion in the New World Order*. Durham and London: Duke University Press, 92–124.

White, Paul, Alexandra Hillman and Joanna Latimer. 2012. 'Ordering, Enrolling, and Dismissing: Moments of Access Across Hospital Spaces', *Space and Culture*, 15 (1): 68–87.

Whiteside, J. 1906. *History of the Wesleyan Methodist Church of South Africa*. Cape Town: Juta.

Widerquist, J. and R. Davidhizar. 2006. 'The Ministry of Nursing', *Journal of Advanced Nursing*, 19 (4): 647–52.

Wilson, M. and A. Mafeje. 1963. *Langa: A Study of Social Groups in an African Township*. Cape Town: Oxford University Press.

Wilson, Richard A. 2001. *The Politics of Truth and Reconciliation in South Africa: Legitimizing the Post-Apartheid State*. Cambridge: University of Cambridge Press.

Wilson, Richard A. 2002. 'The Politics of Culture in Post-apartheid South Africa', in R. G. Fox and B. J. King (eds), *Anthropology Beyond Culture*. Oxford and New York: Berg, 209–33.

Wunsch, James. S. 2014. 'Decentralization: Theoretical, Conceptual, and Analytical Issues', in J. Tyler Dickovick and James S. Wunsch (eds), *Decentralization in Africa: The Paradox of State Strength*. London: Lynne Rienner, 1–22.

Xaba, J. and G. Phillips. 2001. *Understanding Nurse Recruitment: Final Report*. Pretoria: DENOSA.

INDEX